The Art of Perversity

D. H. LAWRENCE'S SHORTER FICTIONS

The
Art of Perversity

D. H. LAWRENCE'S SHORTER FICTIONS

by

Kingsley Widmer

Seattle
University of Washington Press
1962

PR 6023 .A93 Z954

For
Eleanor
whose love goes beyond perversity

Foreword

No, no, my boy, don't be on the side
of the angels, it's too lowering.[1]

THE subjects of this essay are the art and attitude of the more than sixty short stories and novellas of D. H. Lawrence. While I have a large argument to present—an apologia for perversity—those who do not find the argument digestible may still find some small explicatory usefulness in the discussions of the themes, style, motifs, and other characteristics of some of the shorter fictions. For these fictions, I believe, constitute Lawrence's central writings. After recently rereading the shorter fictions of many of his contemporaries, I believe that Lawrence was at least among the best of the writers of short fiction in English in his time (1910–30). Thus the value and importance of Lawrence's stories would seem to justify a relatively thorough discussion. Such modest utility as this study has is that of the "close reading" of a significant body of literature.[2]

But analytical explication should not turn into a higher form of remedial reading. While literary criticism may properly utilize such means, it should do so, I insist, only for larger ends. I am partial to Lawrence's negative views, which have often been underrated and misunderstood, and I wish to explore and partly affirm the perversity that gives much of Lawrence's work its distinctive being. A trio of inversions may suggest the way: Lawrence-the-advocate-of-love-and-marriage denies any ideality to love and any peace to marriage; Lawrence-the-moralist insists on the irrelevance of morality to the more significant areas of life; Lawrence-the-prophet-of-life insists on death and destruction as the basis of awareness and meaning. While we need not make too much of these obvious paradoxes, my theme is that the wisdom of such waywardness reveals the largest existential significance. Lawrence's negative ways to his affirmations provide the cruxes of understanding. His lively pessimism, and his verities of directness, responsiveness, rebellion, polarity, dark knowledge, and passion require a harsh disenchantment with life, especially modern life, and an awareness of the defining extremity of authentic existence. "Brethren, let us go down." [3]

The discussions of the fictions have been centered on the longing for annihilation, the demonic, the social negation of modern woman, the ways of erotic conflict, and religious regeneration—in that order. (Since the stories are grouped around themes and motifs, the index provides approximate dates for chronological arrangement.) While the discussions overlap, they also develop: the concluding discussion of Lawrence's religious tropes is treated as the culmination of the nihilistic awareness with which the essay starts. For the most part, the order within the five chapters is dialectical. The arguments intend to be continuous rather than discrete; the themes, representative rather than exhaustive. Generally, I have assumed, without detailed argument, an "organic" or "contextualist" aesthetic: the art and the argument of the work are one; where the art is best, the argument is most true. However, there are a number of times when this highly useful aesthetic of the practical critic reveals inadequacies, when the truth and the art show significant conflict. I have, therefore, also suggested a few other ways of confronting the work. However, explication for its own sake may end in triviality; explication for the sake of revealing a fundamental view of life may also reveal the inadequate artifice of explication. Perhaps the use of any method, or even art, finally justifies itself only by self-violation. Art, fortunately, is the product of mortal man—flawed, perverse, and obscurely human—and neither the logic of art nor of critical approaches should be taken altogether seriously. The most important qualities remain outside any method or art as such.

If there be any art to criticism, other than engaged individual response, it must include being critical. And to be critical means, I take it, the stance of simultaneously keeping a sympathetic foot in, and an antagonistic foot out of, the subject. Some of my commentary on Lawrence's fictions is quite negative—otherwise the positive would be quite meaningless. This dialectical insistence should not be confused with the academic scientism that Lawrence, in reviewing a somewhat learned work, commented upon: "The author refused to take an attitude, except that of impartiality, which is the worst of all attitudes." [4] While also heeding Lawrence's warning that "the proper function of a critic is to save the tale from the artist who created it," [5] we must assume the *ambiance* and some of the gestures that give the tales their significance. Part of my partiality to Lawrence has suggested doing this by drawing heavily upon his own statements and language in other works, thus engaging as the fundamental entity something larger than the specific work, which can only be adumbrated as "the Lawrencean view" and remains always our ultimate subject.

After reading Lawrence and writing my original discussion of his tales, I read most of the writings on Lawrence—biographies, polemics, criticism, reviews, and even incidental comments. My additions and corrections undoubtedly show a general obligation to other writers on Lawrence, although one rather difficult to specify properly.[6] I am particularly indebted to many writers on Lawrence with whom I emphatically disagree, especially the sentimental moralists and the genteel authoritarians who dominate much academic literary study. For reasons of space, emphasis, and temperament, I have not attempted to provide a commentary on the commentaries.[7] Probably only perversity can justify adding even more to the massive flow of writings on Lawrence.

I am indebted to the editors of the *Kenyon Review, Modern*

Fiction Studies, the *University of Kansas City Review,* the *Journal of Aesthetics and Art Criticism,* and the *Humanist* (American Humanist Association, Yellow Springs, Ohio), and to Harry T. Moore, editor of *A D. H. Lawrence Miscellany* (Carbondale, Ill.: University of Southern Illinois Press, 1959), in which parts of this essay were published in 1958–59. Professor Moore, to whom all contemporary students of Lawrence are obligated, was exceptionally generous and encouraging. I am also much obliged to the patience and precision of the anonymous second "reader" of this manuscript for the Press.

My other debts are also personal rather than institutional. I owe much to the unusual tolerance and encouragement of Professor E. E. Bostetter (and to Mrs. Bostetter) of the University of Washington. Several friends, of such long standing as not to need naming, have contributed by warmly disagreeing with me. One writer, critic, and teacher, Dr. Eleanor Widmer, has endlessly given criticism, understanding, and, with Matthew August and Jonah Lawrence, something much more wise. While I have taken what I could from others, any perversities not due to the subject belong to my times and myself.

KINGSLEY WIDMER

La Jolla, California

Acknowledgment

I wish to thank Laurence Pollinger Ltd. and the estate of Mrs. Frieda Lawrence (London), and William Heinemann Ltd. (London) for permission to quote from the British editions of Lawrence's works; and Alfred A. Knopf, Inc. (New York), and the Viking Press, Inc. (New York) for permission to quote from the American editions. I also wish to thank the Southern Illinois University Press, *Kenyon Review*, *Journal of Aesthetics and Art Criticism*, *University of Kansas City Review*, *The Humanist* (American Humanist Association, Yellow Springs, Ohio), and *Modern Fiction Studies* for permission to reprint previously published parts of this study. Specific titles and editions are indicated in the notes.

Contents

The Art of Perversity

D. H. LAWRENCE'S SHORTER FICTIONS

CHAPTER I

Parables of Annihilation

*. . . and once we are driven right on
to nihilism we may find a way through.*[1]

I

A LEGION of moralists tells us that the Western sensibility suffers from a crisis of values. For some time, our literature and thought have exposed, and often espoused, varieties of anguished nihilism. Depending on which school of despair one studies in, the history of that peculiar suffering starts with willful egotism's destruction of the medieval synthesis, or with science and skepticism's fragmentation of feeling and thought in the seventeenth century, or with revolutionary rationalism's undermining of myth and style during the Enlightenment, or with the industrial revolution's atomization of organic community and human relatedness, or with violent ideologies' deification of the arbitrary and the absurd in the postromantic present. We need not argue here which is the true and proper history for a world "gone to pot," but only note the tacit agreement as to the death of the "old idols" and the painful revelations of subconscious, subatomic, subhuman, and other subterranean powers and desires. Nihilism, at a number of levels, provides an essential focus—one at least to go through, if not remain in—if we wish to recognize our time, our place, and ourselves.

D. H. Lawrence, I hope to show, confronted much of that nihilism, and he attempted to make from it a dialectic simultaneously of destruction and of salvation. In his most intriguing

3

works, his sardonic tales, nihilism often seems to be the one pre-occupation and informing spirit. Elsewhere, the spirit of destruction seems more oblique, with Lawrence displaying the very nihilism he is angrily denying. Put another way, the primary insights and arts of his work reveal themselves in images and gestures that insist on the annihilating, wayward, rebellious, demonic, and contumacious. A number of previous commentators on Lawrence have properly noted these peculiarities, although not, I think, in sufficient depth to give the perversity its full significance. In reading the immense criticism on Lawrence, one comes to feel that it proclaims a moral line, with those who condemn Lawrence and his perversity on one side, and on the other side those who praise him and deny his perversity. In contrast, I shall treat the perversity as matter for praise, as an authentic mode with excellent aesthetic possibilities and considerable human wisdom.

Let us start with a characteristically perverse declaration of Lawrence's, one by no means a lonely extreme, which reveals his attitude toward the act of literature. In affirming his belief in art as creativity, he writes: "You have to have something vicious in you to be a creative writer. It is the something vicious, old-Adamish, incompatible to the 'ordinary' world, inside a man, which gives an edge to his awareness. . . ." [2] Vicious? Might not this be a rhetorical hyperbole just to emphasize the grandeur of the artist's calling? Apparently not; one way and another Lawrence repeatedly makes the linkage of awareness and viciousness, and without late-romantic qualifications that the artist is separate from all other men. A similar point of perverse yoking and alienation appears in his descriptions of the ecstasy that he demands. For example: "Nothing is wonderful unless it is dangerous. Dangerous to the *status quo* of the soul. And therefore detestable." [3] *Wonder,* as we shall see, occurs as a key word and quality in Lawrence's insistence on passionate desire and aliveness. It would seem to mean something quite close to what the traditionally religious mean by *sacred,* on its subjective side. The awful wonder brings the "detestable" shock of illumination. This destroys ordinary values and makes one confront ultimate meanings—and lack of meaning. The world-sundering moments, the fundamental extremes where opposite feelings meet, annihilate all relative and moral values to reveal the deepest affirmations and denials.

Death, then, would be an apt starting point for our analysis. In one of Lawrence's most extreme statements, *The Reality of Peace*—a violent abstract polemic, written during World War I —he insists that "We must *choose* life." [4] Yea-saying? Not quite, for such insistence acknowledges no simple affirmation. When Lawrence speaks of humanity in this essay, he prays for death:

Sweet, beautiful death, come to our help. . . . Purify us with death, O death. . . . Sweet death, save us from humanity. Death, noble, unstainable death, smash the glassy rind of humanity. . . . O death, give us to our single being. Release me from the debased social body. O death, release me at last; let me be by myself. . . . [5]

Quite possibly one could develop the pathological factors in Lawrence and in his relation to World War I to "explain" such statements (there are many others). But, as we shall see, the longing for the purity of death, for the "single being" of annihilation, presents a major theme of Lawrence's. His famous exaltation of intense immediate life has its natural correlative. As he writes elsewhere, "I would die, I would quickly die, to have all power, all life at once, to come instantly to pure, eternal oblivion, the source of life." [6]

Rather than responding to such nihilism with the shock of the rational moralist or the easy righteousness of the antiromantic literary critic, let us follow further this fusion of desire and self-destruction. It is not just that Lawrence, one of the modern soul-confessional artists, displays the undeniable "death instinct." He also asks and answers one of the "eternal questions": What is the answer to death? Let us embrace annihilation with ecstasy. [7] This, like the doctrine of immortality, or the making of a Stoical "good end," or the communal apotheosis of the sacrificial hero, provides one of the "great" answers, which has analogous forms in Chuang Tzu, certain Medieval heresies, nineteenth-century European nihilism, and parts of modern atheistic existentialism.

Clearly, Lawrence concerns himself with religious values, however unamenable to all official religions. The art of his best fictions has the same logic of emotional extremity as *The Reality of Peace*. Embracing annihilation provides Lawrence with a crucial ingress into certain forms of confused longings in the fictions: "This is the root of confusion, this inability of man to admit, 'Now I am single in my desire for destructive death.' " [8] And this is but part of a larger principle that works in Lawrence's perception of life: "One should go to the extremity of any experience," [9] though he adds that one should not, and cannot, maintain life at the extremes. But literature is not life; it is a form of knowledge about life, and Lawrence's literature directs our attention to the knowledge of extremity, which is the knowledge of annihilation.

II

Some of the shorter fictions will show more exactly than Lawrence's frequently suggestive but angry and obsessive arguments the insights premised on the longing for annihilation. Two stories centering on a death agony—one early and one late work—will suggest the paradigmatic knowledge of extremity. *The Prussian Officer* [10] is a pre-World War I tale, written in Lawrence's early manner of sensuous elaboration of a melodramatic episode. In the simple plot, a young peasant orderly hates his superior officer, a sadistic Captain; he rebels, kills the officer, flees, and dies in his flight. The concluding scene of the officer and the orderly "together, side by side, in the mortuary" emphasizes the obvious irony of similarity in death for warped authority and desperate rebel.

The story is usually commented upon as a revelation of Prussian militarism and, with some niggling by genteel critics, as showing an exploratory concern with homosexual sadism. This seems true enough, although hardly sufficient. Covert homosexuality is a major element in Lawrence's fictions. (There appears to be very little acknowledgment of it in Lawrence's statements, other than a general recognition of the significance of sexual warpings and a repulsion to inverts.) The Captain is actually a full-drawn example: he dislikes women, is moved "like a warm flame" by the nearness of the youth's body, develops a "deep" and "undiscovered" physical interest in the youth, becomes obsessed with a scar on the youth's hand, tries to stop the youth from having anything to do with a girl, flies into jealous rages, tries to hide "the passion that had got hold of him," obtains "intense gratification of his passion" by brutally beating the youth's posterior, and so on. The very brutality of the aristocratic officer produces in the peasant orderly a personal emotion that is quite new, and "he felt at once a thrill of deep pleasure and shame." Despite his conscious wish to remain innocent of both fascination and hatred, the youth is trapped in the "chaos of sensations" that characterizes the Lawrencean lover and the extremity of alienating experience. His new emotions separate him from his fellows until he feels that there "were only two people in the world." This is the world of love and hate, which tests one's deepest nature.

There is something more than homosexuality here. The sexual sadism of the officer-servant relation rests on the covert sexual basis of all authority, but the narration emphasizes the subjective change in the youth as his innocence loses contact with home, fellows, sweetheart, obedience, and certainty. Forced to the extremity of feeling, the youth's rebellion becomes gratuitous murder. The "passion of relief" with which he chokes the Captain to death and his solicitude for the destroyed body have strong sexual elements, but the revenge is subordinate to his loss of purpose and inversion of reality. The image of authority is dead, but one-fourth of the literal narrative remains to explore the subjective abyss of simple innocence as well as the unresolvable

fatality that always marks the confrontation of Innocence and
Authority—the antitype of tragedy.

A sensitive reading must account for the style and metaphoric
order of the work as well as for the psychology and archetypal
pattern of action and character. The opening paragraphs of the
story display characteristic Lawrencean intensification of physical sensation:

> . . . the valley, wide and shallow, glittered with heat; dark green
> patches of rye, pale young corn, fallow and meadow and black pine
> woods spread in a dull, hot diagram under a glistening sky. But right in
> front the mountains ranged across, pale blue and very still, snow gleam-
> ing gently out of the deep atmosphere. And towards the mountains, on
> and on, the regiment marched between the rye fields and the meadows
> . . . the mountains grew gradually nearer and more distinct. While
> the feet of the soldiers grew hotter, sweat ran through their hair under
> their helmets, and their knapsacks could burn no more in contact with
> their shoulders, but seemed instead to give off a cold, prickly sensation.
>
> He [the orderly] walked on and on in silence, staring at the moun-
> tains ahead, that rose sheer out of the land, and stood fold beneath fold,
> half earth, half heaven, the heaven, the barrier with slits of snow, in the
> pale bluish peaks.

From the beginning of the story, Lawrence's vivid sense of
place and physical sensation shows a metaphoric heightening
that will later be crucial. The repeated "on and on" toward the
cool mountains—the "heaven" in the youth's mind—points the
direction of escape from his burden of hatred; the violated innocent longs to get away from the passion and pain of the "dull
hot diagram" of life and reach nothingness.

But before turning to the latter part of the story, we might recall briefly the significance of the recurrent icy-mountain image
in Lawrence's work. Perhaps inherited from the romantics,
where it was an image of defiant withdrawal (as in Byron and
Stendahl), it also represents for Lawrence the icy idealizing and
dutiful conscience of northern Europe and its Christianity, in
contrast to the warm pagan South. Lawrence writes in one of
his travel sketches: "The very pure source of breaking-down, the

very quick of cold death, is the snowy mountain peak. . . ." [11]
In the fictions it so appears in *St. Mawr, Women in Love, The Woman Who Rode Away, The Princess, The Captain's Doll,* and others.

At almost all points Lawrence's style insists that we be aware of the relation of person and natural scene, and it is his aesthetic as well as his metaphysical principle that everything in life must be "one living *continuum* with all the universe." After the young soldier has been carried away from normal life into the extremes of love and hate, only the image of authority has any relation to him. When he kills that he loses his last relation to the living universe. He no longer desires "to save himself"; and "nothing . . . could give him back his living place in the hot, bright morning." Thus, all reality is lost: he is "disembowled, made empty, a shadow creeping under the sunshine." He was only his passion; with that dead he is in a "blackish dream." The very ripeness of the summer scene, maintained from the opening paragraph of the story, turns to dissolution: "The air was too scented, it gave no breath. All the lush green-stuff seemed to be issuing its sap, till the air was deathly, sickly with the smell of greenness." The human order dissolves with the natural order. A Dostoyevskean aloneness is his greatest pain: "He would not have minded anything, but he could not get away from the sense of being divided from the others." Later in his wanderings, thirsty and in need of help, he sees a peasant woman, but "he had no language with which to speak to her. She was the bright solid unreality."

At great length, in proportion to the story as a whole, Lawrence develops the youth's break with the natural and human continuum. As the youth wanders in a surreal forest of green and gold, light and shadow, horror and fulfillment, he achieves an ecstatic vision. At one point he describes to himself the metaphysical scene of the forest:

It was peace. But now he had got beyond himself. He had never been here before. Was it life, or not life? He was by himself. They were in a big bright place, those others, and he was outside. The town, all the country, a big place of light; and he was outside, here, in the darkened open beyond, where each thing existed alone.[12]

To be the existentialist outsider, to be completely in the beyond of pure existence, is the most profound state of subjectivity and awareness, but it is also fatal. Wandering in the forest, the youth achieves a vision of wonder and magical knowledge: ". . . thick-golden light behind golden-green glitterings, and darkness further off, surrounding him, growing deeper. He was conscious of a sense of arrival. He was amid the reality, on the real, dark bottom." In the flight from the horror of injured innocence, the youth has found what the idealists call the "really real"—nothingness. There is one final image of light and longing, three times repeated—the snowy mountains with which the story opened:

. . . looking down the long, bare grove whose flat bed was already filling dark, he saw the mountains in a wonder-light, now far away and radiant. Behind the soft, grey ridge of the nearest range the further mountains stood golden and pale grey, the snow all radiant and pure, soft gold. So still, gleaming in the sky, fashioned pure out of the ore of the sky, they shone in their silence. He stood and looked at them, his face illuminated.

The ecstasy of identification with the mountains continues the next morning:

There, straight in front of him, blue and cool and tender, the mountains ranged across the pale edge of the morning sky. He wanted them— he wanted them alone—he wanted to leave himself and be identified with them. They were still and soft with white gentle markings of snow. Finally, in his death throes, he stared at the gleaming mountains. There they ranked, all still and wonderful between earth and heaven. He stared until his eyes went black, and the mountains as they stood . . . so clean and cool, seemed to have it, that which was lost to him.

The guilty longing for the ultimate beauty, innocence, and purity beyond life becomes the annihilation of life.

The literal-minded reader may wish to explain the insistent cosmic metaphors as part of the "realistic" motivation in the story—the youth's delirium during his fatal flight from his crime. But that will hardly account for the opening of the story with its vision of the mountains as the heaven; nor for the then disproportionate emphasis on weird wandering; nor for the odd intensification and repetition of the magic qualities of the mountain goal—gold, soft, clean, tender, radiant, pure, wonderful, and endlessly desirable. Lawrence's subject in the story is the destructive wonder of extreme experience. As the author comments in the story, it is the tale of a youth who "had gone out from everyday life into the unknown and he could not, he even did not want to, go back." A figure of primordial innocence has been taken, by the extremity of desire and rebellion, out of his conventional self of obedience-home-friends-sweetheart-prudence-belonging to his deepest self of passion and violence and ecstasy and death.

Many years later, and after many other violent and amoral parables of the limits of experience, Lawrence is still using the same thematic crux and image, but the subjects are more sophisticated, the form more logical, and the style less sensuous and more sardonic. The fatal flaw becomes idealism, instead of innocence; and the dangerous force is escape, instead of authority. The flight into annihilation of *The Man Who Loved Islands* [13] forms one of Lawrence's most precise fictions. It suggests syllogistic organization—three actions, three islands. On the first and largest island the hero is "the Master"; on the second and middling sized island he becomes the ordinary—and trapped—man; and on the third and smallest island his own logic and the elements master him. He who is a master of men is also a man, and therefore mastered.

The story opens with the detached tone of the fable: "There was a man who loved islands." Then comes a brief sketch of the "superior" Englishman, by birth and nature an islander in all the connotations of withdrawal into private means, Englishness, and rationalized sensitivity. He finds his native isle too complex and too crowded, and so he "wanted an island all his own . . .

a world of his own." But the desire for a pure and private world has a hidden destructiveness, and on his very first island the hero begins to learn the metaphysical "danger of becoming an islander." Alone, one is liable to be cut off from the flux of tangible life and thrown back into the "dark mystery of time." The hero, with the usual idealist's naiveté about a man's inner company, learns that withdrawal into the simple self brings forth complex fears from the unconscious; and he is haunted by nightmarish images of violence and sacrifice.

The rationalist escapes from primitive solitude by way of an ideal community. The man who loved islands creates a willed utopia, mostly of employees, in which he wants everyone to be happy and "the little world to be perfect." "But," says the mocking narrator, "anyone who wants the world to be perfect must be careful not to have any real likes or dislikes. A general good will is all you can afford."

The mode of the Lawrencean fable is usually statement, followed by a brief action commenting upon the statement. General benevolence must confront the tangible desires that it obscures but does not eradicate. The crux, once again, is authority: the goodness of "the Master" merely breeds his own "egoism"; this in turn raises the defensive "malice" of the "servant." Authority masked as virtue, power that pretends to be benevolent, creates the personal deceit and the general destructiveness of rebellion that becomes "symbolic of the island." The atmosphere of the island utopia is to be found in its symbolic tone— the Lawrencean "spirit of place"—not on its rational surface. The Master's benevolent plans increasingly rely on economic prudence, but neither benevolence nor bookkeeping will stop the cow from falling over the cliff. Nor can rational goodness and authority produce the desires that create human community. The sensitive Master admits defeat when confronted with the breakthrough of the covert self, the subterranean and primitive past, which is always discounted in principles of benevolence and of rational social order: "Strange floods of passion came over you, strange violent lusts and imaginations of cruelty. Uncanny dreams, half dreams . . . fears." The benevolent rationalist has been defeated by the covert malignity of place, principle, and self; and the utopian island—with typical Lawrencean sarcasm —is sold as a resort for honeymooners.

The second island, his next alternative, provides the sensitive and intelligent man a withdrawal into the purity of private life (Anglo-Saxon practical idealism). This small island has no past, no community, no economic purpose except simple comfort and quiet living. In his small house with a couple of servants, he is now "mister" instead of "master." Simplicity, solitude, study (a compendium of classical flower references), and an end to ambition, benevolence, and rational and social pretension make the hero safe. "The island was no longer a 'world.' It was a sort of refuge."

Purely private life creates a sort of harmony and he is "without desire, without *ennui*." But a lingering doubt of self-consciousness raises a question: "Is this happiness?" He answers himself: "I feel nothing, or I don't know what I feel." Lawrence thus shows that such harmony can hardly be distinguished from mental and emotional stupidity. But the actual world remains to belie tricks of consciousness. The needs of the body rather than the needs of the rational mind this time defeat the man who loved islands. Out of "a kind of pity," he becomes the lover of the girl who waits on him, and then realizes that his own abolition of will is not enough. He wills nothing, and so becomes the girl's lover because "*she* willed it." The assertion of willed order brought failure on the first, utopian, island; the negation of will brings failure on the second, escapist, island. Manipulation of the *will* as such simply won't do.[14]

The man who loved islands is, however, a Lawrencean who explicitly believes that sex is "one of the great life mysteries." Like Lawrence, he also believes in the quiescence of sexual desire.[15] Yet in the story the escape to a "stillness of desireless-ness"—a typical Lawrencean tumor of phrasing that mars an

otherwise lean prose—leads to the trap of sexual "automatism."
Apparently willed benevolence and willed escape have sapped
some essential quality of being, so that the Lawrencean belief
is inadequate for Lawrence's hero. He wishes, later, to transform
his relation to the girl, but somehow has not the strength to
combat the usual female who wants dependence rather than
desire, selfish submission rather than the integrity of passion.
He dutifully marries the pregnant girl; and the independent
man now has an island peopled by a wife, a daughter, a mother-
in-law, and a nurse. In the comfort of matriarchy, in a "refuge"
that has turned to the fatuousness of a "suburb," all selfhood
and desire become burdensome, even "nauseous." Here we see
Lawrence's diagnostic image of the pervasive morality of comfortable duty, ending in disgust.[16]

This sardonic tale hovers on the edge of the absurd at many
points, as is often true of Lawrence's mocking fictions, and the
grotesque failures of the "good" sensitive man provide endless
possibilities; but it is also characteristic of Lawrence that the
third, final, and shortest episode of the fable becomes vehement
psychological denouement. The hero still has enough of his
"finer distinction" that he can bring himself to flee the destructiveness of ordinary life. Truly alone at last on a barren third
island, except for a cat and some sheep, his quest for harmony
and perfection has left the human realm. His obsessive consciousness is fictionally maintained by a systematic denuding of
the scene. As in *The Prussian Officer*, the style depends upon
turning psychological realism into a surreal magnification of the
details to give the logic of the obsessive emotions. Thus, when
"all interest had left him," each fact of life becomes grotesque.
He finds the bleating sheep of his pastoral escape "repulsive,"
"degrading"; he finds the "intrusion, the clumsy homeliness" of
the fishermen who bring his supplies, sickening; and he even
finds indirect reminders of his humanity and identity so upset-
ting that he "hated to read his own name on an envelope." The
longing for the ideal has become self-hatred and self-destruction.

"He felt ill, as if everything were dissolving. . . . Everything was twilight, outside, and in his mind and soul." Oneness has been reached.

The man who loved islands of the mind rather than the actual world ends by destroying all marks of the mind: he tore "the brass label from his paraffine stove . . . [and] he obliterated any bit of lettering in his cabin." His only pleasures are nihilism —the removal of the sheep, the disappearance of the cat, the cessation of supplies, the winter disappearance of the sun, and the final blanketing of the whole scene in snow. Nothing left but himself, the self becomes nothing: he achieves mystic dehumanization and ceases "to register his own feelings."

Negation is the final ecstasy. "Soon, he said to himself, it will all be gone, and in all these regions nothing will be alive. He felt a cruel satisfaction in the thought." His final assertion of negative individuality is that self-destruction must override the destructiveness of the universe; this is his heroic defiance, his Lawrencean gesture. He attempts to free his boat from the snow, not with any intention of escaping, but that he may be trapped by "his own choice, not by the mechanical power of the elements." But the nihilism of the cosmos is even greater than that of the ego, and the concluding image is another version of the snowy mountain of the beyond. On the bleak snow-covered rock in the wintry northern sea, there is only more and more "snow rolling over the sea" and "its breath on him." The cold cosmos, the very loss of the warmth of the human animal, provides Lawrence's concluding trope for frigid idealism.

There is an entrancing precision to Lawrence's exitless tale of the sensitive hero's search for the ideal world and his consequent loss of the human, culminating in the pure cold image of annihilation. The rock of Promethean defiance; the sacrificial antihero; the longing withdrawal, both guilty and paradisical, symbolized by the post-Renaissance dream of the island haven; the ecstasy of denial of the intellectual individualist—all are recurrent qualities of fables of *hard* romanticism. This "counter-romanticism," [17] so well known in Blake, Melville, Baudelaire, Conrad, Kafka, and many others, uses the hyperlogical fable not only to mock the adequacy of benevolence and idealism but to create a cul-de-sac in which choice is grotesque and absurd and the longing for annihilation the only certitude.

In *The Man Who Loved Islands* (and is it not also true of many other powerful modern fables?) there seems to be a deep disgust with the physically human—constant repulsion, sexual desire as "nausea"; a total disillusionment with society—it is treated as obvious that the hero flees civilization, and even the utopian society reverses to the malevolent; a degradation of culture—reading is a game, knowledge an esoteric hobby, sensitivity an illness. Nor can this nihilism be separated from D. H. Lawrence, the yea-sayer of life values. The hero is Lawrencean about the sexual mystery, the negation of modern society, the longing for a utopian community, and the doctrine of simplicity and solitude. The man who loved islands even has the old Lawrencean hobby of naming flowers. This story, too, is the "true" Lawrence, all the more so in that it contains implicit self-mockery. [18]

Let us recapitulate. The early story, *The Prussian Officer,* turns the exploration of its authority-innocence theme into heightened nature images of the good and simple youth's longing for destruction. The late story, *The Man Who Loved Islands,* explores the sensitive idealist's benevolence and follows his emotional logic through the covert longing for destruction. The form of the innocence theme is appropriately lavish in sensual and scenic detail; the form of the idealist theme is appropriately discursive and hyperlogical. But the cogency of these fictions goes beyond the apt fusion of theme and form. The yearning for the extremity of experience, and covertly for its destructive culmination, is the crux of much of Lawrence's art. More will be said about this nihilism, but perhaps we might note now that it may be the negations that make Lawrence so pertinently and appealingly "modern," rather than his formal carelessness, woozy passional prose, and sometimes irritable moralizing and prophecy. That Lawrence so vehemently insists on organic relations to person and place may be to counter not only the nihilism of the prevailing social-moral order, but a more ultimate nihilism within himself.

Lawrence is not the only perverse modern artist. The perversity, after all, reveals the effort to turn an awareness of the destructive into something meaningful, to turn pessimistic knowledge to an affirmation. Often Lawrence insists on the destructive aims, as we shall see, as a transvaluation: ". . . once we are driven on to nihilism we may find a way through." [19] But *The Prussian Officer* and *The Man Who Loved Islands* dramatize, with some of Lawrence's best art, innocence and idealism ending in self-annihilation.

III

We shall have to return in more detail to Lawrence's dramatic critique of idealism in its various permutations, since the "perverse" reversal of it not only provides the boundaries for Lawrencean passion but is, in a sense, the passion itself. First, however, let us examine, somewhat more briefly as to detail and artistic method, Lawrence's use of his death fascination as a mode of revelation in some other fictions.

England, My England,[20] a story written during World War I, shows considerable awkwardness in revealing the futility and the death of sensitivity in the "old England." Its materials, which could be viewed historically as Georgian melancholy pastoral, center on a sweet, loving couple—Winifred and Egbert—who lead an expensively simple and idealistically aesthetic life in an ancient Hampshire cottage of William Morris vintage. Egbert is a handsome young man of superior origins and sensitivity, passion, and gentleness. He will have nothing to do with business or any of the other disillusioning vanities of the "modern world," and devotes himself to the simple life at the cottage, raising flowers, and making love. A fine hero? For E. M. Forster he might have been, but for Lawrence he is an ambiguous figure, even a dangerous one. Much—too much—of the story is devoted to a sarcastic exposition of the dubiousness of the sweet and sensitive young man. While Lawrence should have considerable personal attachment to those, like Egbert, who spend their time raising flowers and making love, he also has the detachment to see that some crude positive force is missing. Everything Egbert turns his hand to is "amateurish and sketchy," from his earnest and ineffective repairs on the cottage to his "tampering with the arts." Without profession, without talent, and—much more important—without any deeply serious purpose, any desire to fight his way in the world or against the world, he is incapable of coming "to grips with life." His wife's, and the author's, dissatisfaction with him derives neither from moral nor sexual criticisms but from the simple fact "that he stood for nothing." "To hold aloof" from a bad world is not enough. The sensitive young man quite rightly does not concern himself with making money, for he has a low "estimation of success" as the world knows it, but there is something in a "robust" faith, an "acrid courage, and a certain will-to-power" that transcends sweetness and light.

Some harsher, and, from the language, obviously Nietzschean, vitality is necessary. Oddly, Lawrence insists that Winifred's businessman father displays the qualities that Egbert lacks. This appears to be the one and only time in Lawrence's fictions—or any other writings of his—that there appears a Forster-like good word for a businessman. And Lawrence spends considerably more time in abstract statement of this than in concrete dramatization. The father, Godfrey, a hardheaded success, goes in for "the delightful game of a cultured home." Further evidence that we are not to take him very seriously lies in Lawrence's repeated insistence that, despite his success, he sees the social order as bad; he, too, has "no profound belief in this world of ours, this society which we have elaborated to death at last." That—and there are many similar points—is not how one succeeds in the world of affairs. Moreover, Lawrence has a speech to make, an editorial on the will to power, which he rejects in his later works. Lawrence recognizes that the supremacy of the father over the son-in-law poses a psychological problem. But he mocks the "psycho-analyst" and his "father-complex" and substitutes its Lawrencean-Biblical equivalent—"the old red flame of fatherhood," the "Isaac and Abraham" story, the "paternal godhead," and "male mystery of authority." This rhetoric covers Lawrence's fictional failure in presenting the father, whose business and cultured home the reader never sees.

The failure of Lawrence's hero is not, as casual readers of Lawrence might expect, sexual. Egbert is endlessly desirable to his wife; their marriage is based on passion and has the "wonder" and "lightning" of successful Lawrencean love. Perhaps the fiction has been badly convoluted by elements of the *roman à clef.*

More successfully, Lawrence transforms the wife into the mother, a change from passion to duty also appearing in *Sons and Lovers* and *The Rainbow*.[21] Libertarian Egbert, "the living negative of power," on the other hand, refuses to turn into a father and accept economic duty (he lets his father-in-law pay the bills) or parental responsibility. The central dramatic episode in the story defines Egbert's failure as a father. He is unlucky, which means that his lack of purpose and incisiveness botches things. His best-loved daughter falls on a sickle he left in the yard. ("It was an accident . . . an accident. Why should he feel guilty?") Her leg is carelessly treated and only the authoritative interference of Winifred's father saves it from amputation. The crippling of the little girl embitters the mother, who flees from freedom and her husband into duty and piety. This, in effect, ends the marriage: "There was no need for her to go into a convent. Her will had done it." Guilty and ineffectual Egbert is left with a poisoning sense of "frustration" and "futility, futility, futility."

A frequent temptation for Lawrence is to drop into an expository prose of portentous metaphors. Winifred is now a *mater dolorosa;* Egbert is an Ishmael; she has her gods—the Catholic institution; he has his gods—Baal and Ashtaroth. Lawrence's usual Christian-pagan antithesis this time lacks consistent dramatization. More purposeless than pagan when separated from his wife and children, Egbert goes into a decline.

During this period (ten years after the start of the story) World War I begins. Like his angrily individualistic author, Egbert feels disgust and repulsion, certain that neither side is right, that militarism is a parallel evil to industrialism, and, above all, that modern war is the insanity of "mass feelings." [22] Nonetheless, war as war makes a deep appeal to him, and he joins the army as a private. He hates it; feels bodily and spiritually corrupted by its uncleanness, mass dreariness, and "mechanism"; yet in the combat front finds "quiet" because "many things go out of consciousness before we come to the end of consciousness." He moves, Lawrence tells us, toward the unburdened aloneness of the soul in which there "was the echo of the new, deep sound, deeper than life."

Lawrence's rhetoric in the death scene is mixed with a graphic sense of the artillery bombardment. To a shell that knocks down some red berries near him, Egbert says from his unconscious: "Whither thou goest I will go." The next shell is a dark bird flying home, taking life—and eternity—with it. But this is not the end of the story. It takes eleven paragraphs for Egbert to die. Lawrence, as we have noted in discussing *The Prussian Officer,* is fascinated by the death agony. Egbert's "fate," even in dying, is to linger ineffectually, reviewing "the moment of death." His final identification with his own pain, his "unutterable sick abandon of life," his "doom" of knowing his wound, his horrifying loss of the stars and the world, and his total mergence into "the thick darkness of blood in agony" culminates in absolute longing for death.

There had been life. There had been Winifred and his children. But the frail death-agony effort to catch at straws of memory, straws of life from the past, brought on too great a nausea. No, no! No Winifred, no children. No world, no people. Better the agony of dissolution ahead than the nausea of the effort backwards. Better the terrible work should go forward, the dissolving into the black sea of death, in the extremity of dissolution, than that there should be any reaching back towards life. To forget! To forget! Utterly, utterly to forget, in the great forgetting of death. To break the core and unit of life, and to lapse out on the great darkness. Only that. To break the clue, and mingle and commingle with the one darkness, without afterwards or forwards. Let the black sea of death itself solve the problem of futurity. Let the will of man break and give up.

What was that? A light! A terrible light! Was it figures? Was it legs of a horse colossal—colossal above him: huge, huge?

That final image of overpowering immediacy is only the enemy, who find the body. "No Winifred, no children"; they have long been lost. "No world, no people"; Egbert longed for this from the start. "Let the will of man break and give up"; thus the recurrent Lawrencean death longing. The death scene explains what Lawrence's earlier rhetoric in the story did not: the hero's sensitive withdrawal from life; his failure as a man despite his sensitivity and goodness and love (or even because of them); his nostalgic dream of a purer past (the old England)—all are but the surface to a deeper nihilism and a longing for death.

Earlier in this chapter was quoted an incantation to death from one of Lawrence's essays of about the same period; it says essentially the same thing. While there is no need to identify completely the author with the protagonist in *England, My England*—even art as personal therapy must allow for some selection and transformation of the material—Lawrence must be understood as at least partly his own Georgian hero of ineffectual sensitivity demanding universal destruction. Since our concern is not biography, we need not document the nonliterary aspect of the theme, but to any reader of most of Lawrence the agonized death longing should be evident. We need not read this as a denial of the commonly accepted view of Lawrence as a prophet-of-life. The nihilist may be affirming the irreducible and poignant desideratum left after the destruction of the phantasmagoria of ordinary and ideal beliefs. What remains is not skeptical doubt, but certainty as to the annihilating limits that define the precarious fact of life.

IV

"The tragic consciousness," Lawrence writes in one of his essays, "has taught us . . . that one of the great needs of mankind is a knowledge and experience of death. . . ."[23] In *Odour of Chrysanthemums*,[24] we can see Lawrence's pursuit of this knowledge operating at yet another level—social and thematic—than those so far examined. This story combines a "realistic" study of a domestic scene and a poetic statement on the relation of death and passion. A sense symbol links them— the flowers that the miner's wife, early in the story, puts on her dress, and about which she later says: "It was chrysanthemums when I married him, and chrysanthemums when you were born, and the first time they had ever brought him home drunk, he'd got brown chrysanthemums in his button-hole." This time the "wan flowers," which Lawrence also uses elsewhere as a death trope, presage the end of the self-destructive miner and a shattering moment of illumination for his embittered and unyielding wife.

The harsh domestic scene of the black-browed and unbending pregnant miner's wife and her two children develops with forceful physical immediacy. Unlike Lawrence's almost invariably satirical portraits of middle-class life or his rhetorical and ideological pictures of vestigial aristocracy, his presentations of lower-class life have a poignant realism unusual in literature because of the almost complete avoidance of sentimental and patronizing stereotypes. Much more than Tolstoy or George Eliot, Lawrence is psychologically as well as physically exact in catching the complexity of the ordinary embittered wife's resentment, self-pity, and covert affection for her children when she indirectly questions them about their father or scoffs at their imaginings. The Lawrencean style avoids sentimentality by giving the domestic drama a kind of cosmic impersonality. Part of this may be noted in such scenic effects as the opening description of the mining countryside, with a glimpse of an anonymous woman "insignificantly trapped between the jolting black wagons and the hedge. . . ." And part of the eloquence comes from a realism infused with Lawrence's dominant thematic metaphors, not only the chrysanthemums, but the recurrent images of darkness and fire, which come to equal death and passion.

The first half of the story builds up the pervading domestic tone of anger, resentment, self-pity, and anguish while the family awaits the return of the miner. The wife alternates in moral indignation at her drinking husband and fear of some great pathos. By careful melodrama, Lawrence prepares for the miner again being carried home, amid the cold smell of chrysanthemums. This time he is dead, smothered by a mine cave-in. The long, ritualized revelation scene of the miner's wife and his mother preparing the dead body culminates in the wife realizing his remoteness in death as the final statement of what he has always been to her—"utterly inviolable." To deny this dread isolation she embraces the corpse: "She seemed to be listening, inquiring, trying to get some connection. But she could not. She was driven away. He was impregnable." This is a double revelation—of her failure in love, as a wife and person, and of the absolute aloneness and defeat that is the limiting condition of life.

The eyes, half shut, did not show glazed in the obscurity. Life with its smoky burning gone from him, had left him apart and utterly alien to her. And she knew what a stranger he was to her. In her womb was ice of fear, because of this separate stranger with whom she had been living as one flesh. Was this what it all meant—utter, intact separateness, obscured by heat of living? In dread she turned her face away. The fact was too deadly. There had been nothing between them, and yet they had come together, exchanging their nakedness repeatedly. Each time he had taken her, they had been two isolated beings, far apart as now. He was no more responsible than she. The child was like ice in her womb. For as she looked at the dead man, her mind, cold and detached, said clearly:

"Who am I? What have I been doing? I have been fighting a husband who did not exist. *He* existed all the time. What wrong have I done? What was that I have been living with? There lies the reality, this man."

Years of marriage and domesticity, children (who "did not unite them"), a way of life, yet "There had been nothing between them." They "had met in the dark and fought in the dark," not knowing each other, not accepting each other. The reason was partly sexual: "She looked at his naked body and was ashamed, as if she had denied it." She admits to herself that as a wife and a woman "she had been wrong." She has denied the "heat," which is the only barrier against the "ice" of fear and death. The rigid and righteous wife has, in both a sexual and in a more general sense, denied her husband's manhood and his individuality, so the failure is more than that of the joint identity which is marriage. "They had denied each other in life." While "grateful to death, which restored the truth," she still resides in the sense of defeat. As the story rhetorically concludes, she has found the ultimate failure of herself: "She knew she submitted to life, which was her immediate master. But from death, her ultimate master, she winced with shame and fear." [25]

For Lawrence—as for this wife who has learned her own failure and denial—the love ethos depends on knowledge of death and its absoluteness. The man, too, was trapped in life as he was trapped in the dark mine in death. Death restores the "truth" of the moments of limited and direct importance in life. It is the confrontation of death, as in the passage quoted, which raises the questions: "Who am I? What have I been doing?" For Lawrence, the answers almost always illuminate a denial of immediate life. But most of the time, Lawrence holds, for most people, this truth is too painful to be recognized. Thus, he must insist on the harshest fact of reality—death, an absolute meaning in, as well as of, life.

But should not the author of a family-generation saga (*The Rainbow*) and of the most famous modern tale of salvational eros (*Lady Chatterley's Lover*) be understood as a sensualist life-affirmer? Not in any simple sense. When we look at one of Lawrence's few fictions about a sensualist, *The Primrose Path*,[26] we see how he restricts the value of the "black-sheep" sensualist uncle. By narration, Lawrence confines the story to a somewhat priggish (and autobiographical) nephew, unlike the uncle who is "at outs with respectability." Even the hearty uncle's starting point rests on a negation. When the nephew tells him that his favorite sister just died of cancer, the rebel uncle replies; "What, lad, do you see any God at the back of that? I'm damned if I do." The uncle's response illustrates the traditional objection to a divinely ordered universe: the dead woman had been an exceptionally good person, but no relation exists between justice and her suffering. The uncle then points up his realistic view by gesturing toward the crowd in the city street: "You've only to look at the folk in the street to know there's nothing keeps it going but gravitation."

What keeps the uncle's world going is the dialectic of sensuality and terror, Lawrence's perpetual polarity of love and death. The uncle once married a beautiful woman who lacked "warmth"; later he cast off the frigid wife and fled to the colonies with another woman. That sensuality also turned to fear, and the uncle ran away again, this time back to London to establish a ménage with a young woman. We see the close relationship of sexual longing and death in the story's main episode of the uncle and nephew's visit to the uncle's first wife—also dying of cancer, as do so many of Lawrence's frigid and moral women, from his mother on. The uncle's fear of death—and this is the denouement of this small story—drives him not to piety but to sensuality.

Returning to the uncle's latest ménage (the young girl and her mother as the servant), the moralistic narrator gives the reader the details that affect a genteel young man—the uncle keeping his coat on (as in a bar), his bullying defensive manner, etc. However, he also notes the authentic basis of the relation. It is not social or moral continuity but amoral passion: the uncle sees in the girl "something impersonal, the female, not the woman." And the girl is "playing with passion, afraid of it . . . because it left her, the person, out of count." Not life but passional conflict provides the Lawrencean affirmation. Behind that lies annihilation, for when the uncle comes into contact with the girl there comes "into his bearing, into his eyes, the curious smile of passion, pushing away even the death-horror. It was life stronger than death in him."

The bones of annihilation give the flesh both purpose and pathos. When we compare the hardness of Lawrence's aye-saying but obsessed and anguished sensual protagonists with those of, say, Joyce Cary, Jean Giono, and Nikos Kazantzakis, we see how much less sensual and how much harder and psychologically more penetrating Lawrence is. Not that *The Primrose Path,* as the pat mockery of the title warns us, amounts to much; it suffers from superficial Anglo-Saxon moralizing by the narrator-nephew, who concludes the story with an intrusive leap into the future to prove his prediction that the girl will leave the uncle. As presented, the ethical constantly vitiates the passional. In Lawrence's search for transcendence of nihilism via the passional, rather than for sensual acceptance, imposed moralizing perhaps becomes inevitable.

Whether viewed biographically or thematically, Lawrence, the raging, dying wanderer, reveals nihilism and a lack of balancing organic continuity. For example, most of Lawrence's heroes and heroines no more raise children and find the biological continuum of life than did their author. The personal malaise may have strengthened the insight. At any rate, Lawrence perceives that eros has existential meaning separate from generation. Furthermore, the generations no longer appear as the crucial image of values in a mass society. Thus, children are significant in the novels only in the past generations—*The White Peacock* and *The Rainbow*—or in a projected, but necessarily incomplete and uncertain, pastoral-utopian flight from society—the pregnancy endings to *The Lost Girl* and *Lady Chatterley's*

Lover. For Lawrence, the family rests on some deeper image of meaning, some heroic quality of purposive maleness, which (as we see in the collapse of the family in *England, My England*), does not exist in "the hard white light of our fatherless world." The death of god and the father gives primacy, in the whole direction of Lawrence's work, to regeneration over generation.

In some of Lawrence's best fictions, such as *The Virgin and the Gipsy* and *The Horse Dealer's Daughter,* the regenerative waters open the salvational eros. With proper irony, then, Lawrence's more literal baptismal story, *The Christening,*[27] has generation without regeneration. By that agonizingly clear perception of family life so alien to the sentimentalist, Lawrence reveals the familial bond as proud hatred. The family of a retired and disintegrating coal miner shows violence, "hard pity," and an obedience "more intolerable than the most hateful discord." Each child shows the scars—the sensitive older daughter, a schoolteacher with heart disease who keeps up the family pride; the rough bully of a malicious son; and the younger daughter resentfully mothering her bastard by a man that she despises. In Lawrence's objective but intense narration of this primordial family, the ritual of baptism simply certifies the bastardy of the willful and well-to-do collier and his self-willed children as the legacy unto the third generation.

We dramatically see the irrelevance of the Christian ethos to the more primitive image of authority in the big, ugly, and nervous clergyman who comes to the house for the christening: he is "full of gentleness, but he seemed as if he could not see distinctly, could not get things clear." His "unseeing" eyes and "vague tenderness" give no strength when confronting the patriarch. Between the clergyman and the father—the New Testament and the Old Testament—tenderness must go down before authority in a harsh reversal. The violent father preaches to the preacher; the slobbering self-willed wreck of a man makes the prayer after fiercely naming the bastard child for himself:

"Lord, what father has a man but thee? . . . Thou art father of this
child as is fatherless here. . . . I've stood between thee and my children.
And they've grown twisted, because of me. Who is their father, Lord,
but thee? But I put myself in the way, they've been plants under a
stone, because of me. . . . It would ha' been better if they'd never
known no father. No man is a father, Lord. . . ."

True to the old man's confession, the children have no father;
authority has destroyed all spiritual and emotional life. The
clergyman sits uncomprehending while the children harden
themselves against "the whole emotional business," "discon-
nected" and "bewildered by the stone" of the old man's confession. The story ends with a bitter tribute to the curse of authority that creates emotional bastardy:

The father sat big and unheeding in his chair, his eyes vacant, his
physique wrecked. He let them do as they would, he fell to pieces. And
yet some power, involuntary, like a curse, remained in him. The very
ruin of him was like a lodestone that held them in its control . . . in
his dissolution even he compelled their being. They had never lived;
his life, his will, had always been upon them and contained them. . . .
The day after the Christening he staggered in at the doorway declaring,
in a loud voice, with joy in life still: "The daisies light up the earth, and
clap their hands in multitudes, in praise of the morning." And his daughters shrank, sullen.

Within the old authority, baptism can produce no rebirth into
the daisy-filled world of joyous morning. For regeneration, the
father must die; but with the loss of the extreme, Old Testament
power and joy, where, in the fatherless world, can there be
generation? Lawrence searches for the old authority and affirmation of life against death, but also for the break from that same
wrecked power so as to allow the new life and dispensation. He
must thus follow out his very personal and penetrating destructive obsessions. The cost is extremity, but one hardly expects this
kind of intense truth at a lesser price. Lawrence aphoristically
notes: "In order to think, man must risk himself."

V

Lawrence was willing to adventure far indeed—much further than his sentimental readers usually admit. In pursuing the destructive, the most obvious, and obviously repulsive, extreme is represented by what has often been labeled Lawrence's "primitivism." The paradigmatic fiction here is *The Woman Who Rode Away.*[28] In this, Lawrence writes *primitivistic* art but is not a *primitivist* in the sense of making a moral affirmation of a past or less civilized culture.[29] Probably Lawrence in some ways wanted to be a moral primitivist, but both personal ambivalence and an amoral aesthetic lucidity did not allow any such simple affirmation.

Typical of the Lawrencean view—the notorious "blood knowledge"—is his comment in *Mornings in Mexico* that peasants and Indians have "a sort of richness of the flesh. It goes, perhaps, with the complete absence of what we call 'spirit.'"[30] As with most writers in the vitalist tradition, Lawrence's use of the primitive almost invariably expresses a criticism of "spiritual values," by which he generally means moral and rationalistic idealism. However, this is not a simple moral choice of the primitive over the civilized; it is characteristic of Lawrence to note his own alien and negative response to the primitive: ". . . all savagery has a touch of squalor, that makes one a little sick at the stomach."[31] Or to take another example from a defensive essay: "I am tired of being told that I want mankind to go back to the condition of savages. As if modern city people weren't about the crudest, rawest, most crassly savage monkeys that ever existed. . . ."[32] The primitive thus tends to be positive for Lawrence when it provides a criticism of modern civilization—ideal and actual—but when the primitive is taken in itself, or as an actuality of life, it is found to be repulsive.

In one of his fullest comments on primitivism, Lawrence discusses Melville's and Gauguin's desire to escape civilization by going backward in cultural time to life in the South Seas. He insists that one can never "really go back." And he adds, "I know that I never could go back. Back towards the past, savage life." For even if our "forms and systems" are "false and foul," even if the great imperative of Western consciousness is to "smash" our civilization, still "we can't go back to the savages." We can perhaps "be in sympathy" with the primitives, and even perhaps take "a great curve in their direction," but we cannot be "life-haters" and "renegades" from the civilization of which we are essentially a part without decomposing.[33] While this statement appears earlier than the Mexican fictions, which represent his most extreme primitivistic art, the continuity is basic; neither in his literary and social criticism, nor in his autobiographical materials, nor in his fictions does Lawrence clearly affirm those who flee civilization for the embrace of primitive man.

The genesis of this restraint—the distinctive English prudence and realism never too far from hand in even the most extreme aspects of Lawrence—appears less important here than its resulting ambivalence. Lawrence sought out primitive peoples and religions, simple ("primitive") ways of life, authors concerned with the primitive, and prehistorical *civilizations*. As with most modern primitivistic art—from the sophisticated iconography of Klee to the rhetorical mythology of Faulkner—considerable self-consciousness and complexity, rather than simple moral affirmations, seem essential to Lawrence's work. When it comes to savages and peasants, Lawrence is just as often shrewd or repulsed as idyllic or fascinated. His repeated negations of the primitive, like so many of his other polemical statements, may have been part of a continual self-argument. The repetitions emphasize the ambivalence. A few years after the previously quoted rejection of the primitive—and while writing some of his most primitivistic fictions—Lawrence found himself fascinated with the "tribal mysteries" of the American Indians of the Southwest. Not Christianity but the primitive tribal force corresponds to his sense of ultimate power and aspiration.

Within a couple of paragraphs he insists nearly a dozen times
that "we do not need to live the past over again." [34]

But apparently a significant portion of the modern world will
have to do just that. Because of some failure in lived life, a great
many Lawrencean heroines *must* turn to the primitive in its
most extreme, self-annihilating forms. It should be noted at
this point that Lawrence wrote no fictions concerned with the
primitive as such but only with the primitive as it reflects the
need or malaise of civilized and overcivilized moderns. Nor is
there much in Lawrence's fictions that can be judged as a moralistic or sentimental image of either primitive people or places.
Not even Lawrence's more primitive heroes—although they
often have irritatingly inconsistent and compensatory similarities
to their author—receive simple moral or sentimental affirmations: they are usually described as dangerous, predatory, and
amoral, even when they are not rapists, as several of them are.
Similarly, uncivilized natural scenery in both Lawrence's novels
and descriptive writings receives passionate attention and awareness but appears almost always as inhospitable and harsh. In
Lawrence, as in other contemporary artists, the primitive functions in diagnostic or ecstatic insistence on the ominous, hard,
alien, and destructive.

In *The Woman Who Rode Away*, a well-to-do but isolated
middle-class American wife and mother longs for something
different from her ordinary life—the "mystery" that *"lives in the
mountains."* In her hope for something that has "wonder"
(again, Lawrence's key religious term), the woman rides into the
primitive countryside and lets herself be passively taken prisoner
by a lost tribe of primitive Indians for which she has been looking. The heroine—or more correctly, antiheroine—has been
briefly typified as an emotionally "dead" representative of negative middle-class American culture. Her responses, therefore, appear rudimentary and her somnambulistic acceptance of the
Indians simply consists of a ritualistic fascination with their "dark
power" and "glittering purity." No individual regeneration can

exist for such an antiheroine; she accepts without personal hope the tribe's lengthy preparations to use her as a sacrificial victim of "white consciousness" in order to restore the gods of "passional cosmic consciousness." In the final wintry scene, the naked American housewife willingly goes to an altar on an icy mountain, where she is to be killed with a stone knife on the shortest day of the year—Lawrence's adaptation of the Aztec death cult. Perhaps the briefest statement of the theme could be given by quoting Lawrence from another work during this period: "The consciousness of one branch of humanity is the annihilation of the consciousness of another branch." [35]

In *The Woman Who Rode Away* (unlike the closely related and more ambiguous *The Plumed Serpent*), there is, in principle, a complete opposition of the primitive and civilized, and a consequent destruction of the civilized. But this antithesis operates only abstractly. Civilization, even in the debased form of the middle-class American housewife, receives but little development. Nor are the way of life, society, and nature of the primitive tribe very fully developed. In both material and technique, the reader cannot posit a choice between societies, primitive and civilized, nor see one as resolving the ills of the other.

The novella only concerns the reversal of a hypostatization of consciousness, and it is this that the style creates. Despite some of Lawrence's usual scenic and psychological acumen—the woman's relation to her businessman husband, for example, is presented as a sentimental investment—the ritualized prose makes a narrowly obsessional consciousness the dominant element. The synthetic ritualism—dark powers, symbolic costumings, stock priestly figures, a "primitive" scene drawn in primary colors and tonalities, and, above all, the hypnotic repetitions—becomes ponderous rather than primitive in quality. But at the crux of the story, through abeyance of will, ritual preparation, and drugs, the woman does achieve moments of consciousness that contrast positively with her previous ennui and paltriness of feeling: ". . . once . . . she felt she *heard* the little dog conceive, in her tiny womb. . . . And another day she could hear the vast sound of the earth going around, like some immense bow-string booming." This attunement with the vital cosmos achieves the Lawrencean search for new consciousness and the transforming "wonder." However, in this story the animistic empathy and cosmic subjectivity are at the price of total destruction of free personality (the woman's willing captivity), of normal awareness (her isolation and drugged state), and, finally, of not only any selfhood but of existence as well (the ritual death).

Because of this fantastic and undercutting disproportion, there appears to be an overstatement of the theme within the fiction, just as there is a hypnotic repetition of ritual detail to overbalance the lack of the actual. Statements such as "the quivering nervous consciousness of the highly bred white woman was to be destroyed . . . and cast once more into the great stream of impersonal sexual passion" do not fit the action. The somnambulistic American seems decidedly underbred rather than overbred, and quite lacks the "intensely personal and individual nature" that the story demands and claims to negate. Only the doctrinaire could read this strident assertion for a dramatic fact. While Lawrence's recurrent misogyny toward emotionally dead middle-class Anglo-American women (which we shall examine in more detail later) may have caused him to overstate his theme of the failure of consciousness in this story, the fiction pointedly demonstrates that the longing for a more primordial awareness really covers a desire for annihilation in the fullest sense.

The author's final point about the rape-murder sacrifice, that it will insure the "mastery that man must hold, that passes from race to race," intrusively attempts to justify the author's misogyny. But we can apply to the repeatedly heroine-identifying Lawrence, and to his heroine, one of Lawrence's own insights: in the "civilized" person, "cruelty lust is directed almost as much against himself as against his victim." [36] Thus the "vicious-ness," which is part of the "creative" of which Lawrence spoke, may bring defeat as well as awareness.

We may, however, give *The Woman Who Rode Away* its due, though it is far from being Lawrence's best—either on its own terms or with respect to any unique insights or aesthetic qualities. The lucidity of the fiction's extremity persuasively shows the longing for a richer and unitary consciousness in a representative figure. And the suggestive use of a primitivistic ritual form, although somewhat synthetic, does eliminate the qualifying social, moral, and ideological considerations that would be present in "realistic" fiction and would tend to obscure the central fact of self-destructive longings. While the longing for both primordial awareness and for self-destruction is surely self-evident in the middle of the twentieth century, Lawrence's presentation remains remarkably stark and central. Unlike, for example, the crucifixion of the heroine in T. S. Eliot's *The Cocktail Party*, no stock Christian ideology glosses the violent longing.[37] And unlike liberal ideologists, who explain mass self-destructiveness by political rationalizations and individual self-destructiveness by psychic aberration, Lawrence shows the annihilation of selfhood and life as an amoral need and desire of the representative individual consciousness.

Lawrence's somewhat arbitrary use of various primitive and pagan materials aims to present images of prerational richness of feeling. But this may be less important to the distinguishing qualities of his fictions than his diagnostic images of need and his stark logic of consequent behavior. His fictions, that is, are rooted in the absoluteness of the emotions and their inexorable logic, which he believes in as well as perceives. "The essence of tragedy, which is creative crisis, is that a man should go through with his fate, and not dodge it and go bumping into an accident. And the whole business of life, at the great critical periods of mankind, is that men should accept and be one with their tragedy." [38] (Lawrence's usual use of "tragedy" seems to be in the broadest rather than in the formal sense; he also insists that "tragedy really ought to be a great kick at misery.") [39] Thus, the death of a Lawrencean protagonist is neither gratuitous nor the result of external forces; it is his or her fate, as well as a "kick" at the modern world—a willed and destined conclusion to a state of being.

VI

The primitivistic aspect of Lawrence's art deserves careful attention, not only because it confuses unsubtle readers but because it presents "consciousness," not moral or social forces, and is thus concerned with decadence more than with primitivism. Decadence comes from the self-consciousness and inner nihilism of sensitive individuals. It should be distinguished from the more social failure that Lawrence comments on, degeneracy: ". . . the collapse from the psychology of the free human individual into the psychology of the social being." [40] In life as well as art, though he would be disinclined to allow the distinction, Lawrence is obsessively concerned with decadence, the failure of civilized consciousness, and its symbolic or actual suicide.

Lawrence dramatized an important decadent type in his *Portrait of M. M.* In some senses this is not a short fiction, since this novella-length prose sketch is the "Introduction" to Maurice Magnus' tedious, and apparently dishonest, *Memoirs of the Foreign Legion.*[41] It gives Lawrence's encounters with, and some reflections upon, a man he knew for a year, and might be taken as another instance of that expertly cultivated modern "free-form" art, the familiar travel sketch, which Lawrence did so often and so well. But no virtue is evident in academic catagories which would separate *The Portrait of M. M.* from Lawrence's fictions. From the opening of the M. M. portrait ("On a dark, wet wintry evening in November 1919 . . ."), through its vivid descriptions of place and its staccato dialogues and characterizations, to the letters announcing M.'s suicide the following November, it utilizes both the techniques and the symmetries of the fictional art. The use of actual scenery—Florence, Naples, Sicily, Taormina, Monte Cassino, Malta; the ruminations on all sorts of tangential matters—religion, money, and war; the use of the epistolary method to unfold elements of the action; the incisive portraiture of minor figures—Norman Douglas and a crafty retired waiter—all may be found in almost equal proportion in such novellas as *The Captain's Doll, St. Mawr,* or in such novels as *Aaron's Rod* and *Lady Chatterley's Lover.* Lawrence the artist and Lawrence the man were much of a piece, and so with his works.

M. was a "cosmopolitan," "a little smart man of the shabby world, very much on the spot, don't you know," who knew equally well all the "short-cuts" and all the "first-class" accommodations everywhere. He was a bounder who wore custom-tailored clothes, had exquisite and fastidious taste, and justified himself as a writer (*"littérateur"* rather than "journalist")—"always talking about his work, even always working, but never properly doing anything." An upper bohemian, the pathetic *persona* of modern culture, he was also an end-of-the-road gentleman, or, rather, the sensitive and mannerly out-of-luck "half-gentleman" desperately staving off his final degradation. Possibly he was a Hohenzollern bastard, definitely an aesthetic convert to Catholicism, probably a homosexual. (Though once married to a woman—who developed an immense "contempt" for him—he is a "rabid woman hater," "mincing" and effeminate in manner, shrill-voiced, perfuming and pampering his body, "fussy . . . like a woman," always caressing men, including Lawrence. He was, as Lawrence knowingly emphasizes, the "adored" child of a beautiful but lonely mother whom he worshipped.) This sensitive intellectual, this swindler and parasite, was legally an American, actually homeless and one of the disinherited race, an "outsider" in Western culture because he so fully revealed its logic.

M.'s principle of spending the most when he had the least, of borrowing from strangers whom he did not ask for loans, of having refined proclivities and swindling actualities, and, above all, of having the imperative conviction that he must travel and live only "first-class," almost forms a comic-rogue story. The tears-in-laughter ending tells how M. drank acid with the police at the door and as a last testament left funeral instructions: "I want to be buried first-class, my wife will pay." Such is the image of M., living with bibelots and sentimental souvenirs, and pomades and custom clothes and manuscripts (autobiographies exposing vice in the Foreign Legion), in the Benedictine monastery at Cassino. He devoutly thinks of joining the order; he simultaneously is hiding from his creditors and the police; and he plays cicerone to Lawrence and argues for the medieval Catholic Church and the superiority of its mental and authoritarian beauty over modern crassness. Lawrence can more readily reject the arguments than the man: Catholicism, like primitivism, is the corrupting appeal of the past; and of Catholicism, like primitivism, Lawrence says: "One can't go back . . . the blood suppressed and going sour—no, it's too late. It is too abstract—political. . . ." Lawrence also makes M. another loan. But argument and charity, just as in Henry Miller's recent portrait of the same type in *The Devil in Paradise*,[42] only turns the superior parasite into a nightmarish appendage, pitilessly pursuing the benefactor and making the most outrageous demands.

Lawrence had a withering contempt for M.'s leprous gentility; he also was aware of what was wrong with M.'s sensitivity, religious longings, and rejection of the modern world, which were so similar to Lawrence's own, yet lacking in the harsh Lawrencean vitality. "He seemed to understand so much, round about the questions that trouble one deepest. But the quick of the question he never felt. He had no real middle, no real centre bit to him. Yet, round and round about all the questions, he was so intelligent and sensitive." This lack of final individuality, of a self-sufficient and purposeful assertion of life, marks the fully self-destructive.

Yet Lawrence is endlessly fascinated with M., writes to him, goes to visit him, makes loan after loan when he himself lacks money. There is of course an obvious emotional peculiarity about Lawrence's involvement with M. He finally rejects M., but after reading the letter telling of the creature's suicide, he said: ". . . the world seemed to stand still for me. I knew that in my own soul I had said: 'Yes, he must die if he cannot find his own way.' But, for all that, now I realized what it must have meant to be the hunted, desperate man: everything seemed to stand still. I could, by giving half my money, have saved his life. I had chosen not to save his life."

But charity is not the moral of this tale. Lawrence replies to his own sympathy without sentimentality: "I still would not save his life. I respect him for dying when he was cornered." While Lawrence weakens the end of the sketch by angry digressions about the war, and by some of the nervous and righteous stridency that mars so much of his writing (M. was a "Judas" and a "loving vampire" and should have "died sooner"), he ends with mixed feelings about M. Although he despises the typically Anglo-Saxon pettiness of *"keeping up appearances"* and hates the futile values of such a life—"God damn his white-blooded gentility"—he nonetheless has a grudging admiration for the man sticking to his grotesque role and playing it out to the bitter end. M. was a "rat," yet "had his points, the courage of his own terrors, quick-wittedness, sensitiveness to certain things in his surroundings. I prefer him, scamp as he is, to the ordinary respectable person."

In his reflections, as in his presentation of the wan character amidst vividly alive scenes, Lawrence shows that M. had to die, just as he had to be at odds with the world and in petty trouble with the police and traveling first class and betraying ordinary kindnesses and suffering his own sensitive horrors. Lawrence concludes that the "tragedy" of M., like that of modern civilization, cannot be understood or resolved by "charity" and "sloppy sentiment and cant." Decent human feelings are all well enough, but what we really need is a deeper knowledge of "the terrified courage of the isolated spirit," which defines the "boundaries of human experience. . . ."

This, as I understand Lawrence, forms his major theme. What are we to do with it? In the *Portrait of M. M.* he says, "take the bitterness and cleanse the blood." Whether Lawrence presents actual life or fiction—and he insists on no final line between the two—he searches out the extremity of experience and what it can tell us. Compassion is cut away in this harsh quest, and the absence of kindness is the most unpleasant quality of Lawrence and his work. We must thus accord Lawrence his own unsentimental treatment. The destructiveness in Lawrence's tales, as in his attitude to M., can only be justified by some such terms as he applied to Poe's tales: "They need to be written because old things need to die and disintegrate . . . the human soul must suffer its own disintegration, *consciously,* if ever it is to survive." [43]

So far our discussion of Lawrencean nihilism has centered on self-destructive longings, and we must look at further developments of such negations. We need also examine such related motifs as the demonic, anti-idealism, the attack on the middle-class social order and modern woman, the insistence on the uniqueness of erotic love, and the reversal of traditional religion. Perhaps the real perversity comes from Lawrence's treating these motifs as ways to affirmation. For despite the dominant nihilism, there appears a positive element in the half-dozen fictions discussed so far. Whether innocent or idealistic, decadent or moralistic, the character's destructive act may indeed be his true fate, the moment that simultaneously destroys and sets free. Perhaps for that moment, when his life achieves purpose and pattern and illumination, he truly realizes himself.

But are not all these tales diagnostic studies of psychic malaise, faulty consciousness, weakness, and failure? Clearly so, but such states universally pervade life, if we are willing to see them. As to proportion, we shall see that the Lawrencean moments of heroism show an essential destructiveness toward ordinary morality, society, and self, in which the nihilism of the heroic simply reveals more defiant courage than does quotidian self-destruction. Heroes accept and exalt the nihilism of all life. Thus, the hero rushes to the extreme awareness; the ordinary must be dragged.

This reaching beyond any possible illusion for the ecstasy of the authentic and actual necessarily remains exceptional, and so Lawrence must demand a unique awareness. His terms aim at annihilation—the "extreme," the "unknown," the "dark gods," the "wonderful," which rule a dangerously heightened life-and-death force. But only by such perverse awareness does one break-out of "conventional feeling-patterns," as Lawrence demands, and thus achieve "separate individuality" and "a new world outside." [44]

CHAPTER II

The Demon Lover

*The devil and anathema of our forefathers
hides the Godhead which we seek.*[1]

I

OF THE strange welter of thoughts and feelings from the past
which provide the sources of modern art and attitudes, perhaps
those least adequately acknowledged are the demonic. Arguments praising the merit and significance of our major cultural,
moral, and religious traditions have been most peculiarly and
benignly selective in deciding what constitutes our heritage.
Religious aesthetes who delight in finding Christ heroes in the
incidental symbolism of literature have ignored an even larger
number of exalted devil heroes.[2] And Christian apologists for
literature have been particularly remiss about noting the actual
poetic depths of the past. Earnest pietists not only sketch an un-
lived and unlivable past but blandly recommend for our enlightenment and succor orthodoxies whose very demise resulted,
in good part, from heterodoxies of which the pietists appear to
be unaware. Then literary moralists apotheosize a "great tradition" of delicate academic sensibility which lacks most of the
heroic excess and peculiar passion that provide the major qualities of both tradition and greatness.

This becomes especially shocking when we reflect that one
of the main burdens, and certainly one of the major dialectical
functions, of many modern literary efforts comes from a re-

pulsion to blandness, piety, and orthodoxy in any form. The "modern" in "modern literature" may almost be equated with the spirit of denial—denial of historical and intellectual progress, of moral and cosmic benignancy, of our usual and public affirmations. Though obvious in much of our art, sometimes full awareness of the perversity and negation requires some subtlety. When confronted with the bland mirror of some art we must, as Lawrence once advised, "look through the surface . . . and see the inner diabolism." [3]

But usually this does not demand a very elaborate subtlety. One aspect of the demonic that can hardly be overlooked is the Satanist tradition in modern literature, though the frequently obsessive identification of our nineteenth-century literary ancestors with the devil and his powers and problems appears to many contemporary critics as "minor pathology" or as "embarrassing" gaucherie. Romantic Victor Hugo's efforts to get Satan back into Heaven, diabolic Baudelaire's prayer-poems to Satan, nihilistic Rimbaud's descent into Hell, witty Corbière's dallying with the devil, or skeptical André Gide's conversations with the "evil one" are but a part of a positive treatment in French literature of orthodox Christian evil. We might add the work of Musset, Vigny, Verlaine, Nerval, Huysmans, France, Valéry, Sartre, and Genêt, among others, to note how emphatic the Satanist traditions appear in French literature in the past century and a half. French literature, like French painting, has keyed most modern artistic movements. Analogous German traditions run from Heine to the late work of Mann; Russian literary diabolism can be traced from the minor romantics through Artzybashev; and Anglo-Saxon glorifications of the devil and demonic appear in Blake, Burns, Byron, Shelley, Melville, Swinburne, Shaw, and Santayana, among others, and may still be found in stories and plays in the 1950's. Perhaps, also, we should add the peculiar treatment of the devil types to be found in Hawthorne, Twain, Dostoyevsky, Conrad, and some more recent novelists. Romantic and related views of Cain,

Prometheus, and other outcast heroes simply show variant forms of the demonic—as do the excesses of Hart Crane and many similar literary rebels from the romantics through the "beatniks."

Nineteenth-century Satanism and its later variations appear as modified forms of ancient demonic traditions—our most fundamental religious heritage—which sought the dark powers of death, rebellion, and forbidden desires. The rites (and rights) of primitive shaman artists, of the Dionysian and other erotic mystery religions, of many of the medieval heresies, of the major pagan literary-religious tradition that produced romantic love, and of the derangement of the ordinary practiced in Symbolism, Dadaism, surrealism, and more recent "irrationalisms" constitute much of our cultural heritage. Since most of them depend on inversions of public values, they may be conveniently called demonic, though the "devil" may no longer be a central image of the demonic process. The modes of knowledge and experience that will not well fit into our touted humanistic, scientific, and Christian traditions are indeed vast. May we not, then, assume a sustained and rich demonic heritage, which has been, and still is, antithetical to official cults (which seek to obscure it) and to the institutional moralities (which seek to repress it)? Certainly much of the best and most interesting literature cannot be understood in terms of rationalistic or Christian forms—nor can considerable areas of our desires and activities.

We need, then, some sense of the demonic tradition—as a prerequisite for accurately understanding Lawrence.[4] Otherwise, willy-nilly, the reader will base his expectations, as have so many writers about Lawrence, on morality rather than amorality, order rather than rebellion, and on moderation rather than intensity.[5] Or perhaps we may put it this way: the reader of Lawrence must recognize the nihilistic way to knowledge as the arcanum of the Lawrencean lover and hero. As Lawrence summarizes the hero of *The Border Line* (discussed below), he was a true man and the living proof that "only the cold strength of a man, accepting the destiny of destruction, could see the human flow through the chaos and beyond to a new outlet. But the chaos first, and the long rage of destruction." This is a demonic dialectic.

II

Perhaps this negative way to wisdom may be clarified by first examining one of Lawrence's simplest fictional inversions of the usual values. *The Blind Man* [6] is a moral fable that reverses the usual moralistic distinctions: for Lawrence, the world of "darkness" reveals a deeper truth than the world of "lightness." [7] It is the blind man in his permanent darkness who has the "rich positivity" of physical and personal awareness, and Lawrence's hero, unlike such traditional literary blind men as Tiresias or Gloucester, shows strength not because of "blinding" moral acumen or intelligence but in spite of it.

In one of Lawrence's characteristic triangular erotic contests, the blind man duels—at a not quite conscious level—with a pale, cerebral figure from the "light" world of society, success, and rationalized intellect. Implicitly he struggles also with the part of his wife that has allegiance to that man and those values. The characteristic Lawrencean villain—intelligent and impotent—is Bertie: skeptic and barrister, permanent bachelor and cosmopolitan, and longtime Platonic friend of the blind man's wife. The slight action of the story consists of the visit of the worldly Bertie to the isolated and self-sufficient farm world of the blind man and his wife. The blind man's wife, dramatically pivotal in objectifying the values of the conflict between the two men, longs for both the intimacy and organic relations represented by her husband—sex, fusion, farm, social isolation—and the intellectual relations represented by Bertie—ideas, detachment, gossip, the world at large. Early in the story she sees her blind husband as "a tower of strength." But this very strength is oppressive, and at times the intensity of her life with her husband "made her almost desperate." Thus she looks forward to Bertie's visit.

The blind man is a sexual figure; Bertie is one who "could

not approach women physically." Lawrence's recurrent theme of virility versus impotence points up several principles of awareness. For example, the blind man praises his blindness: "You cease to bother about a great many things." Bertie is honestly puzzled: "What is there in place of the bothering? What replaces the activity? . . . when there is no thought and no action, there is nothing." [8] The following episode in the barn, as well as Lawrence's style, attempts to adumbrate the "something else" below or beyond the intellectual and social "bothering"— touch and physical awareness, a mysterious selfhood, a nonverbal and noncerebral relatedness to place and person, and the pervasive *felt* quality of experience.

In the barn, in the blind man's sensate world of animal warmth and darkness, the blind man, withdrawing from social intercourse, engages in the mindless task of pulping turnips for the stock. He requests friendship from Bertie, which, since the usual intellectual and social marks of relation have inadequate meaning in the dark world, must take the ritualistic form of physical contact—the touching of each other's faces in "the passion of friendship." "Passion" as a relation between people is totally alien to the man of the world, and so is physical contact, particularly since the blind man insists on acceptance by having Bertie touch his scarred face. The blind man grabs the reluctant and shuddering Bertie's hand and forces it against his scars. There are touches of the grotesque in this scene with its sexual overtones of "passion" between two men, and in the saint-kissing-the-leper trial of love.

The two men return to the woman in the house, the blind man jubilant in his belief that an act of emotional depth and intimacy has taken place. However, the story ends with the blind man's wife viewing the two men through images that reveal what has happened to Bertie and what the wife's choice is between the dark and light values. The blind man appears to his wife "like a strange colossus." The other man, shattered inwardly by the alien and primitive act of intimacy, is the literal and the metaphoric antithesis of the blind man. "He," the wife sees, "could not bear it that he had been touched by the blind-man, his insane reserve broken in. He was like a mollusc whose shell is broken."

The nerve-rubbing Lawrencean heightening is in the style as well as the theme—the repetition of "broken" and the vehe-mence of "insane." This triumph of the passional dark develops the usual Lawrencean moral, but it also reveals the usual harsh ambiguity. The dark and isolated world of physicality, intimacy, sightlessness, and emotion *is* oppressive in both meaning and style. Not only does it make the wife "desperate," it also makes the blind man desperate. Early in the story we have learned that the blind man, despite his passional belief, often falls back into the "chaos inside himself, when he seemed at the mercy of his own powerful and conflicting elements." The "rich positiv-ity" of the dark forces is a precarious affirmation, which lacks "control or surety" and slips over into the annihilation that gives the dark values their characteristic quality.

Lawrence's insistence on chaos, passion, withdrawal, the organic, and the acts of emotional violence, stand against self-consciousness, rationalized thought, social activity, and "norma-tive" behavior.[9] But we must not leave out of account the under-cutting and cruel irony to be found in the blind man's feeling that his passional ritual succeeded and that he gained friendship when, actually, he merely destroyed the would-be friend.[10] There is a fundamental incompleteness, pathos, and failure—in the worldly senses, at least—for the dark passions, even when they win.

Almost exactly the same points can be made about a quite different, weaker, and much longer fiction, *The Ladybird*.[11] Again, the story involves the dominant figure of the dissatisfied woman and the two allegorical males. Here, however, the hus-band is the figure of lightness, the visitor the figure of darkness —a more usual Lawrencean situation, and autobiographically closer to the author, with the demonic figure as the alien. Once more the hero of dark passion wins an incomplete victory.

The *ménage à trois* form of the story serves also as an allegory of the divided nature of the modern heroine's soul. But there is rather considerable extraneous material. We have the mocking treatment of the heroine's family, Earl and Lady Beveridge, the regal but passé aristocrats. This is tepid social comedy. The other parts of *The Ladybird* are myth, and rather stickily learned and literary in language. Lady Daphne (for allegorical purposes the nymph of that name) falls in love with an enemy prisoner of war, Count Dionys Pasanek (allegorically the outlaw, Dionysius in the Nietzschean sense). Lawrence's version of the Daphne legend puts Dionysius in place of Apollo —passion in place of wisdom. Count Dionys, emphatically a figure of death as well as of virility, has been wounded in spirit as well as body by the World War; Daphne has been wounded by that other major modern disease, ennui.

Daphne is not only the nymph of that name, she is also Artemis, Atalanta, Astarte, Cybele, Isis, and Venus. Dionys, too, is a literary compound—a Bohemian aristocrat, a Teutonic hero, a "dark" mystic and ritualist with his scarab and snake symbol of Egyptian ancestry ("the Ladybird"), and several kinds of primitive. Lawrence also puts Biblical language in the mouth of Dionys, particularly a favorite and rather misplaced touch of the author's, the postcrucifixion agony of Christ. Boris, Daphne's husband, a more "realistic" figure, is defined on the social rather than the mythic level—officer, politician, and English gentleman, though also a villainous Platonist who symbolizes the bloodless, abstracting, and idealizing intellect.

Our concern with *The Ladybird* cannot be with its aesthetic merits, which are few, but with the direction in which it points. In Lawrence, as in Blake, Yeats, and the other experimenters in self-conscious and synthetic mythology, the material illuminates more by what it intends to do than by what it actually does. Such a rhetorical *mélange de tout* of mythologies and literatures, and its correlative rejection of the modern world and modern liberal rationalism, appears also in Pound, the early Eliot, the late Joyce, and Jungian mythology, as well as in Yeats and Lawrence. Historical and mythological syncretism is perhaps the distinguishing stylistic direction of "modernism" between the two world wars.

The effort to mythicize the bored and purposeless upper-middle-class lady tends to suggest a nymph at a quite unmythic level. Unfortunately, the effort at poeticizing seems forced and produces a tawdry language in which the lady has "pearl-like beauty," is a "hot house flower," etc. There is a similar rhetorical paucity to the action of this long fiction, which simply consists of the lady's visit to the hospitalized Count, and his visit to the lady at the end of the war.

In the final action of the story, after a mystical communion has been established between the pure Lady Daphne and the dark Count Dionys, the lady is seduced. Boris, the moralistic English husband, implicitly encourages the seduction of his wife—a perceptive point Lawrence makes about more than one husband. The necessity for the lady's seduction derives not only from her revitalization but also from the failure of white-moral-ideal love, that of the husband who believes in a "higher state of consciousness" and a "higher plane of love." This goodness makes Boris a successful and socially beneficent figure, but it produces, Lawrence declaims, "adoration-lust" which is destroying the lady. The criticism of idealizing love never becomes very specific, but the opposite love displayed by the Count appears to be more mysterious and thus more attractive, though the emphasis is upon his rhetorical rather than his sexual prowess. However, the Count can only be the night lover. Soon he must leave his mystical union with the lady and go to meet his uncertain but fated destiny. He is to return at some indefinite future: an eternal cycle of return and regeneration—Lawrence's version of the romantic-legend form of demonic passion and death.

At the end, the husband, too, has turned against the modern, active world and is going to spend the rest of his life "brooding through eternity"; he seems, therefore, to deserve his wife's loyalty at least in the daytime. The lady is to remain forever divided between her day lover, the husband in the actual and social world, and her night lover, the dark outsider in the world of eros and death. The figure from the "shades" has brought passion, but passion is only an exalted and furtive moment in the actual world. The real consummation, as Dionys repeatedly tells the lady, is that "when you die you are mine." Thus Lawrence, despite the moralists, affirmed the traditional love-death passion. As he wrote in one of his polemics: "Death is the only pure, beautiful conclusion to a great passion. Lovers, pure lovers, should say, 'Let it be so.' " And Lawrence adds: "And one is always tempted to say, 'Let it be so'. . . . let it be a great passion and then death, rather than a false or faked purpose." [12]

We may view *The Ladybird* as an uneven Tristan and Iseult romance—Boris as Mark, Dionys as Tristan; the strange wound; the eternal return without issue; Iseult's divided fealty; and death as the ultimate consummation of love—which sharply brings in focus the being in "eternal solitude" broken only by the powers of "dark flame." These most basic Lawrencean images, as well as the declamatory and portentous tone of this mythic story, recur in the other heavily religious works of Lawrence, such as his theocratic novel, *The Plumed Serpent*. Like Cipriano in that novel, Dionys has a considerable burden of doctrinaire principle to carry as the true leader, the last aristocrat, a figure of authority as well as the dark lover. He is little, primitive, heroic, dark, semidivine, has animal attributes and magical powers, and avows his belief in the sensate soul and the "under-conscious." But he also insists on his masculine power in the social realm, on aristocracy, and on an ethic that includes "obedience, submission, faith, belief, responsibility, power." In his myth, as well as in his polemics, Lawrence insists upon the necessity of the aristocratic principle, as do most of the other mythicizers of "modernist" literature.[13] But in this crux of "authority" I find both a serious contradiction in Lawrence's thought and a fundamental incoherence in his art.

The dark hero is emphatically "the outsider." From where, then, his sense of power and authority? It comes from legend, myth, the unconscious, as well as from a literary Bohemia, but most importantly from the "Kingdom of Death," for he is "King of Hades." This figure of furtive passion, fire, and rebellion, this black magician of the ladybird scarab with its demonic snake, undergoes, in his nocturnal communion with the lady, a peculiar regeneration that cannot exist in the daytime and actual world and that must remain "like death, risen death." He leaves with the words and powers of death still on his lips.[14] The resurrection of the hero from the shades with his war wounds and despair—like the resurrection of the upper-middle-class lady from ennui and respectability—is, in a phrase of Lawrence's, from a crucifixion "with the head down." Dionys' power is demonic.

Can the demonic outsider be a figure of social authority? Not, surely, if he is to remain the outsider, the rebel, the force of seduction and flame, mystery and darkness, passion and death. Lawrence, in the works of his middle period, covered by the novels *Aaron's Rod, Kangaroo, The Plumed Serpent,* and *The Boy in the Bush,* continually tried to make the rebellious outcast a leader and master. In his last works—*The Virgin and the Gipsy, Lady Chatterley's Lover,* and *The Man Who Died*— social authority for the hero was rejected. There is little reason to argue with those critics who find the interesting but strident and hortatory "leadership" works to be aesthetic and intellectual failures. Perhaps basic artistic failure shows itself in the forced pastiche of literary myth and social realism. This produces a synthetic language and a pretentiously literary and allusory style. The attempt to transform a rebel from the actual world into a semidivinity depends on an ideological artifice which denies art. This failure, I would like to suggest, rests on the refusal of the rebel—Dionys and Lawrence—to play the true role as perpetual outsider—and pay the lonely and profound price.

III

Fortunately, Lawrence made other, and aesthetically better, explorations of similar material, which do not sully the demonic theme by playing at the god of political authority who remains the fundamental anathema of Lawrencean insight. For the point of all the dark heroes is that the world of passion must be alien to the domestic and social order. The intense desires connected with the deepest knowledge of sexuality and death reveal an ultimate chaos and the denial of all authority. Love and death are final ontological entities, things-in-themselves. Such insight into pure being is not how one wins and rules the daily world.

From the start, Lawrence's work centered on the demonic. One of his simplest and earliest demonic works was the story *A Fragment of Stained Glass.*[15] This brief tale, with its rather awkward device of multiple first-person narration, starts with an undelineated narrator visiting a curate, who reads his dinner guest a passage from a fifteenth-century manuscript in which a monk describes a visit of the devil on a winter night. The "jump at God" by a devil with "face flaming" broke the "lovely image of the glasse," a chapel stained-glass window of a crucifixion. The inverted resurrection of the devil coming through the crucifixion image is explained by another narrative, the first person account of a horse serf who was the "fiend."

The serf struck a horse, got bit in the mouth in return, then retaliated by killing the horse with a hatchet. In punishment, the serf was brutally flogged by his master; he revenged himself by firing the stables and the manor house. All this violence occurs in two short paragraphs. But despite some awkwardness in the handling, the remaining dramatic narrative has an effective physical intensity with all the sharp delineations and contrasts of a "primitive" painting. The agonized serf seeks help from his girl, a miller's daughter with red hair, called "the fox." At the mill he crawls into a pigsty and suckles himself, for both food and warmth, on a brood sow. This figure of violence, crime, and degradation is a hero of passion.

The serf takes the girl with him to join the outlaws, "lest being alone were worse emptiness than hunger." The images of their love link with violence, such as the blood from his wounded mouth each time he kisses the girl. The fleeing lovers come upon an abbey in a snowstorm, and the girl asks her lover to pluck the "scarlet flower" from the lighted stained-glass window, behind which midnight services are being conducted. The serf breaks the stained glass window, cuts himself, and obtains a piece of the red glass. In the process his wild and flame-lighted face appears through the opening as a devil to the pious worshippers below. The lovers flee again and spend the night clasped together in the snow. In the morning the serf takes from his bosom the piece of "coloured light" but finds that by day-light it has lost its "magic" and is now "black and rough." The girl insists that the glass is still really "red and shining" and, with her faith in the power of passion, asks the serf not to be afraid. He answers:

> "It is bloodstone. . . . It will hurt us, we shall die in blood."
> "But give it to me," she answered. . . .
> "It is my blood," I said.
> "Give it," she commanded, low.
> "It is my life stone," I said.
> "Give it me," she pleaded.
> "I gave it her. . . . I took her. . . ."

Such blood-and-life giving with its consummation ritual reappears later in Lawrence in the cosmic poetry of "blood-knowledge." The consummation is both an end in itself and the end. The lovers fall asleep and wake to "the sound of wolves." Here ends the improbable narrative of the serf. Back in the initial modern scene, the curate hurriedly adds to the narrative:

". . . they lived happily ever after." But that is not the right ending to a demonic fairy tale, and the visitor has the final word, "No."

Though too crudely simple to be important art, this Gothic fantasy of demonic passion shows Lawrence's basic metaphoric pattern of the lover as the destructive fiend, along with all the related fire imagery—fox, bloodstone, devil face, etc.—and the amoral rebellion. The "life stone" will not save the nihilistic lovers, and the religion of eros is defeated, on the surface. But the story, which undoubtedly owes much of its coloration to pre-Raphaelite medievalizing, has a larger religious significance for Lawrence: the curate narrator calls it "the Bible of the English people—the Bible of their hearts." The Mexican or Mediterranean paganism of Lawrence's later works changes the scene but not the gospel story of sacramental rebellion and passion.

A later and more sophisticated version of Gothic demonism is the story *The Border Line*.[16] We have the by-now-familiar pattern of two antithetical men and a love that is at the border of death. Only here the heroine dominates the narrative. Katherine Farquhar is married for the second time to Lawrence's impotent type, "a clever" lawyer and intellectual. Philip, though intelligent and successful, is dependent, "doggy," a success by "fawning power," pathetic. This contrasts with Alan, his late best friend and Katherine's first husband, who displayed an aristocratic "over-bearing manliness," unconventionality, harshness, independence, and passion. To vitalists such as Blake, Nietzsche, and Lawrence, pathos warps emotional authenticity; and the pity that weak men demand produces, says Lawrence, "panic-love." This weakness, and even compassion, deserve demonic wrath.

The story opens with the aging Katherine making a trip through the border area of post-World War I Germany. It appears to be a journey to death in which "the wintry landscape realized itself in her consciousness." At the multiple border line —of consciousness, Germany, war, and winter—the story

turns from realism to allegory as the heroine undergoes an in-
verted religious experience. In the winter dusk she is staring at a
Gothic church, which she sees as a living and threatening
"Thing":

> There it was, in the upper darkness of the ponderous winter night, like a
> menace. She remembered, her spirit in the past used to soar aloft with it.
> But now, looming with a faint rust of blood out of the black heavens, the
> Thing stood suspended, looking down with vast, demonish menace,
> calm and implacable.
>
> Mystery and dim, ancient fear came over the woman's soul. The
> cathedral looked so strange and demonish heathen. And an ancient,
> indomitable blood seemed to stir in it. It stood there like some vast silent
> beast with teeth of stone, waiting, and wondering when to stoop against
> this pallid humanity.
>
> And dimly she realized that behind all the ashy pallour and sulphur of
> our civilization, lurks the great blood-creature waiting, implacable and
> eternal, ready at last to crush our white brittleness and let the shadowy
> blood move erect once more, in a new implacable pride and strength.
> Even out of the lower heavens looms the great blood-dusky Thing, blot-
> ting out the cross it was supposed to exalt.

This is not Lawrence's best prose, but, as in Yeats and Faulkner, the Latinate rotundity stylizes the emotion of the apocalyptic vision. The bloody and phallic beast of the second coming,
the primordial urge in the blood, the demonic, heathenish
black heaven, and the ancient fear of the implacable menace
and mystery reveal essential aspects of the Christian tradition,
only partly obscured by the Christian symbols of religious love.
Furthermore, as do Melville and Yeats and Faulkner, Lawrence
here presents a demonic attack on the sentimentalist and rationalist sensibility.

At the conclusion of her ominous vision, Katherine sees a
man, "dark, with a dusky glow" and "duskily ruddy," "a man
who came from the halls of death to her, for her relief." This
demon lover, the ghost of her dead husband, takes a walk
through the dark streets of the border-area town with her. The
next day Katherine finds the same church "cold and repellent,"

without its demonic "Thing" in the prosaic light of day. But with her new demonic knowledge, she finds the wintry, war-beaten scene no longer "ashy." She continues her trip, and the cold landscape appears now "strong and barbaric," with "a frozen, savage thrill in the air." The exhilaration created by the apocalyptic and demonic, so basic to Lawrence's dramatization, is repeated sexually.

At the end of her literal journey Katherine meets her present husband, Philip, now craven, sick, and whining. She leaves him alone to walk in the snow of the mountain forests—the snowy mountains as representing the longing for annihilation have been discussed in the previous chapter—and she again meets Alan's ghost. To this demon lover she "yielded in a complete yielding," and he "took a complete possession of her." With the other-worldly brutality of the love-death passion, she can hardly endure the sight of her present and living husband when she returns to him. In his illness, Philip complains: " '. . . it's murderous cold! It's murdering me!' " "She did not mind. She sat abstracted, remote from him, her spirit going out into the frozen evening." With great reluctance she embraces her sick and terror stricken husband. At the same moment the figure from the shades enters the room, and the living husband dies with a "ghastly grin," a "thief caught in the very act." The story concludes: "Alan drew her away, drew her to the other bed, in the silent passion of a husband come back from a very long journey."

Lawrence's fictional technique compounds the major points of his theme. The style itself is repetitious, and the plot employs parallelism and recurrence: the demon lover repossesses his former wife not once but twice, and the love and death emotions are parallel and recurrent. The very lack of passionate relation between Katherine and Philip—the agony of many of Lawrence's more "realistic" stories—is here overcome by symbolic supernaturalism in the return of the dead husband. With considerable malice, the unmanly husband is killed off, and a total fulfillment of passion consummated. But it takes the fullest force of death—wintry nature, a war-end world, an apocalyptic vision, the death of the present husband—to achieve the consummation with the demon lover.

Lawrence carries the theme of the demonic a malicious point further in a later, and insufficient, supernatural story, *The Last Laugh*.[17] This short piece is obviously a satire on some of his friends—one of the introductory characters is a thin, red-bearded "satyr" named Lorenzo, Lawrence's nickname. The villainously laughing and mocking Marchbanks of *The Last Laugh* is the same figure as the "satanic" and monkish Matthew, in the trivial and fuzzy anecdote of *Smile*, who compulsively grins at the corpse of his wife. The miracles of *The Last Laugh* during a London night of apocalyptic snowstorm are only indirectly sexual: a mysterious, virile, and transforming "eternal laugh," heard from a bush and a smashed church, cures a deaf woman of both her deafness and "soul," gives a policeman a crippling clubfoot, and, finally, kills Marchbanks, the mocking intellectual. Pan-devil, recognizable in his bacchic laughter and the lascivious pagan smell of almond blossoms, comes back to "alter all the world immediately." But Lawrence hasn't bothered to provide much world, or character, to be altered; shattering churches, policemen, and intellectuals remains supernatural trickery. Quite properly, the Lorenzo who proclaims a "new world" when he sees the fresh snowy scene—in contrast to the "weary, sardonic" friend who sees only "whitewash"—does so "ironically."

The demonic serves Lawrence, as it has much of the Western tradition, as a way out for the intellectual, as transcendence for his irony. By carrying disenchantment to its perverse extreme— the godless universe becoming totally bedevilled—the ironist gets back to a sacred sense of wonder. But demonic sorcery creates only a pyrrhic last laugh when it fails to relate to a living world.

IV

The works so far discussed in detail in this chapter affirm the dark forces traditionally associated with the demonic. However, they comprise only one aspect of Lawrence's art. Other, more "English" fictions, are frequently taken as the healthy center of the Lawrencean view. With the perspective provided by the works just discussed, we can examine the demonic theme when its rhetoric is subordinated to a relatively realistic—rather than fantastic—set of simple characters in a lower-middle-class English milieu. Here Lawrence displays a full sense of time and place and thus contributes to the tradition of English fiction one of the "inside" views of simple life, without sentimentalizing it. The most powerful effects of Lawrence's realism come from projecting his peculiar religious-erotic melodrama into the crucial moments of ordinary life, so that simple and common love has all the turbulence of the demonic myth.

In *You Touched Me*,[18] a youth, Hadrian, has returned from the wars to visit his father by adoption and his two foster sisters in a Midlands town. This disruption of the "gray" lives of the old-maid sisters shows class conflict between the "ordinary" charity boy and working man and the now genteel daughters of the tough and whiskey-drinking father, a successful and retired brick-maker. Hadrian, presented as seen by the sisters, is "sly," "contemptuous," lacking all "refinement," and "full of plebian energy"; the former "truant" from school, who ran away to Canada at fifteen and later enlisted in the army, hates all class distinctions and authority. On his return he is a man, but one held "at bay" by the restrictive society of middle-class England. His air of self-possession makes him appear "common" and "dangerous" to the genteel virgins. The women are obsessed with the young man, suspect him of having returned to get the dying father's money, and feel that he is "a thing of evil," "a sliving demon," and "malevolent." The author adds: "Hadrian had some of the neatness, the reserve, the underground quality of the rat." Such a hero is not intended as flatly admirable; however, he also "had his courage, as a rat had indomitable courage in the end." The Lawrencean heroes are antimoral, even immoral, but have an older sense of "virtue." [19]

The crux of this simple story is evident when the most refined of the sisters dramatizes her unconscious sexual desires. One night in a state of "entranced" misery, when she is thinking "of her father, only her father," who may need her in his sickness, she goes to the father's room. She has forgotten that the father has insisted on giving his room to Hadrian. She touches the sleeper, awakens him, and is shocked to find that her somnambulism has put her in a crucial physical contact with the young man. "Well," said her calm and weary mind, "it was only a mistake. . . ." But the regenerative physical desire is never an accident, and "she could not reason her feelings so easily."

The covert emotional linkage of the father and the youth has all the disproportionate ramifications that constitute fate. Hadrian's arousal shows him the "same glamour" in the daughter as in the father. He bluntly decides that he must "possess her," and is quite willing to do it in an "unscrupulous way." Hadrian gets the father to order the daughter to marry him, her foster brother. The tough old man complies and threatens to disinherit his daughters if one of them does not marry Hadrian. The father's motives, too, are subterranean and marked by Lawrencean misogyny: he had a "strange desire, quite unreasonable, for revenge upon the women who had surrounded him for so long, and served him so carefully." (So, of course, had D. H. Lawrence.) The basic pattern of the author—the mixture of love and hatred, the probing of covert incest and misogyny in family life, the amoral passionate conflict—gives ordinary reality demonic extremity.

The power of physical contact in the unconscious—the fairy-tale motif of the awakened sleeper—traps Matilda. The fiction seems to emphasize that the sight of "death not far off" in the father forces the daughter to acquiesce. The psychodrama of the son replacing the father as master of both money and sex is emphasized in the concluding scene on the wedding day: the dying old man murmurs approval to his foster son for forcefully marrying his daughter. Lawrence's demonic negation of gentility and decency also has the primitive motif of ritual succession. By such dramatic cruxes, the ordinary reveals a deeper, demonic, and unconscious vitality; and *this*, rather than class sentimentality—so often emphasized by critics of Lawrence—is why the lower class shows more vitality than the rationalized and restrained middle class.

The Fox,[20] a novella, has similar materials and motifs more elaborately developed, though the emotional triangle is not father-daughter-son but a man and a lesbian couple. In *The Fox*, utopian-yet-antiutopian Lawrence elaborates a negative analysis of the two girls in their "artsy-craftsy" return to the land, a small and isolated farm. The desire to create a private world makes all the more crucial the problem of vital personal relations; the two women are "losing hope" because they "seemed to live too much off themselves." Furthermore, in Lawrence's fictions homosexual relations defeat hope and love, perhaps because of a narcissism that lacks the creativeness of genuine polarity.

The masculine girl, March, robust in a forced way and "pinched as if in pain and misery," shows a "natural warmth." The more feminine Banford is genteel middle class, fearful, and dependent. March's emotional incompletion and oddity bring the symbolic forces of the unconscious into action, particularly in the form of her obsession with the malignant fox that preys upon the chicken farm. The demonic animal usurps March's consciousness: when he "looked into her eye," her "soul failed her"; "spellbound," she cannot shoot the marauder; his image fills her with dreams and reveries; "her heart beat to the fox, the fox." The red totemic image is likened to a devil, a serpent, a demon that seems malign at the conscious level but profoundly necessary to self-realization.[21]

The demon lover, foretold by his fox totem, comes along to destroy the unvital harmony of the farm retreat. He is the soldier-grandson of the now dead former owner; and he is also the romantic outsider—the runaway youth, the exotic hero returned from Canada and Salonika, the strangely "knowing" and "wild creature," who, like Hadrian in *You Touched Me,* amorally desires both the property and the confrontation of the aging virgins. The lower-class hero is given symbolic portentousness by being made consubstantial with the demonic fox: they have a similar ruddiness, flaming smile, devilish qualities—the traditional marks of the satanic beast.[22] And to March, Henry "was the fox . . . she could not see him otherwise."

But perhaps we should define more exactly what we mean when we speak of the fox as functioning "symbolically," since the word is used these days in so many different senses. For Lawrence, a symbol points neither to an ultimate reality of another order nor to a unique entity within apparent reality; a symbol is simply an ordinary fact showing transcendent subjective meaning. Thus when March loves Henry, his red face looks like that of the fox, but when March is negatively influenced by Banford's genteel and selfish ideas, Henry's red face (the fact does not change) becomes alien and inanimate—"a red chimney pot when looked at objectively" and "remotely." For Lawrence, there is only *one* reality, but the meaning of it depends on the relation of the person to it, and subjective immediacy is only reached by the removal of obstructing moral and social ideas. The fox itself is an actual object that has become a figure of representation or displacement for the most fundamental desires. Thus, the night of the youth's arrival March has a dream of the fox singing in the darkness, and when she goes to him he bites her and whisks his brush across her face so that "it seared and burned her mouth with a great pain." This dream of sexual anxiety parallels her responses when Henry actually kisses her and she feels burned and wounded. Her other dreams relating to the fox—such as covering the dead Banford in the firewood box with the fox's skin—show the same subjective significance and repeat the demonic pattern of sexuality and death, the fox and the fire, and desire and destruction. (Such metaphoric details as Banford—who insists on harassing the lovers—appearing with chrysanthemums, stand for unfulfilled death, as in *Odour of Chrysanthemums*.) Put in the form of an argument: the crucial subjectivity that constitutes individual fate or destiny cannot be realized in terms of rational statements or abstract codes; it must be realized as immediate sense experiences to which the individual has given full emotional response, since ultimate awareness is simply the fullest immediacy.

Thus, too, Henry's relationship to March does not become significant until she physically engages his awareness, and he sees her not as a personality but feels her as female "vulnerability." To accept such subjectivity is to have purpose and commitment, far more than through any "idea": "She was his heaven and hell on earth, and he would have none elsewhere." Henry's reaction to this burden of fate, this total engagement, is "rage" in which all lesser, objective, ethics become irrelevant.

Engaged by his demon, Henry frenziedly returns to the farm he has briefly left, where March is once again under Banford's repressive control and middle-class ideas. As with Lawrence's recurrent double heroines (*You Touched Me, Women in Love, Daughters of the Vicar,* etc.), the moralistic woman is the objective and rejecting side of the self and must be violently negated to allow vital completion. When the youth arrives, he finds Banford ineffectually chopping away at a dead tree; he takes over to destroy the dead past, and, impelled by his love commitment, he carries out a destructive ritual. With sly propriety, he warns Banford that the tree may hit her. Because he said it, she refuses to move—as Henry expected—and he intentionally cuts the tree down in such a way as to kill her.

As with the other symbolic procedures in the story, the killing appears actual as well as symbolic. Such is the harshness of destiny and the perversity of love. Banford dead, March is emo-

tionally free and, with the romantic ordeal completed, marries
Henry at Christmas. When the ritualistic sanction of murder
for the fulfillment of life destiny occurs in *Sons and Lovers* it is
perhaps less clear, because the mother is dying anyway and because Paul Morel has been developed as an exceptional and
artistic youth. But in *The Fox,* and similar works, the violation
of morality and human life dramatically develops in terms of a
simple, nonintellectual, and nonartistic, hero. The implication
remains that not only the unique hero but Everyman must
transcend morality to achieve love and destiny.[23]

This violent religious quest, this romantic journey out of
ordinary behavior to the doom of love, receives part of its amoral
focus by a recurring image, the *hunt,* which points to the predatory nature of desire inherent in the love quest.[24] When Henry
first picks up the axe and solemnly prepares to cut down the
fatal tree, he looks to the sky "like a huntsman watching a flying
bird." When the tree limb strikes and kills Banford, "he watched
with intense bright eyes, as he would watch a wild goose he had
shot." The hunt image has been developed early in the novella,
with Henry hunting for game; hunting, killing, and skinning
the totemic fox of passion; and making the agonized decision to
pursue March and kill her negative self (Banford) so that the
"inner necessity of his life was fulfilling itself."

He would have to catch her as a deer or a woodcock when you go out
shooting. . . . It is not so much what you do when you go hunting, as
how you feel. You have to be subtle and cunning and absolutely fatally
ready. . . . Your own fate overtakes and determines the fate of the deer
you are hunting. . . . Your own soul as a hunter has gone out to fasten
on the soul of a deer, even before you see any deer. . . . It is a subtle
profound battle of wills which takes place in the invisible. . . . The
bullet's flight home is a sheer projection of your own fate into the fate of
the deer. It happens like a supreme wish, a supreme act of volition.

As we have already noted, Lawrence's symbolic mode consists
of "the projection of your own fate" into the living object. One
of its traditional forms is the huntsman-in-spirit notion, which

we usually consider part of primitive animism, a subordination of the factual world (but without denying its factualness) to subjectivity. It is an essential part of Lawrence's non-Christian, nonrationalist, nonethical religious view: the transcending of morality and reason so that one may will the destiny of desire depends on "how you feel" in the "supreme wish" of love-and-death.

But, all-too-characteristically for Lawrence, *The Fox* does not quite stay within the dramatic unfolding of the destined love pattern, nor does it stay within its logical architectural limits, i.e., it does not end with the marriage resolution. A strange coda of two pages (it may originally have been longer), more abstract poetry than fiction,[25] is almost a guilty refutation, or at least a denial of any simple affirmation, of the subjective quest for fulfillment. March finds something missing in marriage, something for which striving is impossible, we are told in summary statement. Apparently, this is not the result of Banford's death—rather brutally dismissed as necessary for Banford's own sake. March displays a "ghastly reaching, reaching, striving for something that might be just beyond." While March has not dramatically shown this yearning in the story, it seems obvious that Lawrence wishes to condemn a romanticism of endless longing and dissatisfaction (*bovarysm*), which might be confused with the demonic quest of subjective destiny. For true fate is not to be misunderstood as the "awful mistake of happiness":

The more you reached after the fatal flower of happiness, which trembles so blue and lovely in a crevice just beyond your grasp, the more fearfully you become aware of the ghastly gulf of the precipice below you, into which you will inevitably plunge, as into the bottomless pit, if you reach any further. You pluck flower after flower—it is never *the* flower. The flower itself—its calyx is a horrible gulf, it is the bottomless pit.[26]

This *symboliste* prose poem lacks dramatic integration with the character of March and with the marriage pattern of the main action, but its attack on the pursuit of happiness is relevant to the theme of the fiction and to defining the distinctive mode of

Lawrence. Not only does love remain an agony but the leap over the barriers of society and morality and emotional restraint to fulfillment does not produce any final happiness or goodness. The joy is in the very necessity of the leap—nothing more. We quoted Lawrence earlier as saying that one should go to the extremity of an experience but that one cannot live there all the time. Here is the fictional statement of the same point: the demonic breakthrough to the deepest needs and the destined sense of life must be achieved if life is to be meaningful, but the demonic cannot itself provide the order or continuity of life.

V

Lawrence has other, and even more extreme, demon lovers than those so far discussed, such as Romero in *The Princess*, the gypsy in *The Virgin and the Gipsy,* and the Christ figure in *The Man Who Died,* as well as some of the heroes of the novels —Cipriano in *The Plumed Serpent* and, in part, Mellors in *Lady Chatterley's Lover.* The type of the fiction—mythic fable, Gothic fantasy, ghost parable, "realistic" story—is less important for understanding the art than the recurrent demonic dialectic. Most of Lawrence's positive figures have at least some of the major aspects of the demon lover, but rather than discuss these here—we shall touch on some of them in later chapters—we might summarize his peculiar hero type, and then look for a more basic meaning to his demonism.

Like the traditional devil, the demon lovers are strangers, aliens, outsiders, to the prevailing order of society. They depend, one way or another, upon the primordial or dark world of sensate knowledge and magical power, and this almost always turns about a special knowledge of death and nothingness. The demon lovers—figures of "black desire" and "fiery" destructiveness— always violate the moral norms through incest, hatred, seduction, violence, adultery, murder, wrath, and rebellion. Their heroism displays cunning and amorality as well as passion and purposiveness; both tenderness and rage express their virility.

Others view such figures as dangerous intruders and see them in animalistic, demonic, and inhuman terms. The metaphors for the demon lovers draw upon their historical antecedents—the less reasonable primitive and pagan deities and the Christian Satan. The motives of the demon lovers can never be understood fully by rational or self-interest psychology and finally turn on religious images—"mystery" and "destiny," or simply "darkness" and "fire." These demonics show particular historical (late romantic) forms in their rejection of modern society, its wars, machines, masses, and middle-class order. Such absolute individualists not only show indifference to many of the usual "goods," they also throw in doubt much of normal reality. The demon demands that experience be intensified to the point where the uncertain lines between chaos and order, good and evil, love and death, submerge in the sense of vivid and intense life. As Lawrence once noted: ". . . the hero is he who touches and transmits the life of the universe." [27]

This "life of the universe," of course, cannot be everything but must be some distinguishing aspect or tone. When Lawrence called upon the mysterious "thing," the fiery "destiny," the "black demon," "blood knowledge," or the "dark gods," he asserted some primal vitality reached only through incisive negation and intense purpose. Like Lorca's *duende*—that dark power which comes "to life in the nethermost recesses of the blood"— Lawrence's demonic reaches for the rare but rich quality that transforms a form, an event, an act, or a man.[28] This demonic intensification, rather than the ordinary form and character, provides the unique aspect of most of Lawrence's fictions. The demon lover represents the vitalistic *ascesis,* but the demon power also appears in Lawrence's descriptive language of darkness, fire, and incantation for describing the ordinary world. And behind the pervasive excitation there moves a positively agonized metaphysic of the universe, an ultimate flux excitingly alien and mysteriously negative. "There is that which we cannot love, because it surpasses either love or hate. There is the unknown and unknowable which propounds all creation. This we cannot love, we can only accept it as a term of our own limitation and ratification." [29] The opposite of most mysticisms, Lawrence's demonic is a religious ecstasy—the joyous acceptance of an unloving and unlovable cosmos.

VI

St. Mawr,[30] an almost novel-length work, includes perhaps the most emphatic images of Lawrence's demonic metaphysic. Here the demonic tropes appear almost everywhere and characterize such diverse matters that aesthetic distinction nearly breaks down. The passionately negative heroine, Lou Witt Carrington, is an "outsider," as is her "malevolent" and "witch-like" mother; so, too, her husband, Rico, who is "a trifle Mephistophelian." The two horse grooms are also demonics: one is an Indian primitive, Phoenix, who retains a dark power that has never submitted to civilization; and the other, Lewis, is a bearded Welsh groom who looks like D. H. Lawrence and believes in solitariness and animistic magic. When questioned as to whether or not he believes in the devil, Lewis replies, "evasively," "I never met him." Even a minor artist-character appearing in only one scene displays the demon in his "tilted eyebrows," "pointed ears," and goatiness of Pan, pagan predecessor of the Christian devil, whom he defends as the "hidden mystery," the rich presence that can only be found in the darkness, "the god that is hidden in everything." [31] But the major demonic figure dominating the first half of the novel is the stallion, St. Mawr, Lawrence's symbol of the passions.[32] This mythical animal of "red-gold colour, and a dark invisible fire," burns with "demons upon demons" in his eyes and always raises the "demonish question" in the mind of the beholder. This "splendid demon," which the heroine feels she must "worship," this "god out of the darkness," this "master of doom," this "menace" and "power" from "another world, an older heavily potent world," has turned vindictive in passional rebellion against the futility and false authority of the modern world.

The largest significance of the demonic horse can perhaps best be seen in the pivotal episode in which the husband reluctantly rides the stallion to a cleft in the Welsh hills called "the Devil's chair." (This gives the heroine the chance to praise "the old fighting stock that worshipped devils," and to contrast them to the modern people who really "don't exist.") St. Mawr rears and falls back on his rider, and also lashes out with his hoofs, injuring another effete young man. While the injured husband and his friends and clergyman believe the horse to be vicious, and gelding therefore necessary, the wife perversely identifies with the horse. Later, she learns that the stallion was not at fault: he reared at a dead snake lying in the grass, and the husband was only injured because he did not let the horse have its head when it needed freedom. Now Lawrence, who repeatedly uses horses for erotic symbolism in his works, appears to be quite self-conscious about his symbols and his attacks on the ideal views of love, which he connects with Plato. Therefore it may not be unreasonable to see fiery red St. Mawr as the equivalent of the horse with the "blood-red complexion" that Plato uses in the *Phaedrus* to represent the passions. In Lawrence's redoing of the Platonic analogy of love, the passions (St. Mawr) have their own good reasons (the snake) for their movements, but the insensitive and willful ego of modern man (the husband, who has been fully developed in this role) forces the passions destructively back on themselves and others. Reason has its own realms, including the understanding of the role of the passions, but when it egotistically and insensitively usurps the passions, the rational ego vindictively destroys—as those with the demonic sensitivity realize.

At the crux of the demonic revelation, Lawrence leaves fiction and turns to the prophetic mode: the heroine has a "vision of evil." This vehement declamation, with its curses on fascism and bolshevism, centers on an apocalyptic vision of the world overwhelmed by "positive evil." In the bourgeois desire to make everything easy and enjoyable without believing in intense reality and experience, Lawrence sees evil "masquerading as the ideal." The "Judas" ideologies, which make comfort and convenience absolutes of faith, belong to the basic purpose of this civilization—"production upon production," the destruction of "natural creation," and the mad longing to "multiply itself million on million . . . until the accumulation of mere existence is swollen to a horror."

One can be highly sympathetic to Lawrence's awareness of a world insanely overpopulated, overmechanized, and overrun by authoritarian and fatuous religions of salvation by quantity without arguing that his vehement and redundant rhetoric provides successful art. Such angry exhortation marks many of Lawrence's longer works and justifies some of the negative criticism of him as a chaotic artist. But perhaps some truths about disorder must remain incompatible with ordered art.

With a subtlety characteristic of certain kinds of romantic thought and alien to Christian thought, the evil and the demonic are contrasted. The same point applies to the demon lovers who clearly act outside the good; they are amoral and impious, but they are not evil. Thus, the answer of the heroine of *St. Mawr* to the "mysterious potency of evil" in the modern world derives not from the traditional panaceas of Christian benevolence or rationalist amelioration but from a kind of demonic saintliness: "Retreat to the desert, and fight." Or: "Try to hold fast to the living thing, which destroys as it goes, but remains sweet."

There develops a fantastic irony, however, when we leave these gnomic utterances and return to the fictional situation and the heroine's either/or: "Who was wrong, the horse or the rider?" The lady chooses the demonic horse over the husband. She is now prepared to justify the demonic stallion against the society. And she sees her husband, not the rearing horse, as "mean" and as one of "mankind's myriad conspirators" who evilly will the "disintegration of all positive living." This raises not a moral but a vitalistic question, and an extreme one since most of the world is "positive evil" and only the inhuman horse represents "positive living." The resolution is the usual Lawrencean one of perplexed and angry flight. Dramatically, the heroine retains no other choice than to abandon noble husband, "emasculated" mankind, and destructive civilization and to flee to the American wilds with St. Mawr. Yet this transcendental sodomy must be viewed as a perverse choice without adequate "positive living" at any literal level. The choice of the demonic always tends to be ambiguous and alienating.

But before looking at the final extension of the demonic in *St. Mawr*, something should be said about some of the other aspects of this uneven but rich fiction, such as Lawrence's portraiture of the heroine's mother. This American matriarch makes a continual assault on English gentility. While horseback riding in Rotten Row, Mrs. Witt looks as if she is "pointing a pistol at every other horsewoman or horseman and announcing: *'Your virility or your life!'* " In contrast are the English "tight mamas who looked as if they were going to pour tea between the ears of their horses. . . ." Mrs. Witt's satiric playing of the *grande dame* in a provincial town, her grotesque fascination with funerals, and her contemptuous mocking of all she comes in contact with suggest a figure of heroically comic proportions. Though Lawrence amuses here, he also relentlessly pursues the negative side of his matriarch, not only by showing the lonely egotistical woman rejected by the groom to whom she proposes, but by commenting directly on the destructive female will: this "fiendish psychologist," who turned her vitality into destructive mockery, really "wanted to be defeated" by "the mysterious, intense, dynamic sympathy" of a deep human "connection." Lawrence's treatment of the matriarch—a mixture of perceptive characterization and author's doctrinaire exemplum—loses comic distance and, finally, we see Mrs. Witt as part of Lawrence's usual condemnation of the woman who refuses to submit to masculine purpose. She even had "a terrible contempt for the

God that was supposed to rule this universe." While the matriarch may be justified in her contempt for emasculated society
and its gods, women who do not submit to male purpose remain
futilely destructive.[33]

Lost in her parody of heroic masculinity, she resolves "to die,
at least, *positively,*" in a neutered world that has no sense of
"power" and "mystery." But toward the end of the novella, as so
often happens with Lawrence, the treatment of the character
becomes cursory, and the conclusion, though significant, lacks
dramatic justification. Back in America, Mrs. Witt suddenly
loses all vitality, now sees all things with "indifference," and
spends her time reading popular novels. Has America defeated
her? The author doesn't bother to dramatize or explain but only
indicates that she, too, becomes quite modern—"crystallized into
neutrality"—and now, contrary to her heroic intelligence, cannot even "decide to die."

What started out as rather satiric social comedy, then, has
turned to attenuated philosophical parable about the impotence
of critical intellect. The development of Rico in *St. Mawr* suffers an even more abrupt eclipse. Like so many of Lawrence's
characters, Rico shows that pervasive modern malaise of the
sensitive: he feels an "outsider." But this poor son of a colonial
baronet is sufficiently "anxious for his place in the world" that
he does not allow his interest in art to interfere with his becoming a fashionable "artist," and he is as "shrewd and sensible as
any young poser could be." He soon has a wealthy wife, a reputa-
tion, and belongs in upper bohemia. Because the portrayal is
negative, and seen only from the outside, it remains satire. Mrs.
Witt mocks unmanly modern man. Rico retorts, "*Somebody*
has to keep up the tradition of the perfect lady." His mother-in-
law makes the personal thrust back at him: "And if the women
won't do it, the young gentlemen take on the burden. They bear
it very well." Rico's purple shirts, brocaded bed jacket, weird
riding attire, along with his flirtatious but nonsexual relations
with women and his supercilious affectations—all belong to

the emasculation used by Lawrence for harsh satire of modern sophisticated men. Sexual introvert and social poseur appear repeatedly to be matching symptoms of modernity for Lawrence. It is inevitable that Rico's relation with his wife would be "a nervous attachment rather than a sexual love. A curious tension of will rather than a spontaneous passion." For Lawrence, such willed relations almost always turn destructive. And no wonder the lady prefers a horse!

With the emigration of his wife, Rico disappears from the story. The salvation of the heroine—the dominant shape of most of Lawrence's novels—again moves out of the social milieu. The heroine, full of revulsion for her society, suffering from negative freedom (she "had her own way so long . . . she didn't know where she was"), alienated ("the lurking sense of being an outsider everywhere"), and aware of the meaningless-ness of the usual success, flees to the wilds.

St. Mawr does not fully probe the psychological genesis of the heroine's desperate ennui, neither in her relation to her emascu-lated poseur husband nor in her extreme dependence on her willful mother. While Lawrence perceptively presents the ma-terials, the actual analysis develops in religious-philosophical terms. Thus the heroine poses the problem of her chagrin: "I want the wonder back again, or I shall die." [34] We have previ-ously noted the cruciality of "wonder" as a religious term in Lawrence's thought. The lack of wonder in *St. Mawr* may be related to the "positive evil" of the heroine's apocalyptic vision: the nonwonderful, dead cosmos results from the rationalistic technological, mass-middle-class civilization. The alternative must be the heroic wonder of demonic awareness.

The characters in *St. Mawr* are not distinguished by their moral qualities—they never are in Lawrence—but by their de-gree of wonder. Sophisticated English society, and Rico, who goes over to it, and Mrs. Witt, with her purposeless intelligence, show a defeating disenchantment. The two manly horse grooms —the Indian primitive and the Welsh animist—exhibit "mystery" and "wonder." The disenchanted heroine remains within the possibility of grace since she responds with wonder to St. Mawr, the symbol of demonic passion. Her quest several times takes form with Lawrence's recurrent animal metaphors: "I don't want to be an animal like a horse or a cat or a lioness, though they all fascinate me, the way they get their life *straight*. . . ." She wants to get life "straight from the source." Lawrence presents not a return to animal existence (we must "still be ourselves") but the need for fuller immediate experience, which has been lost in modern sensibility.

Once again we must note that sex-and-primitivism do not provide the real answer. Though half-attracted to the Indian groom, Phoenix (a psychological and plot parallelism to her mother's attraction to the Welsh groom), because of the "golden" quality of his vitality and nonegotistical harmony with himself, she also realizes the avarice, stupidity, vanity, predatory sexuality, and harshness of the actual primitive. The heroine, like Lawrence, shows simultaneous attraction and repulsion to the primitive.

In her search for a fuller and deeper awareness, both the primitive and the stallion (who now, rather awkwardly, turns into an ordinary horse) are left behind. The heroine does not get beyond the stage of purgation—the hardness and clarity of isolation in which she finds the "wild spirit" for her "mission" of purification. Far from "mechanical" society, from the "cheapness" and the "friction which is the whole stimulus in modern social life," and from dubious efforts at "achievement," she wants to "be very still . . . very, very still, and recover her own soul." Renunciation aims at transforming the disgruntled wife into "one of the eternal virgins, serving the essential fire." It is emphatically not a Christian asceticism. Lou says: "I don't hate men *because* they're men, as nuns do. I dislike them because they're not men enough. . . ." At the ranch, "Las Chivas" (the female goats—last refuge of Pan's nymphs?), she awaits the heroic vision of an uncertain future. As with Lawrence's last virgin serving the "essential fire," the Priestess of Isis who becomes the temporary mate of the Christ in *The Man Who Died,* the scene provides a presacrament preparation for ultimate eros rather than agape, for passionate selfhood rather than moral eternity.

We have leaped over the substory in this rather episodic novella, which shows the relation of the demonic to the final Lawrencean verity. The thematic functions of St. Mawr transfer in the later part of the fiction to the "malevolence that was in the spirit of place." This is the subject of a nearly autonomous story within the story about the ranch the heroine moves to in New Mexico—"man's last effort towards the wild heart of the Rockies."

The history of the ranch centers particularly on a trader and his New England wife, who, with the twin American drives of Protestant labor and the idealistic desire to command nature, struggle against a "curious disintegration working all the time, a sort of malevolent breath like a stupefying, irritant gas, coming out of the unfathomed mountains." (The "savage" spirit of place does not, of course, belong only to New Mexico for we have already met it on the first island in *The Man Who Loved Islands,* and it appears widely in Lawrence's works.) The unaccountable irrationality of the cosmos alternately locates itself in drought, weeds, sickness, accidents, human mistakes, and in the hordes of packrats who become "symbols of the curious debasing malevolence that was in the spirit of place."

The New England wife labors with a "blind frenzy," which shows, says Lawrence, a "sex-passion" for the place. But in front of the cabin she has a "demonish guardian," a large but "non-phallic" pine tree. It marks a deeper frenzy than that of human sexual passion—the "blind will" of the "pre-sexual primeval world." It provides a portal to the grandeur of the mountain and desert scene, the "beyond" of "pure beauty" that signifies the *"absolute"* and the *"ne plus ultra."* Thus the universe is the absolute demonic, the beautifully malevolent cosmos with its totally inhuman amoral force.

Between the absolute and the human lies the "raging, seeth-ing conflict" of life and death. The surrounding sense of cosmic destruction overwhelms the Puritan idealist—the death of goats, horses, chickens, plants, trees, and human efforts and hopes. However, by this very awareness, placed against the absolute negation of the cosmos, one sees the hard "flame" amid the "sordidness" that is the price of life, the violent urge to live.[35]

Again, Lawrence leaves the story for prophetic statement:

Every new stroke of civilization has cost the lives of countless brave men, who have fallen defeated by the "dragon" in their efforts to win the ap-ples of the Hesperides, or the fleece of gold. Fallen in their efforts to overcome the old, half-sordid savagery of the lower stages of creation, and win to the next step.

And every civilization, when it loses its inward vision, and its cleaner energy, falls into a new sort of sordidness, more vast and more stupen-dous than the old savage sort. An Augean stables of metallic filth.

And all the time, man has to rouse himself afresh, to cleanse the new accumulations of refuse. To win from the crude wild nature the victory and the power to make another start, and to cleanse behind him the century-deep deposits of layer upon layer of refuse. . . .

Neither primitive nor decadent, Lawrence here expresses a passionately disinterested balance between savage and civilized sordidness. While the mythology-cum-social-Darwinism of the first paragraph displays Lawrence's nineteenth-century intellec-tual milieu,[36] both the defiance and the faith in the inner vision (rather than in culture and institutions) as the basis of civilization belong to an ancient, and major, Western tradition in which the cleansing force comes from the demonic. For the Puritan pioneer suddenly realizes that *"Jesus and A God of Love"* and "Universal love" are *"nonsense."* There is *"no merci-ful God,"* *"no Almighty loving God."* The universe, both to the pioneer and to the modern heroine, reveals itself as relentless and destructive. Cause for despair? No, for it brings an aware-ness of "life, intense bristling life." As the heroine of the story within a story, and apparently the modern heroine as well, feels: *"This is more awful and more splendid. I like it better."*

Lawrence's awareness that life has no moral or rational or divine purpose except the furthering of intense and harsh life in its splendor of struggle and feeling is, I think, even hopeful, since it requires no illusions. (Unless the bravery of awareness and truth be the greatest illusion of all.) This enchantment beyond disenchantment, this awe after the death of the gods of society and tradition, becomes an exhilarating negation. The arguments of *St. Mawr*—whose fragmentary and frequently awkward scenes and insights have only been partially discussed —insist repeatedly on both the harsh negations and the liberating joys that result from such extremity.

Since it goes outside of love, this ragged but brilliant fiction provides a proper end to the discussion of the demon lovers. The demonics finally long beyond love for the absolute—and a loveless absolute, at that. Desire carries them to, and then through, love, which is one of the great intensifications of experience. They find that ultimate reality reveals destruction, which they come dangerously close to imitating, but they also succeed in stepping into true and vital life by perversely keeping one foot planted on the reality of nothingness.

CHAPTER III

The Destructive Woman

Anything that triumphs, *perishes.*[1]

I

THE Lawrencean pursuit of the nihilistic and demonic forces at the center of life provides an incisive perspective into the lesser destructive impulses of the psyche and of modern society. Destruction is not all of a piece, and we must attempt to distinguish between violence as a condition of existence and violence as a particular sickness. Often this requires subtle distinctions, but the *poet mauvais* is a connoisseur of destructive longings.

Starting perhaps from the Victorian sentiment that a bad man is bad indeed, but a bad woman is worse, Lawrence repeatedly uses the female to dramatize the sicker forms of destruction. Though the dominant role of heroines and feminine sensibility in Lawrence's fictions may partly derive from his sources (novelistically from the Brontës and George Eliot, as well as from the general English moral exaltation of women in the eighteenth and nineteenth centuries), the obsessive quality of Lawrence's interest in the heroine runs much deeper. As we know from the autobiographical *Sons and Lovers,* Lawrence was the sensitive son of a domineering mother with genteel ambitions. The re-enforcement of the Oedipal situation by willed conflict and moralistic repression assumes importance, as will be discussed later, to a specific group of stories. In general, the vehemence with which Lawrence treats the maternal powers would seem to require from the reader an extraliterary sense of why the author so insistently exposes what he called "the obscene love will of the mother." [2]

The heightened Oedipal hatred must also be a major source of his mystical misogyny. But Lawrence's vision of the female as a "nemesis," a "destructive influence," and as the creature most "subtly diabolic," [3] becomes more than a biographical problem. We may assume that the long tradition of literary misogyny from Ovid to Montherlant points to a deep and manifold distrust of the female powers. Even in such drastically different romantic views of love as those of Blake and Baudelaire, woman is diabolic. The Great Whore of decadent civilization derives not only from that lady of Babylon but from the treacherous goddess of many fertility rituals and the civilizing female disrupting almost any primitive masculine paradise. Indeed, most moralizing males in the Judeo-Christian tradition sometime or other write of Woman, like Lawrence, as the "strange serpent-communing Eve." [4] If misogyny is not universal, it is at least a major and inescapable tradition of our culture.

Lawrence's attack on the ever-present Eve rests on principle as well as myth. Antifeminist Lawrence writes: "When a woman is thoroughly herself, she is being what her type of man wants her to be." [5] The destructive women of Lawrence's fictions have invariably failed to submit to masculine destiny and order. The Great Whore substituted civilization for woman's true fertility. Civilized intellectuality marks the real witch: "Teach a woman to act from an idea," Lawrence wrote in one of his psychological polemics, "and you destroy her womanhood forever. Make a woman self-conscious, and her soul is barren as a sandbag." [6]

This male bigotry against women who are not submissive, like the nasty sexual malice of many of Lawrence's fictional portrayals, should not be "explained away." But Lawrence also gives his misogyny a modern parabolic form. At the mythic level he redoes Genesis with a prophetic purpose. "Why were we driven out of Paradise? Why did we fall into this gnawing disease of unappeasable dissatisfaction?" In Lawrence's view of the Edenic parable, it was "not because we sinned, but because we got our sex into our head."[7] Eve's fall represents the inversion of desire from a direct relation between a man and a woman into abstractions in which love becomes clever egotism, generalized idealism, sham sentiment, moral dogma, and all the other obstacles of consciousness that hinder the flow of vitality. Modern and "emancipated" woman, markedly self-conscious and self-aggrandizing, believes in ideas and images of love, in comfort, decency, and happiness, but can neither submit to love nor to any fullness of experience.

Nor is the Edenic "fall" simply a personal failure of love; it is also a parable of "the race," of the fate of a civilization. Genesis tells the tale of willful feminine intellectualism, the decadence of paradise: "Every race which has become self-conscious and idea-bound in the past has perished."[8] The twentieth-century self-conscious Anglo-American woman, the consumer of a culture of "happiness" and comfort, marks the triumph of a civilizing effort that finally brings destruction. Seen more concretely in terms of the materials of Lawrence's later tales, the fallen are the somewhat-cultured and intellectual, frigid, and rich, middle-class women. The bored and willful *haute bourgeoise* lady reveals the end of the Edenic road. For Lawrence, the society of mass technology and mass men may do the actual destroying, but the essential human strength and heart will have first perished from the triumph of petty will and pernicious ideals.

II

In turning to Lawrence's sardonic portrayals of fallen modern Eves, we should be aware that the willful woman actually dominates most of Lawrence's work, though in diverse forms. The extreme post-World War I parabolic figures, which we will emphasize here, were preceded by the harsh wives of his working-class genre stories.[9] For the dialectic about the distinctively modern destructive woman, we might start with one of Lawrence's most extreme types—Ethel, in *None of That*.[10]

This pointed but rather thinly textured story is limited by its "shocker" plot and its forced retrospective narration. An urbane narrator tells some undescribed friend of a woman he knew in Mexico. Ethel, the rich American, reveals our traditional sexual-fantasy type—pale, tall, blonde, attractive but essentially cold, and with that distinctly American "false-innocent" look, to which add a touch of the "diabolic." She also shows archetypal American femininity in her "terrible energy" and her unsatisfied mental "lust": first for literal things—antiques, art works; then, as her sophistication grows, for power over things—politics, important personalities; and, finally, for "ideas" as the biggest things of all—socialism, culture. Always willful and unsatisfied, she has gone through two husbands and a number of lovers but rejects sexual love as such and will have "none of that." Her bodily desires provide the means to abstract ends, and as a consequence she becomes restless and bored; the denial of the affective life has destroyed all spontaneity and *joie de vivre*. For substitute affections Ethel insists on her fervent belief in "soul," "progress," "culture," and, above all, in "the life of the imagination." With no little malice, Lawrence has epitomized the Great Western Ideas as the willful devices of a bored, wealthy, sophisticated, and frigid American siren.

This antiheroine shows no patience with "reality," not because of an authentic idealism, but because she lives in an egotistical fantasy consisting of "an imaginary picture of herself as an extraordinary and potent woman," one who might change "history." With physical revulsion from life as a basis, her faith in the "life of the imagination" becomes a form of refined and sick sainthood:

She said the imagination could master everything; so long, of course as one was not shot in the head, or had an eye put out. Talking of the Mexican atrocities and of the famous case of the raped nuns, she said that it was all nonsense that a woman was broken because she had been raped. She could rise above it. The imagination could rise above it. The imagination could rise above *anything* that was not real organic damage.

By pressuring the argument in a way reminiscent of Dostoyevsky, Lawrence extends his point to an attack on modern relativism. The American woman holds that the power of "imagination" can be used to justify "even the meanest and most bad things," and that one can fancifully transform a sinner into "an innocent child"—as long as you are the sinner. The point gets rather heavily driven home by the otherwise passive auditor of the story who interrupts the narrator to repeat the moral: "It's the modern dodge. That's why everybody today is innocent. To the imagination all things are pure, if you did them yourself."

The rest of the action of *None of That* disproves the cleverly egotistical notion of imagination and of mental tricks that attempt to deny tangible experience. The woman's discussion of rape foreshadows the test of a grotesque idealism that denies the body, and she predicts her own end: "If my body is stronger than my imagination, I shall kill myself." For Lawrence the absurdity of dualistic "idealism" constitutes "the real enemy today." [11]

Ethel, with obscured motives, is attracted to a "nada" character, a "brute" of a half-breed Mexican bullfighter, Cuesta, and to his "inverted passion," which makes him love to "play with death." Cuesta's "joyful cruelty" lacks all imagination, which the lady finds deplorable, but the brutality makes a deeper than conscious appeal to her own destructive longings. Entranced by the primitive's purposeful assurance, Ethel attempts to "imaginatively" seduce the bullfighter. As in some of Hemingway's more sentimental versions of the lady and the bullfighter, the desire for such a figure appears to be the frigid woman's longing for ritualized sexual oblivion. But Cuesta, a spoiled primitive, wants only sadism and money. He toys with Ethel, and succeeds in getting her to visit his home late one evening. Three days later the American woman commits suicide. Her last will and testament leaves half her fortune to the bullfighter.

At this point in the story Lawrence uses the plot device of

withholding a crucial bit of information for the carefully foreshadowed surprise revelation in the concluding paragraph. It turns out that when the lady went to the bullfighter's house he coolly handed her over to the pleasure of half-a-dozen of his bullring handlers. Ethel has her test case of rape. Apparently the lady's imagination is unable to override the body and reality, and she kills herself, as she previously swore to do. The denial of actual life in the name of a spurious idealism collapses, and we see in melodramatic retrospect that a sham "belief" in "imagination" and "will" merely masked a longing for rape and destruction.

This fiction, brutal in both its denouement and its logic, is not, one supposes, what the more sentimental readers of Lawrence think of as representing the author. As in many of his fictions, anti-intellectual Lawrence has brought almost an excess of analytic logic to bear, not only in the melodramatic plot but also in the shortage of particularized detail. Here the parable simply requires a type of wealthy, intellectually pretentious, pseudosexual American as archetype of the modern woman.[12]

The brutality of Lawrence's imagination takes a less clever form in a related and longer story, *The Princess*,[13] where scene and range of perception draw more fully on tangible experience. The Princess (so-called by her father—actually a widespread fashion in the twenties) shows more individuality than the heroine of *None of That*. Child of a late and ineffectual marriage, then isolated by her father's withdrawal (by taste and a small income) from ordinary experience, the Princess is the product of an implicitly incestuous emotional warping where she soon knows "the impossibility of intimacy with any other than her father." But neither the Jamesian milieu of the world of cultivated withdrawal from experience nor the more recent concern with the psychological "case" provides the primary interest in Lawrence's treatment. The progression of the heroine—kept by a mad father, then the mad father's keeper, finally mad and married to a father figure—provides hyperlogical melodrama to embody the theme of nonrational and inexorable fate that goes beyond psychology and milieu.

Lawrence deals with metapsychological dialectics rather than with the social and moral analysis of his nineteenth-century predecessors, except for acute incidental remarks and details. The deracinated, declassé, self-made aristocrat and demonic prophet, Lawrence, projects into three of his characters—the father, the Princess, and the Mexican guide, Romero—pieces of his self-preoccupation with the outsider. But the romantic motif of the alienated hero receives a devastatingly negative dramatization. The description of the father as a refined, reticent, unworldly gentleman, but a "bit mad" and an anachronism in the modern world—"like some old Celtic hero"—provides one version of the alienated aristocratic spirit. The father attempts to impart his unique tone to his daughter, who already is a strangely old-young child, a "changeling, not quite human." The father's legacy consists of a superior ethic, a "great secret" to be guarded from the contagion of the "vulgar," which centers on a denial of the ordinary world of ambitious and vain activity. A metaphysical simile provides the justification:

Inside everybody there is another creature, a demon which doesn't care at all. You peel away all the things they say and do and feel, as cook peels away the outside of the onions. And in the middle of everybody there is a green demon which you can't peel away. And the green demon never changes, and it doesn't care at all about the things that happen to the outside leaves of the person, all the chatter-chatter, and all the husbands and wives and children, and trouble and fusses. You peel away everything from people, and there is a green upright demon in every man and woman; and this demon is a man's real self and a woman's real self.

This extended romantic metaphor (it proceeds for another half-page) almost becomes the subject of the story. There can be little doubt that this "demon" of the "real self" is but another version of the demon-lover theme discussed in our preceding chapter, and that the long metaphoric statement of the father

in *The Princess* constitutes part of D. H. Lawrence's own belief. Or at least of the Lawrence who so insistently writes of
"selfhood" and of absolute individuality as his credo: "The goal
of life is the coming to perfection of each single individual." [14]
As with much of Protestantism, essential selfhood and soul
saving have little to do with human community. Take, for example, the repeated emphasis in the quotation that the inner
demon "doesn't care at all about the things that happen" to the
outer person. This restates a favorite Lawrencean point. In one
of his best short essays, "Insouciance," he writes of the abstract
anxiety about the outside world which marks the failure of almost all modern people: "They care! They are simply eaten up
with caring. . . . They certainly never live on the spot where
they are. They inhabit abstract space, the desert void of politics,
principles, right and wrong, and so forth. They are doomed to be
abstract." [15] Lawrence's attacks in his polemics on "idealism"
and humanitarianism, or the satire on "imagination" in *None
of That,* or the rejection of the abstract anxiety of "caring" in
The Princess appear as variations on the point that life must be
focused on immediate, felt, personal existence. When we return
to the story, however, we see Lawrence's subtle discrimination.
The protagonist's version of the Lawrencean "real-self," insouciance, and demonic knowledge falsifies them into life denial
instead of life enrichment.

In *The Princess* the demonic legacy of the father (and
Lawrence) leaves the lady peeling the onion—but in her own
dehumanized way. Instead of peeling away false anxiety and
care, she strips life of all immediacy. She sees the world "from
the outside"; with the harshest realism, "she seemed to understand things in a cold light perfectly, with all the flush of fire
absent." Lawrence repeatedly insists—even against his own role
as artist and outsider—that the heat of experience, not the light
of knowledge, gives meaning to existence.

Without quite being conscious of it, the Princess finds, like
Ibsen's Peer Gynt (the probable source of the trope), that you

peel away at the onion of life for the secret, and with the last peel the onion disappears. The warped virgin reaches this "nothingness" in her thirty-eighth year when her father dies. The "great secret" gives "only the blasphemous impertinence of her own sterility." But now she must "do," and real "doing" for a woman is *"marriage."* To the Princess, as to so many women, marriage is not an actual experience but a "peculiar abstraction" that "has imposed a spell on her."

The third inverted hero and defeated aristocrat of the story is another of Lawrence's demon lovers, Romero, a Mexican guide. He, supposedly the last of the Spanish-American rancher-barons but now a hired hand at a tourist ranch, is an exceptional figure of virile force, "handsome," with "a strong natural body," "dark," "sinister," "different" from the mass, "proud," and simultaneously a primitive and a "gentleman." As a demonic "death worshipper," he dresses all in black. This satanic figure carries the sexual "spark in the midst of the blackness of despair," and when this "fine demon" enters the story he does so as an absolutist of the spirit "waiting either to die or to be aroused into passion and hope."

The bored Princess, like the heroine of *The Woman Who Rode Away,* desperately wants to see and experience something different, dangerous, wonderful. Now that she has found her demon guide, she decides to make a trip far up into the "heart" of the Rocky Mountains to see the "wild-life." The central section of the story consists of one of those hard and intense descriptions of the New Mexico mountain scene, which mark Lawrence's American period. A Lawrencean landscape functions as an expressionist metaphor as well as a graphic scene. Thus, one of the heroine's reactions to the autumnal mountain landscape implicitly reveals her own "tangle of decay and despair" in the "virgin forests." Later in the journey to the primitive heartland, and above the timberline in the region of cold, black rock and silver-gray spruce copses, the Princess achieves a sense of the "inhuman" force and the "anti-life," which is the "repellent core of the Rockies." This breakthrough into the heart of the destructive cosmos provides the same spirit of place and self-purification that Lawrence developed at such length in the last section of *St. Mawr*. Though the scene harshly threatens, the Princess, like the heroine of *St. Mawr*, finds that "now one of her desires was fulfilled." The crucial experience of confronting the nihilism of the universe will make or break the person.

The Princess and Romero reach their destination—a squalid mountain cabin. That night the Princess realizes her penultimate response to the cold scene and to herself in a dream containing the recurrent snow image of death. In the fearful cold of the mountains and her anxiety dream she longs for annihilation in two contrary directions. She "wanted to be taken away from herself" in fundamental warmth and possession, and she "wanted to keep herself intact, untouched, that no one should have any power over her." Romero, sleeping on the floor of the cabin while the Princess occupied the only bunk, provides the warmth, but to the Princess it was "a terrible animal warmth that seemed to annihilate her." She feels the "victim" of her desire and frigidly denies herself at the moment of coition. It is the ego refusing to accept the act of unity: ". . . she had *willed* that it should happen," but without her being a part of it. Thus she turns herself into a sexual *object* instead of a sexual partner, and this changes the longing for love into the act of rape.

So love reverses to death.[16] In revenge for her own feelings of degradation, and as an assault upon her own desires, the Princess denies the masculinity of Romero. He retaliates by keeping her prisoner and repeatedly raping her to break her will. But she inwardly refuses to yield, refuses all sexual response, and victoriously breaks the man's desire. Will has triumphed over passion; consequently, "they were two people who had died." The inward death is then spelled out in the factual world. Romero, left with only the death-longing half of his passion, recklessly shoots it out with the search party that has come looking for the Princess, and dies. The Princess tells her rescuers that Romero had "gone out of his mind," but the irony is that *she* becomes a bit "mad" and makes up a fantasy to obliterate all reality of what has actually happened. Later, she seems to recover: "She was the Princess, and a virgin intact." And she marries an old man so that, essentially, she remains as she is. The willful woman has killed both desire and the last true man, the demon lover. Neither within nor without remains any demon of selfhood, only the childish and sterile reign of the modern "Princess."

III

Lawrence, commenting on Hawthorne's heroines, insisted that "the half-genuine belief is much the dirtiest and most deceptive thing in life." [17] These two rape stories are ideological melodramas attacking "half-genuine beliefs"—"imagination" and the pursuit of the "real self." Such cultivated notions—like recent pseudobeliefs in the "artist," "tradition," "vision," etc. —adumbrate cultural religiosity, a derivative aestheticized idealism that replaces moral fervor among the nonutilitarian and rootless segments of the middle class. The personal genesis of the half-belief, as Lawrence dramatizes it, comes from warped self-assertion. Ethel and the Princess have violated the non-egotistical principle of their being. Lawrence wrote: ". . . hurt this being mortally at its sexual root, and it will recoil ultimately into some form of killing. The recoil may be prompt, or delayed by years, or even by generations. But it will come, We may take it as a law." [18] The madness, suicide, and rape in these stories unite violation of the law of physical being with cultural religiosity in leisured ladies who represent "high" civilization.

As the reader of Lawrence knows from *The Rainbow, Women in Love, The Lost Girl, The Plumed Serpent,* and *Lady Chatterley's Lover,* among others, the author had a remarkable identification with feminine sensibility, particularly in sexual longings and language. Despite the dominance of this quality, and of heroines over heroes in his fictions, final misogynic masculinity rises from his labyrinthine consciousness. A positive heroine, like the lady of *St. Mawr*, tentatively transcends destruction by a masculine self-discipline and defiance. Really a traditional romantic rebel masked as a woman, she quite lacks the female's essential fusion with the social order. But in most of Lawrence's portraits of modern ladies, the middle-class values become primary elements. Let us sketch Lawrence's assertions on this pervasive social form. "Ownership," the "cash-nexus," and "industrialism" receive the obvious and violent assault from Lawrence.[19] Surprisingly, this Puritan housekeeper and baker of bread also attacks domesticity. This comes from Lawrence's sensitivity to the "spirit of place," his awareness of the rigidity and repression dominant in areas where the domestic virtues are exalted, such as Switzerland, Germany, and his own English Midlands.[20] "It is our domesticity which leads to our conformity, which chokes us."[21] The "new" middle-class domesticities of Australia and America appeared to him even more oppressive with their "popery of sacred 'convenience.'"[22]

The economic basis of the domestic society is taken care of in typical fashion in a letter Lawrence wrote to E. M. Forster: ". . . you *did* make a nearly deadly mistake glorifying those *business* people in *Howard's End*. Business is no good."[23] We have already noted his view of the religiosity of culture (which will also be commented on in later fictions). Against such other bourgeois pieties as technology and progress, Lawrence aptly notes: "Civilization is revealed rather in sensitive life than in inventions."[24] The nature and quality of the emotional life are ultimate, not only as criteria but as *forces*. "After all, it is change in feelings which makes changes in the world."[25]

What, then, of the feelings of the all-pervasive middle class? As Lawrence wrote to a friend, the "bourgeois *milieu*" turns its own virtues of "morality and family and affection and trust" into something "suspicious and repulsive" by making virtue so "loveless, so materialist."[26] It is not, Lawrence repeatedly indicates, a question of the moral sense but of the emotional sensibility: ". . . the middle-class is broad and shallow and passionless." [27] Their attenuation of substantial feeling of course has *felt* sources: ". . . the modern bourgeois consciousness . . . turns upon the secret poles of fear and hate." [28] Thus, both in and out of the fictions, Lawrence praises primitives, peasants, old-style workingmen, aristocrats, Italians and other Mediterranean peoples—indeed, just about anyone without the Protestant and urban middle-class emotional ethos. In Lawrence's heroic—if violent—stand for the richer emotional life, the middle-class qualities and tones of life almost invariably come off badly. "The most evil things in the world, today, are to be found under the chiffon folds of sentimentalism. Sentimentality is the garment of our vice. It covers viciousness as inevitably as greenness covers a bog." [29]

Lawrence is not so much attacking sweet old ladies—though he finds most of them despicable—as applying an absolute standard of emotional validity to a civilization that is blandly destructive and prettily sordid. However suspicious the rational moralist may be of feelings as criteria, the personal deadness and the public counterfeit of much of feeling in the contemporary West can hardly be denied.

The emphatic Lawrencean negations of the cash nexus, domesticity, security, business, culturism, technology, convenience, and sentimentalism clearly constitute a rejection of middle-class values. One of Lawrence's metaphysical dialectics may suggest a more specific characterization of the middle-class mind. "It is not," he writes, "exactly the triumph of the middle-class that has made the deadness, but the triumph of the middle-class thing." [30] This thing-consciousness may relate to money, machines, dehumanized people, manipulative techniques, or works of art, so long as a dead object has replaced an active awareness.

A sharp but brittle satire, the short story *Things*,[31] provides an elaboration of thing-consciousness. This tale mocks the enlightened middle-class device of the aesthetic-spiritual escape

from materialism and conformity. A young couple, "true idealists, from New England," well-educated and well-intentioned
in "a mutual love of beauty," inherit the freedom to pursue the
good life. In other words, they are fuzzy-minded middle-class
Americans with a private income and the religion of culturism.
For a while they lived in Paris, where they "both painted, but
not desperately"; when life in Montmarte was no longer "thrill-
ing" enough they took up "Indian thought." Later they fled to
Italy, pursuing the "priceless treasure" of "freedom" with
"beauty." The ennui of cultivated tourism—which has taken on
such major proportions since Lawrence's time—defeats the
aesthetic idealists. Not so young any more, they realize that
Bohemian Paris and majestic Italy

. . . hadn't given them quite, not *quite,* what they had expected. Europe was lovely, but it was dead. Living in Europe, you were living in the
past. And Europeans, with all their superficial charm, were not *really*
charming. They were materialistic, they had no *real* soul. They just did
not understand the inner urge of the spirit, because the inner urge was
dead in them, they were all survivals. There, that was the truth about
Europeans: they were all survivals, with no more getting ahead in them.

The caricature here depends on stylistic parody—as if the author
were, with a touch of exaggeration, reporting overheard conversation. As so often with angry art, however, the apt caricature
sometimes disappears as scorn submerges the object; for example,
the supposedly American colloquialism of the cultivated husband: "Europe's the mayonnaise all right, but America supplies
the good old lobster—what?"

Another technique of this satiric fiction depends on the juxtaposition of principle and contrary action. Thus, while the
"idealistic" Americans have become disillusioned with the "materialistic" Europeans, something has been happening to them as
they gathered in their "things" of beauty:

Yes, unknown to themselves, the lives of the idealists had been running
with a fierce swiftness horizontally, all the time. They had become tense,
fierce hunters of "things" for their home. While their souls were climb-

ing up the sun of old European culture or Indian thought, their passions were running horizontally, clutching at "things." Of course they did not buy the things for the things' sake, but for the sake of beauty.

The sarcasm directed at these twentieth-century Romans might be contrasted with the Jamesian treatment of the same theme. Where James would consider this a problem for endless moral exploration and ambiguity, Lawrence treats it as not a question of morality at all. The truth of people's lives may be seen in how their passions, not their aesthetic or moral aspirations, run. For all their superior idealism and sophistication, the American couple have quite a pile of Venetian bookcases, Sienese curtains, expensively bound books, and the other artifacts of somebody else's dead culture. Such cultivation opposes the rougher vitality that creates real culture.

Lawrence usually develops his fictions with all the nasty logic of a fundamentalist. Hence no saving graces appear in his Americans. Approaching middle age, the American idealists could take no more of the artistic life; so they "left Europe behind, but they took as much of it along with them as possible. Several van loads, as a matter of fact." And for Lawrence, this hypocrisy comes from the inherent logic of idealism: the "full and beautiful life" for idealists means a superior "attachment to *something*." It is a particularly apt point when applied to Americans—as we know in literature from some of James's characters, Fitzgerald's Gatsby, etc. As Lawrence writes elsewhere: "Your idealist alone is a perfect materialist." [32]

After briefly covering other escapes for the characters (the simple life, the contemplative life, Europe once more), and forcing the fiction's tone until the urbane figures sometimes sound like Babbitt, Lawrence shrewdly uses American academic life as the final natural refuge for the "horizontal" idealists. The husband becomes a teacher at a university in Cleveland, the best place for the "things" since "all looked perfectly out of keeping, and therefore very impressive." The former artist feels caged, "but it was safe inside." The conclusion tells of the keeper of the cage—and returns us to our theme of the destructive woman—for the wife of course would *"never* part with the 'things'. . . collected with such passion." While "religions, continents, cultures and hopes" might pass away, there still remains the implacable force of the self-crucifying middle-class woman and the things to which "she was nailed."

"How beastly the bourgeoisie is—" starts one of Lawrence's poems; and such shrewd sarcastic stories as *Things* spell out the author's view that the idealizing, cultivated middle class ends in just as beastly a manner as the less "enlightened." The mode of consciousness and feeling of modern society, whether gross or cultivated, cannot be transformed by ideals or culture or any other form of liberal amelioration. Lawrence, from the liberal moralist's point of view, commits himself to an unreasonable and dangerous demand for demonic negation and passional renewal. Furthermore, the extremity of such demands for authenticity of feeling may well be antithetical to society—any society, except perhaps the ideal one that Lawrence for years quite unsuccessfully proposed to various friends.

Lawrence intends to be unreasonable and extreme, in contrast to the rationalistic and ameliorative. As for his utopianism, it has a function within any actual society. Lawrence writes: "There is deep inside one a revolt against the fixed thing, fixed society, fixed money, fixed home, even fixed love." [33] The revolt against the fixed-thingness of life is hardly peculiar to Lawrence, though it may be peculiarly masculine and antithetical to feminine sensibility—which may partly account for Lawrence dramatizing his attack against middle-class thingness primarily through women. The denials of the flux of reality and of subjectivity, the full externalization of possibility and desire, destroy individual purpose and the immediacy of life. Moreover, the total objectification of life energies by identification with the state or the family or business or science or art becomes destructive. "What was once the breath of inspiration becomes in the end a fixed and evil form. . . ." [34] If a significant part of life does not operate from "inspiration" rather than "form," regardless of the danger and chaos (so often overrated), life disappears. Deadness results from even the best order: "Anything that *triumphs,* perishes."

IV

Let us examine some of the other fictions in which the middle-class matriarch has triumphed. While these stories do not deal with the state bureaucracy and the industrial machine—the larger order of things that men appear to control—the fictions nonetheless concern the basic social order. Not only do women maintain the mass sentiments that create human identification with the largest things, they also translate the rule of things into the area of personal relations. (Lawrence generally dramatizes his industrialists—Gerald in *Women in Love* and Clifford in *Lady Chatterley's Lover*—as emasculated men.) Thus the female psyche expresses the deepest currents of contemporary society for Lawrence. Three stories, all relatively late fictions— *The Rocking-Horse Winner, The Lovely Lady,* and *Mother and Daughter*—show the modern matriarch turning sons, love, and self into things.

The Rocking-Horse Winner [35] is one of Lawrence's best-known and most praised stories. This neat piece utilizes, in a Balzacean sense, a money plot and theme. In a letter written about the time of the writing of this story, Lawrence said: "Perhaps it's really true, lucky in money, unlucky in love." [36] This old adage, with its antithesis of love and money, which so appealed to Lawrence, appears to be the literal source of the sardonic fairy-tale theme:

There was a woman who was beautiful, who started with all the advantages, yet she had no luck. She married for love, and the love turned to dust. She had bonny children, yet she felt they had been thrust upon her, and she could not love them. . . . She herself knew that at the centre of her heart was a hard little place that could not feel love, no, not for anybody. Everybody else said of her: "She is such a good mother.

She adores her children." Only she herself, and her children themselves, knew it was not so. They read it in each other's eyes.

They were a boy and two little girls. They lived in a pleasant house, with a garden, and they had discreet servants, and felt themselves superior to anyone in the neighbourhood.

Although they lived in style, they felt always an anxiety in the house. There was never enough money.

The mockingly simple exposition, with its devices from the children's story of the beautiful lady with the hard heart and the doubled pronouns for clarity, schematically pictures an upper-middle-class family attempting to keep up appearances and expensive tastes. The mother explains her version of magic to her son: "If you're lucky you have money. That's why it's better to be born lucky than rich. If you're rich you may lose your money. But if you're lucky, you will always get more money." Using another fairy-tale technique, Lawrence dramatizes the inner consciousness of his characters by projecting their feelings into inanimate objects. Thus, the stylish house itself whispers: *"There must be more money! There must be more money!"*

Appropriately to the form, the hero is a child, Paul, with "uncanny cold fire" and heightened sensitivity. Paul, the not-truly-loved child of an avaricious mother, may be a parabolic version of the autobiographical Paul of *Sons and Lovers*. In both fictions the exceptional son wishes to stop the whisperings of anxiety and prove himself to his mother. He forlornly hopes that by some magic of money success he can obtain love, but false magic leads only to death.

The child, "absorbed, taking no heed of other people . . . went about with a sort of stealth, seeking inwardly for luck." The "secret of secrets" resides in his rocking horse. Though past the age of such a toy, the boy insists on having it in his room at the top of the house (the fairy-tale magic tower?) and justifies it to his mother with the "quaint answer" that he wants the rocking horse until he can have "a *real* horse" because he likes "to have *some* sort of animal about." For Lawrence, we recall, horses symbolize the passions. The rocking horse provides the masturbatory toy counterfeit of passion in the middle-class world, as the modern gambling race track provides the public counterfeit of the heroic riders of the past.

Paul "madly" rides back and forth on his rocking horse in a trance-like state until "sure" about what horse to bet on in the big races. The terrible inner strain of such magic does not always succeed, but when the boy "knows" (*feels* certain) he bets heavily, with the help of the horse-playing gardener, and wins. The boy's Uncle Oscar, a "mildly cynical" horseplayer, and one of those people with money luck, shows the usual shrewdness of the lucky; he worms out Paul's secret and joins in on the betting. Uncle Oscar also arranges Paul's gift to his mother of five thousand pounds from his winnings. Paul hopes the money, disguised as an anonymous legacy, will bring love instead of the whisperings of anxiety to the house. But the money only makes the mother more "cold, determined," more extravagant, and greedy for yet more money. Instead of joy, the house goes "mad" with a crescendo of "there *must* be more money . . . more than ever!"

Paul rocks away for magical luck in the Derby, the biggest horse race of all. On the last night before the race, his mother, with a sudden illumination of maternal anguish at a party, rushes home to find her son frenziedly swaying on his rocking horse. Paul screams out the name of the Derby winner, and the gardener and uncle place the bets. But for the boy delirium ends the sexually mad race for money, briefly interrupted by the knowledge of winning seventy thousand pounds, and his last words: "Mother, did I ever tell you? I *am* lucky." He dies, lucky in money but not, in this paradigmatic bourgeois home, lucky in mothers or love.

The cruel irony of the conclusion comes in the money-lucky uncle's comment to the mother: "You're eighty-odd thousand to the good, and a poor devil of a son to the bad. But, poor devil, poor devil, he's best gone out of a life where he rides his rocking-horse to find a winner." And so he is—but how else do poor devils make money? Or even well-to-do ones, like the uncle who has made a tidy sum from Paul's magic which he so disdains? Good and decent people all—the bourgeois are decent and affectionate, Lawrence allows—and no one really believes in going *that* far to make money. However, as a matter of fact, the good and decent mothers and uncles do go that far to make money, both because it provides the only full passion of their lives and because only through such total commitment can money really be made.

The Rocking-Horse Winner, a "well made" fiction, "objectively" imparts most of its vital information dramatically by the boy's dialogues with his mother and uncle. The shrewd dialogue, the economical delineation of figures in a set milieu, the allegorical neatness of the whispering house and magical rocking horse, the lack of the usual Lawrencean editorial intrusions, and the precise irony of the luck not worth having, make this a superior story. However, such aesthetic neatness is also a limitation— Lawrence, after all, has turned his magical perception of reality to haunting a house and a hobby horse in order to turn a moral —and the admirable attributes of the "well made fiction" should not be used to denigrate other and quite different fictions of Lawrence's. The artistic detachment and precision of the Flaubertian and Jamesian traditions,[37] and of *The Rocking-Horse Winner,* create one kind of fiction, but not the sole criterion for imaginative prose.

Two of the premises implicit in *The Rocking-Horse Winner* —the negative power of money and the poignancy of the mother and son relation—receive even harsher exploration in a longer story, *The Lovely Lady.*[38] In both of these mother-son stories it appears that Lawrence, like many artists, played agonized variations on one of his nuclear personal experiences. Because of this, the stories implicitly ask the reader to accept the rather extreme convention of cannibalistic mothers. In *The Lovely Lady,* Lawrence does not really develop an explanation of the "mother

murdering her sensitive sons" so much as he draws the consequences of the hidden matriarchal crime. We are told, almost
casually, that Pauline, the mother, murdered one son by despis-
ing his love and fighting his sexual desire for another woman.
This is just what happened to the elder Morel boy in *Sons and
Lovers*. And like Mrs. Morel in the novel, Pauline then turned
to the lesser and weaker younger son, Robert, as a substitute for
the dead son.[39] While we may contrast the early and earnest
novel of lower-class life, with its expressionist prose and youthful struggle for fulfillment, and the later story of the *haute bourgeoisie* with its almost brittle sophistication and nasty exposé of
obscene will, the matriarchal curse of family life remains constant.

Pauline is one of Lawrence's most vicious examples of the
destructive matriarch, and her maternal attitude to her neutered
son and to her dependent niece shows utmost contempt. The
matriarch's emotional cannibalism keeps up her facade to the
world, just as the mother in *The Rocking-Horse Winner* pursued
keeping-up-appearances. This lovely lady is a real grotesque:
seventy-two years old, she is a self-made *objet d'art*—a shrewd
businesswoman, *objets d'art* have been her specialty, and the
source of much of her wealth. Pauline is so well "preserved,"
so "chic," so able to "don her youth," that in "the half-light" she
can pass as much younger and much more beautiful than an old
woman has any right to be. For this violation of nature there is a
considerable price to be paid, by others as well as herself. Pauline
is a living death, as Lawrence mockingly emphasizes in the opening description of her "exquisite skeleton" and "skull." The
loveliness and the charm are a trick, a "little wire" of "will,"
which Pauline pulls, thus making herself a puppet. We are in
the realm of demonology with this "devil of a woman"; and her
inevitable collapse shows the real person, "haggard with a look
of unspeakable irritability, as if years of suppressed exasperation
and dislike of her fellow men had suddenly collapsed her into an
old witch."

The artifice of self-violation takes its toll of coy women, who, in their very effort to avoid it, achieve the grossest old age. With all the thoroughness of hatred, Lawrence dwells on the immense efforts of a woman to achieve the paltry goals of appearances. The lovely lady uses her plain niece to set herself off to advantage, and she uses the erotic appendage of her son to give her yet another illusion of youth. The artfully done country house and settings, the elaborate manners, and, indeed, anything that money, ingenuity, or emotional robbery can come by, create the empty epitomization of "high" culture. This woman is the key representation of the society's will to the artificial and purposeless mechanism. In an important sense Lawrence is the most exact of artists, for his hollow men and women suffer from no indefinite malaise of metaphysical or traditional despair, but from a precise failure of character, which they systematically compound into a denial of direct life.

Guilt remains the only real emotion left to those trapped within their "shell" of artifice. The shell "breaks" when the niece uses a "diabolic trick" on the fearful Pauline. Cecelia accidentally discovers that she can make "ghostly" accusations down a drain pipe to frighten the sun-bathing Pauline about her lurid past, her dead son, and her past illicit liaison with a priest. The impact of the guilt turns Pauline's artifice against herself, so fragile is the construct and so unrelated to the actual person, and all her usual efforts at grace and beauty only result in a "dreadful caricature" of a lovely lady. For "once a definite thrust of condemnation" is made, there remains no power to resist. Power of character is not a cultivated mechanism of nerves. No longer able to sleep, Pauline takes a strong dose of sedatives, which kills her because "her heart was weakened."

The "supernatural" device that reaches Pauline's sense of guilt in a moment of weakness is a plot technique of the same order as Paul's racing hunches gained from riding his rocking horse, the trick of satanic laughter in *The Last Laugh,* the use of spirits to arouse sexual desire in *Glad Ghosts,* and the return

of the dead husband in *The Border Line*. Lawrence's naturaliza-
tion of the Gothic tricks of his romantic predecessors makes for
effective moral melodrama. But the very use of such plot artifice
to expose artifice has its ironic limitation. And in *The Lovely
Lady* the trick reversal is rather pat and mechanical.

At the end of *The Lovely Lady* appears a set dialogue between
the son and the niece, apparently to extend the moral of the tale.
This pathetic pair are would-be lovers, but the niece's efforts
to take the "ever-lasting lid" off the house of artifice and repression will not work since the son "rebels when it is too late." The
couple discuss the moral of the episode: Pauline had no love in
her and had only the vicarious desire for "power to feed on
other lives." But their conclusion turns the psychological point
to its external form—money. The victimized niece and son are
the genteel poor. In Lawrence's sardonic style, the problem of
the poor barrister son is "a secret but very deep mortification; he
earned about a hundred pounds a year. He simply couldn't get
above that figure, though it was rather easy to get below it." The
wealthy mother had always helped out with "a *lovely* and *undeserved* present . . . presents are so much nicer when they
are undeserved, Pauline would say." Oddly for a Lawrence
fiction, the problem of the would-be lovers ends as a problem of
money. We are to assume that Pauline ruins their possibility of
marriage by not leaving them any money—certainly a trite and
un-Lawrencean view of passional fate, but Lawrence is here not
concerned with passion, only with the negative moral. The final
statement of this stands out in Pauline's last testament to false
cultivation. The matriarch has left everything for the formation
of the "Pauline Attenborough Museum" for her antiques.
Lawrence's portrait of a lady raises the question of whether the
culture consists of living monuments or egotistic tombs.[40]

In *The Lovely Lady*, Lawrence's lovers, as well as the matriarch and the culture, are dead. Has the moralist stuck too
close to his fervor against the "cash-nexus" to allow much richness of life? Lawrence inveighs against such flat negation and

moralistic distortion in other novelists, such as Tolstoy. True fiction, writes Lawrence, has the "passional inspiration" to present not the moralist's "thumb," but *"life as it is!"* [41] This mockingly intelligent fable presents a moral truth but not enough of the vibrant larger sense of life-as-it-is.

A related story, *Mother and Daughter,*[42] suggests another aspect of the destructive woman. Early in the story the author insists that the relation of the mother and daughter has "nothing to do with parental authority," but is rather a problem of "a strange *female* power." The main analysis in *Mother and Daughter* turns about that peculiarly modern urban phenomenon, the "independent woman," and Lawrence's moral that no such creature exists. This story, like *St. Mawr,* explores a daughter's fate in relation to her willful matriarch, and only incidentally in relation to her mate. In what the reader now recognizes as the late and sardonic style of Lawrence, we are told that Virginia is a very "modern" young lady: ". . . so elegant and yet a slut. It was her charm, really." A career girl, finally head of a governmental department that Lawrence does not particularize, this modern woman succeeds in her simulation of the world of male power only at the price of a great tension and by living "on her nerves alone." Though talented and clever, she depends on men to tell her what to be talented and clever about, since "she didn't *really* know anything, because anything and everything was interesting to her for the moment, and she picked it up at once." As Lawrence repeatedly dramatizes, the difference between men and women is not a question of talents but of *"purpose,"* and the deepest masculine purposes of seriousness, dedicated conviction, and unique creation are alien to women, who may imitate but not originate the basic ordering of the world.

The modern Virginia is not all virgin and once had a man that she lived with for some years, but, with the aid of her mother, she dominated him. The balance of masculine and feminine opposites that constitutes love is destroyed; and man must use his perversity to save himself.[43] Lawrence briefly develops several examples of the female power at work (one, of course, centering on the man's clothes), and then summarizes the man's retreat as he "saw himself simply reduced to nothingness by two women, an old witch with muscles like the Sphinx, and a young, spell-bound witch, lavish, elfish, and weak, who utterly spoiled him but who ate his marrow." He finally manages to get out from under the two "witches." The man "saved his life, but he had lost, he felt, a good deal of his youth and marrow. He tended now to go fat, a little puffy, somewhat insignificant." The covert emotional struggles make and break one.

Eventually the witches, both manless, "set up married life together," and take a long-term lease on a dramatically stylish apartment. Women will have marriage, and if they can't bear men they will—just as two women will dance together—defiantly marry each other.[44] In their mimicry of the male order, both women act the man—the daughter in her career, the mother in setting the "positive" tone. Since the shrewd and cultivated mother is no longer lovely, she stylizes herself after a more forceful type, that of the eighteenth century, but "that she was Monsieur le Marquis rather than Madame la Marquise made her really modern."

Part of the ostensible purpose of the female ménage is to find a proper husband for Virginia. But this "double Circe" (Pauline in *The Lovely Lady* was also a Circe) destroys all men. The men they entertain although ready and willing to fall in love with Virginia, feel "afraid," "shut-out" by the "magnetic connection" between the two women, and so "in some way, annihilated." One of the man-destroying weapons of the matriarch usually takes the form of sophisticated humor, a "knocking everybody and everything humorously on the head." As with the similar Mrs. Witt in *St. Mawr,* this reveals the mother's "lust and passion" for negative will, her "mission" of "destruction."

The mother made the daughter her *"alter ego"* in urbane and civilized nastiness. But the daughter, in a rather late and decadent revolt, decides to marry in a way that denies female authority. She picks a fat, sixtyish, gray, and widowed grandfather—a "tribal father"—for a husband. This crafty and sensual Armenian businessman, a humble indestructible patriarch with the "subtlety of serpents," displays a rather grotesque version of the Lawrencean demon lover. To the mother the lover is the "Turkish carpet gentleman," but her sophisticated contempt no longer touches the daughter. When Virginia is "caressed softly and paternally" by the Armenian grandfather, her modernity, her "old irony," and all her "independence" and will are negated. The father figure treats her as a child, and she achieves the longed-for escape from purposeless freedom and ambition and can now repose "with no more effort all her life." The mother slashes out at the daughter about to marry the "Armenian grandpa": "You're just the harem type." Virginia accepts this picture of feminist horror, and adds that "perhaps daughters go by contraries, like dreams." The unconscious need behind the modern "independent woman's" revolt has been to move from the matriarchy to the patriarchy. In this mocking fiction the style and action are negative and show very little of the heroic individuality of some of Lawrence's other works. However, his usual theme of the passional law also functions in this story. Despite the civilized decor, the sophisticated mother, and the decidedly modern career girl, the action resolves in primitive need. The modern woman must flee the sterilized matriarchy and masculine imitation and submit to male purpose. Only thus will she achieve that which all must seek—a "luxurious sense of destiny, reposing on fate."

V

It would be unjust to leave the emphasis so fully upon the almost manless fictions that have been discussed in this chapter so far. The focus of criticism is never quite the focus of art, and we have separated out one extreme of Lawrence's dialectic between the sexes. The erotic conflict basic to all of Lawrence's work shows woman as most destructive when least confined by the male polarity. We might, therefore, take some intermediate fictions as a transition between the decadent woman and Lawrence's love stories (the subject of the following chapters). In many of the marriage fictions we still pursue those strange females who are less engaged in courtship, marriage, and domesticity than in rebellion, adultery, flight, erotic anguish, ritual sacrifice, and self-destruction.[45]

The very title of one of Lawrence's long and fervid early stories, *New Eve and Old Adam,*[46] suggests much of the issue. While the story grows out of the primordial Adam and Eve conflict, the modernity of Eve receives emphasis. Thus the beautiful, modern, sophisticated wife of a wealthy man in this story appears primarily in her *bovarysm,* her subordination of sexual desire to self-aggrandizement and endless, petty, willfulness. The agonized and ineffective husband concludes to himself:

> There was no core to the woman. She was full of generosity and bigness and kindness, but there was no heart in her. . . . He began to understand now sirens and sphinxes and other fabulous Greek female things. They had not been created by fancy, but out of bitter necessity of the man's human heart to express itself.

Lawrence's version of the modern fatal female turns back to the destructive nature of Woman and her permanent perplexity to man.

In terms of the rather heavy-handed action of *New Eve and Old Adam,* the estrangement of man and wife unfolds around the trick plot of a misdelivered telegram, which erroneously convinces the husband that his wife plans an infidelity.[47] But what should be a Latin comedy situation becomes, in characteristic Lawrencean handling, a frame for agonized psychic exploration. For example, we have Lawrence's descent into the subrational subjectivity of his character—the notorious "blood consciousness."[48] The well-to-do husband in his hotel room, after having fled his supposedly unfaithful wife, attempts a regenerative bath: "All the life was accumulating in his mental consciousness, and his body felt like a piece of waste." The bath, however, does not succeed in restoring his fundamental sense of self-unity. Alone in bed, the conflict of "mental consciousness" and the "elemental male" self becomes more pronounced: ". . . the dark, unknown being, which lived below all his consciousness in the eternal gloom of his blood, heaved and raged blindly against him."

His later return to his wife appears sexually successful, yet the final "elemental male" longing remains defeated. As with Paul Morel and Lawrence's other autobiographical lovers, the ultimate male craving for unity of the flesh and total commitment by the woman cannot be satisfied. "Flesh of my flesh," he says to his wife: "For him it was almost an agony of appeal . . . flesh of my flesh—a wife?" The male demand for a transcendental union of the flesh, an absolute eros to end the duality of love, must go unanswered, as Lawrence himself insisted elsewhere. Yet in this story the final separation of husband and wife suggests that the selfish independence of the modern woman is at fault. She, in a recriminatory letter, insists: "Your idea of your woman is that she is an expansion, no a *rib,* of yourself, without any existence of her own." The husband's concluding reply is that the woman loved only herself. The persistent Lawrencean conflict about the ultimate union of the woman with the man—the compensating reversal of the mother-son unity of the flesh—here peters out in ambiguous uncertainty about whether it is the milieu of sophisticated modernity or the primordial Edenic alienation that has sundered the modern Adam and Eve.

All that remains certain, especially in the earlier fictions, is the witchlike destructive power of Woman with her explosive combination of traditional sexual power and modern will. In an obviously early and forced melodrama, *The Witch à la Mode,*[49] we see that part of the woman's power to injure results from sexual guilt on the man's part. The witch in this short story first shows her meanness in a rather trite episode of mistreating an old lady. Her lover, a married youth guiltily divided between "pitying tender love" for his wife and "fire" mixed with "hate" in his illicit passion for the willful witch, rather simply illustrates a quite literal version of the adage that those who play with fire will get burned. The conflict between the lovers culminates in an inflammatory good-by kiss, in which the very yielding, for a moment, of the woman somehow causes the lover to "involuntarily" knock over an oil lamp. The youthful adulter ends the story by running away from the modern witch "with burning red hands held out blindly."

The very clarity of much of Lawrence's later fictions depends on the apparent separation of the two themes of absolute Eros and the modern destructive woman. Three stories of destructive women in marriage—*The Blue Moccasins, Two Bluebirds,* and *Wintry Peacock*—will illustrate also several techniques pointing to the larger perspective of Lawrence's valuation of the passion that can match the destructiveness.

The Blue Moccasins [50] starts in the hard discursive manner of so much of the later Lawrence: "The fashion in women changes nowadays even faster than women's fashions." And the fashion in female destructiveness presented belongs to an older type of "independent woman"—the "superior" kind who intended to have "no nonsense with men." Lina, well-to-do, traveled, artistic in the genteel sense, and aging, obscenely falls—as such women always do in Lawrence—from feminist grace. Almost at the age of menopause, her maternalness, tears, suggestion, and a handy but harmless poor male orphan, twenty years younger than herself, result in the momentary leap of wartime marriage.

Superior and independent Lina, however, does not really marry. Marriage and a man seem to her a burden, a "humiliation," which she will triumph over by an act of will. And so, to a point, she does: ". . . she managed him [her husband] with perfect ease." Any difficulties she explains to herself as resulting from the social disparity of having married "beneath her." But Lawrence delights in focusing harshly on the more basic inadequacy underlying a social rationalization. Lina was afraid of her husband and his "clumsy but violent sort of passion," which makes her both shrink away and insist on a sterile higher plane of feeling. For in Lina's view, her husband's passion "was just his indiscriminating desire for Woman, and for his own satisfaction. Whereas she was not just unidentified Woman. . . ." The frigid woman's denial of the impersonality of male passion reveals the denial of her own fundamental role as Woman. As a result, she not only becomes a rigid "unused woman" in her ideal independence but also rejects all common life thus ending in the nihilistic cul-de-sac of idealism—"a world of her own." In Lawrence's imaginative logic, the final result of denying reality is the very destruction of the real self—Lina even falsifies her own image in the mirror.

This time Lawrence reaches the denouement by following the change in the husband, Percy, who has turned increasingly to the outer world of common life. With his overeagerness to please—the displaced eroticism so essential to modern middle-class achievement—he becomes a moderate business and social success. Though married, this branch-bank manager acts the genial bachelor type that "men secretly pitied," the "nice, harmless fellow" who could be turned loose with one's daughters. "Good-looking, and big, and serviceable, he was inwardly remote, without self-confidence, almost without a self at all." His affability is not goodness but inertness, showing that "in his will, in his body, he was asleep." Or, as the thirtyish and perky widow who has taken an interest in Percy wonders: "How *can* a man be so nice to *everybody?*" Niceness, not passion; blandness, not distinction; good-nature, not vital nature—such are the qualities of the sleepers of life, the somnambulistic victims of frigid idealizing Woman.

Part of Lawrence's smooth technique in *The Blue Moccasins* develops through the almost casual symbolism of the title. Remote, blue-eyed Lina—blue eyes stand for the cold, idealizing, northern moral culture of Europe—purchased the blue moccasins from an Indian during her American travels. They took on symbolic import for her because Percy ardently assured her that they were lovely blue like her eyes. Lina hung the moccasins in her husband's room; much later, she goes to look for them; they are missing, and her husband assures her he doesn't know where they are. In her desperate loneliness she unexpectedly appears at the community theatricals in which Percy plays, and she sees on the feet of the widow, who plays harem girl to Percy's sultan, her pure moccasins of "the sacred blue color, the turquoise of heaven." Consciously, Lina feels more upset by the degrading contact with common life than by jealousy toward her lying husband. But the scene becomes heavily sexual; the widow has aroused Percy—and arouses Lawrence's woozy passional prose ("her limbs were suave and molten, as her young sex, long pent up, flooded even to her finger tips . . . living liquid"). Lina, now aware of a "new naked clang" in her husband's tone, implicitly recognizes her own defeat when the action of the play requires the other woman to kick off the blue moccasins of sacred and heavenly purity, and sing, as she makes love to the stage Percy: "Away, shoes of bondage, shoes of sorrow!"

Righteously sure of moral superiority and oblivious to all else, Lina interrupts the play to demand the return of the blue moccasins. Later, between acts, she insists that her husband take her home, but he, for once not submissive and impotently nice, sends his wife home with someone else. With his maleness finally aroused, he damns his "holy-holy-holy, all to herself" wife, and explains to the other woman:

"Why, she's never once touched me to be fond of me—never once—though she pretends sometimes. But a man knows—" and he made a grimace of contempt. "He knows when a woman's just stroking him, good doggie!—and when she's really a bit woman-fond of him. That woman's never been real fond of anybody or anything, all her life—she couldn't, for all her show of kindness. She's limited to herself, that woman is; and I've looked up to her as if she was a God. More fool me! If God's not good-natured and good hearted, then what is He—?"

This heresy, which would turn an impotent husband and bland bank manager into a figure of passion demonically defying the ways of the universe, is never completed. The story ends with the final act of the amateur theatricals yet to be played. The life-denying marriage has been exposed, along with the false idealism and egoism of the blue-eyed, white-headed Woman of the moral North. However, the defiance and passion (the other woman "was like an open, dark doorway to him") are kept at a comic distance as an intrascene in an erotic holiday farce in the suburbs.

In *The Blue Moccasins* the antiheroine is the "independent" woman, the self-defeating product of nineteenth-century moral idealism. To be thus independent, Lawrence sarcastically noted, was to be without a man, in contrast to the later sophisticated female who had lots of men, but still no man. The wife as antiheroine of the even more sardonic *Two Blue Birds* is the latter type of self-sufficient woman who insists to her husband that she has the right to *"live."* [51] This means that she wants expensive clothes, travel, lovers, and all the rest of the "vehement pursuit of enjoyment." The opening of this inverted fable of the bluebird of happiness—"There was a woman who loved her husband, but she could not live with him"—suggests that marital antagonism, like the monster in the fairy tale, just *is.* The monster, however, turns out to be born of modern sophisticated intelligence.

No man—to redo an old adage—is a hero to his wife; but that, for Lawrence, is the fault of the wife.[52] She "knows it all." Thus, desire and wonder become a sardonic and ineffective knowledge that allows only purposeless pleasure.[53] However, the story is not really doctrinaire about the submission of the wife to the husband in marriage. For the novelist-husband's slavishly adoring secretary, who has put herself and her whole family at the man's service, provides only an ersatz wife and a cloying "health and comfort." Lawrence, narrating through the wife's eyes, sees both sides—the sense of "deep satisfaction" and "mission," which comes from devotion and submission, as well as its destructiveness. The wife perceives the commonness and blandness that infect the adored male. She says to her husband: "I suppose you are perfectly happy?" He replies that he is "perfectly comfortable," and she pointedly asks if that isn't bad for him and his art. While no one, any more, can reasonably deny comfort, its adequacy as the basis of significant awareness and of human relations becomes quite another matter.

But the intelligence to perceive the inadequacy of the modern dogma of comfort does the wife no good. She, too, has the same tired ends, and intelligence itself cannot restore the sense of life. This is presented metaphorically by her response to the spring scene:

She went down into the garden in the warm afternoon, when birds were whistling loudly from the cover, the sky being low and warm, and she had nothing to do. The garden was full of flowers. . . . Lilac and snowball bushes, laburnum and red may, tulips and anemones and coloured daisies. Lots of flowers! Borders of forget-me-nots! Bachelor's buttons! What absurd names flowers had! She would have called them blue dots and yellow blobs and white frills. Not so much sentiment, after all!

There is a certain nonsense, something showy and stagey, about spring, with its pushing leaves and chorus-girl flowers, unless you have something corresponding inside you. Which she hadn't.

The rising irritation with the flowers in the first paragraph, then the rejection of any emotional connotation, and finally the rejection of spring and the denial of natural reality ("stagey"), defines a failure of sensibility. ("Which she hadn't" is the to-be-expected Lawrencean intrusion—a kind of stylistic irritability and sarcasm that mars so much of his writing.) The passage on the wife's response to the flowers not only desentimentalizes nature, it reveals her loss of the living sense of the universe, a turning of rich sensation into "dots" and "blobs" and "frills," and a failure to reach outside the abstracting and negating self.

The withdrawal from immediate experience is the ultimate Lawrencean sin. In the same garden on the same spring day the wife withdraws from her marriage. In the scene of confrontation between wife, husband, and devoted secretary, however, no one has any life vitality. The husband, for example, is dictating an article on the future of the novel and displays a formalist and un-Lawrencean literary pompousness about the "architecture" of literature.[54] Nor does the secretary of the villainous literary critic show true life: she devotes herself to the literary figure, not the man.

Enter then the symbolic figures, two fighting blue-tits—"the blue-birds of happiness" in the wife's sardonic mind.[55] Are we to understand happiness and marriage as impassioned conflict? The two bluebirds rip each others' feathers out. The wife interrupts her husband's dictation of the critical article, mocks his writing, mocks the secretary for not getting her due as a person instead of as a dictating machine, and mocks even herself by urbanely inviting the secretary to tea. Both the wife and the secretary come to tea in blue dresses, but Lawrence sets up the parallel with the bluebirds only to undercut it. Instead of fighting like one of the real bluebirds, the wife gives up her husband to the vulgar and devoted little secretary. As for herself, she is too intelligent to allow any man to have "*two* blue-birds of happiness to flutter around his feet, tearing out their little feathers."

It must be taken as an empty victory for the adoring and submissive secretary. The reader realizes the unromantic triad through the knowing though sterile intelligence of the wife, and thus perceives the husband's literary fatuousness, his exploitation of his secretary, and his bland substitution of comfort and convenience for all vitality. The reader also perceives, with the wife's eyes, the "birdish" little secretary as an inadequate bluebird of happiness. While much of the failure of this modern marriage resides in that mocking, superior, willful, and intelligent self-consciousness that makes the wife unable to act and react authentically, the same mocking, superior, willful, and intelligent self-consciousness provides the whole mode of the fiction itself. Intelligence mocking intelligence, as Lawrence was quick to point out about the work of Gide, Mann, and Huxley, displays a *"perverse* courage which makes the man accept the slow suicide of inertia and sterility. . . ." [56] Lawrence's ironic inversion of the fairy tale cuts both ways, and by pursuing the bluebird through the literary garden he mocks the modern woman and her modern author.

VI

We shall look more fully in a later chapter at the negative perception of marriage so dominant in such stories, but an earlier story of marriage and misogyny may suggest both the artistic and erotic crux of Lawrence's destructive woman. Formally viewed, a competent but not outstanding fiction like *Wintry Peacock* [57] falls between Lawrence's two fictional poles of parabolic melodrama and genre realism. The wife and destructive woman of this piece, represented by the bedraggled and unpleasant peacock that she erotically fondles, shows characteristic touches of Lawrencean demonism—"witch-like," "dark," "malevolent," "ominous," a "devil" of defiant passion and amorality. The fuller significance of the bird trope for the woman can be seen in Lawrence's first novel, *The White Peacock*. There the peacock appears as both "voluptuous" and "ugly" when, with a rather pre-Raphaelite symbolic portentousness, it perches on a statue of an angel in an abandoned church. A bitter and isolated philosophical gamekeeper (who reappears as the hero of *Lady Chatterley's Lover*) provides the commentary on the peacock: "That's the soul of a woman—or it's the devil." "That's the very soul of a lady . . . the very, very soul." And: ". . . the miserable brute has dirtied that angel. A woman to the end, I tell you, all vanity and screech and defilement." [58]

Though less explicitly stated, the same misogyny informs the recurrence of the trope in *Wintry Peacock*, where the witch wife attempts to get the best of her soldier-husband when he returns from the war after fathering a bastard in Belgium. The wife is a harsh creature—and apparently all the more sensuously attractive to the husband and the narrator because of it. She knows of her husband's infidelity by having a stranger, the narrator, translate for her the Belgian mother's pathetic letter to her husband. The returned husband, who shows no concern with the plight of the Belgian girl and his child, took a shot at his wife's peacock on the night of his return home. The violence against the soul symbol of the woman (part of "the contest with his wife") frightened away the peacock. The lost bird of the female witch is found and returned by the narrator, because he, too, is attracted to the soldier's wife by her mixture of malevolence and sexual submission ("which makes a man lord of the earth"). But in the end even the narrator's loyalty belongs on the masculine side of the war with the female soul. He asks the husband about the Belgian girl; the husband explains that she was like his wife, and, struck by the repetition in the war of love—a recurrent Lawrencean insight—lets out a "loud burst of laughter that made the still, snow deserted valley clap again." The harsh and defining natural scene echoes approval of the tamer of the female soul, and so does the narrator as he concludes the story. Shouting with laughter, he leaves the "handsome figure of a man" standing proudly on the wintry hillside. The amoral and primordial conflict of man and woman, not some sentimental norm of domestic piety, constitutes the center of marriage. And only by the genuine, self-desired, submission of the woman's soul will her malevolence be tamed to erotic mating.

Yet the peacock does not provide a satisfactory image, nor does this story adequately illuminate the transcendent Lawrencean eros. Lawrence's erotic bestiary provides the perspective. For example, the wry crux of *The Blue Moccasins* as the neutered husband and the widow reach for common vitality was represented by the wife's image of them sitting together "like two rebuked sparrows on one twig. . . ." Similarly, the double and degraded bird of happiness as two fighting blue-tits in *Two*

Blue Birds sets the limited and suburban significance of that story. When we turn to the larger range of Lawrence's work, we find the mythical and demonic flying forces of the religion of love in the "ladybird" in the novella of that name and in Quetzalcoatl in *The Plumed Serpent*. Then there is the "gorgeous" life-assertive and magically superior "escaped cock," identified with the resurrection of the Christ in *The Man Who Died*, and the "lustrous" black cock, whom it would be destructive for the heroine to deny in *The Virgin and the Gipsy*.[59] Pervasively, there appears Lawrence's personal symbol of passionate regeneration, the mythical phoenix. Instead of the desexualized nightingales and skylarks of desire in romanticism, Lawrence's positive birds show more assertion, heroic passion, and extremity. True love between a man and woman, to take another of his bird images, must be like two eagles embracing in mid-air, and if either one stops beating his wings the embrace will plummet both to the rocks below.[60]

Thus, the bedraggled peacock of the woman's soul, the fighting blue-tits of modern happiness, and the pathetic common English sparrows on their suburban twig come from a part of Lawrence's aviary far distant from the mythic hybrids and the cocks, eagles, and phoenixes of passionate eros. The overreaching extremity of passion and awareness, not ordinary morality and immorality, provides the strength for the heroic flight of love.

But the heroism must be reserved for later treatment. The antiheroines discussed above only represent the legion of such figures in Lawrence's long and short fictions—and in his essays and autobiographical writings, as well. The genesis of Lawrence's obsession with the destructive woman may be explained by various factors—Oedipal hatred, the literary traditions of misogyny, the ambiguous Judeo-Christian view of women, unpleasant experiences with cultured middle-class American ladies, and so on. These have their relevance; so, too, do several of Lawrence's artistic intentions with the willful woman. He self-consciously attacked the nineteenth-century Anglo-Saxon moral idealization—and earlier beatification—of the female as part of his encompassing critique of idealism. He satirized the bourgeois lady in his assault on the despised middle-class values—or lack of them. And, finally, the destructive woman provides the apocalyptic image of modern decadence. Lawrence insisted repeatedly that "the whole of modern life is a shrieking failure." [61] Many of the heroines appear as inseparable from triumphant modernity, in its social, erotic, and metaphysical peculiarities. In a popular article, "Do Women Change?" Lawrence suggested that women have changed in modern times, but added: "Modernity or modernism isn't something we've just invented. It's something that comes at the end of civilizations." [62] Lawrence, who believed in the traditional and conservative role of Woman, usually treated women as archetypal figures of feeling and emotional consciousness rather than as persons of ideas, actions, or purposes. The basic nature of Woman is lost because much of our civilization is "irreparably lost: abstracted into non-physical, mechanical entities whose motive power is recoil, revulsion, repulsion, hate, and ultimately, blind destruction." [63]

Furthermore, for Lawrence, most modern ideals and sentiments—again, an area dominated by women in Anglo-Saxon society—only further the destruction, since "love, joy, hope, true indignant anger, passionate sense of justice and injustice, honour and dishonour, and real belief in *anything*" have been replaced by "the loud and sentimental counterfeit of all such emotion." In this Age of Counterfeit the "higher emotions are strictly dead. They have to be faked." [64] Thus the modern Whores of Babylon support "art" and "morals" and the "public good." As Lawrence clearly intended, his fictions take the places where moral and cultural and religious ideals are most in evidence, as precisely the areas in which to uncover the corruptive and destructive longings of the individual and the society.

But is this a sufficient explanation of why Lawrence so insistently treats the woman and mother as a figure of futility and destruction, rather than fertility and delight? Behind the dialectics against counterfeit idealism and the middle-class way of life resides an extremity both more characteristically personal and more pervasively general than the specific image and argument. A persistent sense of shock and indignation underlies Lawrence's repeated revelations of the paradoxical nature of Woman. In its more universal qualities, his image of Woman belongs to the mode of fabulous female monsters, and of the female as the mother-whore, the savage sentimentalist, the vampire love, the submissive mistress, the murderous fertility goddess, the delicate beast, the beautiful witch. Neither Lawrence's didactic directions nor his artistic particularities obscure his Archimedean center in the universal perversities of the human passions.

While no doubt some societies, such as ours, put a premium on inner emptiness—the basic "sin" of the antiheroine—the inner emptiness of the modern woman (not so well hidden as in the more exhaustively active modern man) is in its nature both local and general.[65] As we follow Lawrence through various fictions, milieus, and tropes, we begin to sense that his pursuit of the destructive has more than a local habitation and name. The absolutist of emotional authenticity constantly rediscovers that "our will to live contains a germ of suicide." [66] But how did the germ become a plague? And why did an artist who insisted on his belief in "passional purpose" and the life verities write so many harsh, satiric, and often nasty and brittle stories of the damned souls of women fallen from life in an empty civilization? Perhaps the author, too, expresses the triumph of the modern lust for inner emptiness. Yet he also aims, with the usual perverse twist of heroic negation, at another sort of triumph: "One gradually gets a new vision of the world if one goes through disillusion absolutely." [67]

CHAPTER IV

The Extremity of Eros

. . . perfect union in opposition. . . .[1]

I

Most of Lawrence's fictions are "love stories." When love itself does not appear the primary concern, the love element nonetheless provides much of the interest, the motivation, and the focus of revelation. This characterizes not only the work of Lawrence; for centuries our literature has been dominated by love. Even if we grant—contrary to the moralists—that heterosexual relations provide the nexus of being, and even if we add—contrary to the fundamental Christian traditions—that immediate human responses remain the primary meaning of the erotic, the overwhelming concern with love in our heritage still seems strange. No doubt love grew strained and problematic because of the peculiar historical arrangements of our moral and religious traditions, but there is more to it than this. There must be deep conflicts and perplexities in our affective life at many levels. Perhaps erotic obsession and perplexity provide a defining characteristic of the Western sensibility. Certainly, much of our literature insists above all on the problems and barriers and agonies of eros, and Lawrence is most insistent of all.

There are, I think, two dominant perplexities in Lawrence, in our love literature, and in the general sensibility, which we may conveniently label *counterfeit love* and *erotic religion.* Counterfeit love, which many of Lawrence's fictions and polemics aim at exposing, arises in part from what has been called our cultural pluralism—the amorphousness of our love forms. Courtship, for instance, has served, and still serves, as the ritualistic preliminary to marriage and the domestic order, as a technique for achieving temporary erotic relations, as a method for concluding agreements and exchanging property, as a system for reaching toward a cryptoerotic religious ecstasy, and even as a stylization of ideally disinterested conduct. When prospective husbands, seducers, entrepreneurs, mystics, and courtiers use the same courtship pattern, strange emotional compounds are more than likely. A religion of adultery, divine coitus, and libidinal salesmanship, not to mention some rather peculiar marriages and ambiguous seductions, appear as but a few of the permutations within the confused emotional logic of our erotic traditions. Thus, too, Christian ministers and confidence men, chi-chi poets and soap-opera heroines, benevolent internationalists and psychiatric quacks can all call upon the universal power of love.

The serious critic of love like Lawrence must first, then, set out some negative limits. By love Lawrence emphatically does not mean Christian mysticism, genial and salable personality, aesthetic sentiment, social benevolence, Platonic idealism, or any other form of generalized and neutered intercourse. Love is sexual love, though this is not to be taken in the narrowest sense, which Lawrence calls "sensation" or "mechanical sex." The passionate relation between individuals which Lawrence treats as the one valid love must remain distinct from generalized sentimentality and reductive biology, as well as from the aggregate pretenses called "normative behavior." Lawrence repeatedly calls love a "mystery," and we may take it in a somewhat theological sense as a quality—rather than a thing, method, or act—but one that cannot be separated from the total, physical, person.

The abstracting methodologies of the natural, social, and moral sciences would only falsify the awareness of the uniqueness of love. But while the romantic notion that "love is lawless" may well be true—and, properly understood, provides the Lawrencean view of love—the lawlessness of love refers to the ostensible laws of logical, ideal, moral, and social rationalism, and not to any lack of shape and limits in erotic experience. The laws of love, like the laws of art, are not, fortunately, the same as the laws of citizenship. In Lawrence's fictions, all forms of love other than that of individual man and woman are treated as dangerous counterfeit and as obstructions to true eros. His view cuts an extreme path: self-love, parental love, homosexuality, group and communal love, humanitarian, religious, and ideal love not only abstract from the unique man-and-woman relation but falsify it and often become pernicious.

The stringent limitation of love to what we more often think of as *passion* has its perversities. Passionate love reveals such drastic limits that even Lawrence, as we will note later, could not always accept them, for they turn courtship into an agonized initiation into life, marriage into a never-ending cosmic conflict, and the actuality of love into an isolated and isolating quality surrounded by violence and agony in its painful independence from our wills and minds. There is, after all, some reason why so many counterfeit eros into the chameleon forms of sentimentality.[2]

As a theologian of the religion of eros, Lawrence insists on an ultimate law, a "limit to love": "The central law of all organic life is that each organism is intrinsically isolated and single in itself." [3] While love reaches out of isolation and singleness, it also intensifies them; a complete fusion—personal, social, or religious—becomes suicidal. As Lawrence restated the point many years later: "To yield entirely to love would be to be absorbed, which is the death of the individual: for the individual must hold his own, or he ceases to be 'free' and individual." [4] Motivated, no doubt, by the Protestant salvational emphasis upon individualism, but also by a longing to find an extreme and unrealizable mergence in love, Lawrence intellectually insists on the inherent limits of love and the "recognition of abysmal

otherness." [5] As we shall see in the stories, the very intensity and
depth of love relate to the difference and otherness that exist
between lovers. Passion rarely evolves in marrying the girl-down-
the-street, since the painful and incommensurable leap of desire
toward the strange and ultimately unknowable constitutes passion. Between lovers, ordinary as well as legendary, there exists
an "irreparable, or unsurpassable, gulf," which causes the agony
and ultimate incompletion of love.

But the very separateness of the lovers provides realization,
the crucial "knowledge of the *limits* of the self." [6] Thus Lawrence usually reaffirms the conflict: ". . . love, as a desire, is
balanced against the opposite desire, to maintain the integrity of
the individual self." [7] Or, as Lawrence put it many years earlier:
"Love is a coming together. But there can be no coming together without an equivalent going asunder." [8] Or, yet again,
love alternates two modes—"the sympathetic and the sepa-
ratist." [9] This variation on the traditional romantic dialectic of
union and separateness, the one and the many, recurs in various formulations. When Lawrence writes of lovers that "they
must be two complete in opposition," or, elsewhere, speaks of
"perfect union in opposition" (compare William Blake's key
aphorism, "Opposition is true friendship"), he lays the ground
for perceiving and dramatizing love as extreme conflict; this
"opposition," or "polarity," provides *the* law, metaphysically as
well as psychologically, of eros.

Thus, for Lawrence, that which denies the deepest opposition
and difference denies love. Generalized forms of emotional al-
truism, such as humanitarianism, which Lawrence contemptu-
ously calls "the sterilized milk of human benevolence," won't
do. [10] (Perhaps hating humanity—particularly in its mass forms,
as Lawrence so violently did—achieves opposition, and hence a
truer passion than loving humanity.) The psychological side of
this rejection of benevolence was summed up in Lawrence's remark: "I shall hate myself with madness the more I persist in
adhering to my achieved self of brotherly love." [11] The various

forms of *caritas* depend on the suppression and denial of the passionately responding, opposing self, and thus result in inner hatred. The religion of charity and the religion of passion remain antithetical.[12]

When Lawrence wrote, "I shall always be a priest of love," [13] he was speaking of immediate, sexual, individual love, and of a religion of eros long antagonistic to religions centering on *caritas*, agape, or humanism. Along with the polarities of passion, we find in Lawrence an insistent emphasis upon desire: "In its essence, love is no more than the stream of clear and unmuddied, subtle desire which flows from person to person, creature to creature, thing to thing." [14] This animistic extension of desire to the entire cosmos points not only to the heightening of sensation—realized in his expressionistic descriptions of nature—but also to the religious ultimacy of his view of love.

The subtle but necessary distinctions between true and counterfeit and big and small desires become part of the dialectical order of the fictions. While desire can hardly be defined in any positivistic sense, we may discern some of its qualities. Desire is only relational—between, from, and to—and thus has no independent existence; it is the "flow," the "flux," of vitality, which expresses the unified being; it is fusion of the body-mind—thus Lawrence's terms "blood-consciousness," "phallic-consciousness," etc. Desire cannot be a product of the reason, the will, or fantasy: ". . . desire is beyond the control of the ego." [15] Desire realizes itself in a state of heightened aliveness ("wonder") and provides the final vitalistic sanction that breaks through the anxiety of time and renews individual experience. Therefore love cannot be formed—only misformed— by social, moral, and rational laws. The final significance of love resides in the release of desire, and the formation of that which can desire further.

"It is a destructive fire, the profane love, but it is the only fire that can purify us into singleness, fuse us from the chaos into our unique gem-like being." [16] Besides the odd mixture of Protestant individualism and pagan hedonism (à la Pater and nineteenth-century vitalism), there lurks something more ominous behind such statements. The chaos and the fire—repeated tropes in Lawrence—frequently go beyond intelligible style to obsession. The "destructive fire" of absolute eros burns as well as purifies, and Lawrencean love cannot be separated from its demonic nihilism.

Now the demonic, heroic, amoral, and legendary passions—such as those of Antony and Cleopatra, Héloïse and Abélard, Troilus and Cressida, Aeneas and Dido, Tristan and Iseult—dramatize the most intense form of eros as necessarily outside and antithetical to the social and moral order. In his basic commitment, as in his mythic tales such as *The Ladybird, The Virgin and the Gipsy,* and *The Man Who Died,* Lawrence exalts the illicit passion outside marriage and the domestic order, even though he refused to treat love as tragic or heroic in the grand manner: "The love between man and woman is the greatest and most complete passion the world will ever see." [17]

Yet the majority of Lawrence's love stories do not appear to be about the uniquely exalted passion, the religion of eros spelled out in his aphoristic comments and his more mythic tales. Indeed, much of Lawrencean eros shows a characteristic provincialism in several senses. Not only are many of the love stories set in the English provinces, far removed from the centers of style and power, which Lawrence hated, but they also concern apparently simple, representative, even ordinary, lovers. However, the distinctive quality of these fictions can only be recognized if we see that in them, as well as behind them, appears Lawrence's violently paradoxical effort to link extreme passion and ordinary life.

Also in and behind Lawrence's provincial love stories appears much of one of the heroic forms of passion, the English pastoral tradition, with its floral-ritual scenes, impassioned ladies, tender swains, aristocratic ironies, and idyllic-utopian longings for a world created in the image of lovers. (Lawrence's major pastoral,

of course, is not his early work but *Lady Chatterley's Lover*.)
Thus, when we fail to recognize the fundamental Lawrencean
eros, we incline to the easy fallacy of the historical critic, and
emphasize the moral and social realism of provincial life that
Lawrence inherited from George Eliot, Thomas Hardy, and, no
doubt, more popular and less meritorious sources. Despite some
of the materials and techniques of English realism, Lawrence's
obsessive tropes, the insistent rhetoric of subjectivity, the expressionistic heightening of the love theme, the subordination of the
social and moral to his distinctive view of love become crucial.
All reality—whether of the English Midlands, nineteenth-
century English fiction, or Lawrence's life—submits to Lawrence's extremity of eros.

II

The dominance of the erotic absolute clearly appears even in
his earliest and simplest novella, *Love among the Haystacks*.[18]
The opening description of the two farm youths stacking hay
in the Midlands summer landscape shows, as we would say of
painting, more "magic-realism" than social and moral realism. In
the "golden-green glare" of the lucid summer day we find a
ritualistic scene centering on the haystack—"an altar reared to
the sun"—which, following traditional rural lore, provides the
fabled phallic scene for the two brothers "roused for the first
time in passion." In the evening one of the young men bathes
near the haystack:

As he dried himself he discovered little wanderings in the air, felt on
his sides soft touches and caresses that were peculiarly delicious: sometimes they startled him, and he laughed as if he were not alone. The
flowers, the meadow-sweet particularly, haunted him. He reached to put
a hand over their fleeciness. They touched his thighs. Laughing, he gathered them and dusted himself all over with their cream fragrance. For a
moment he hesitated in wonder at himself: but the subtle glow in the
hoary and black night reassured him. Things had never looked so personal and full of beauty, he had never known the wonder in himself
before.

The purificatory act creates a subjective unity with the cosmos and a total absorption in the living moment of desire and "wonder." The permutations of the same scene, from the surreal brightness of day through the magically luminous evening and the dark night and its regenerative rain, ends in the shrunken world of morning reality. The heightening, not the ordinariness, of reality reaches the real.

The dramatic action of the novella develops on a Cain and Abel motif. Geoffrey, the elder of the two brothers, suffers from an "inflamed self-consciousness," which makes him "morbidly sensitive." The dualism of consciousness paralyzes him erotically—this appears to be the basis of most of Lawrence's attacks on cerebral consciousness. His handsome younger brother, Maurice, the mother's favorite, has gained the interest of an exotically sensual foreign girl, Paula, a governess at the near-by vicarage and a "wildcat" full of "ferocity," "languor," and "radiance." Geoffrey, in a fury of jealous self-pity, knocks his younger brother off the high stack. The "accident," though not serious, emphasizes both Lawrence's complex view of "simple" emotion and his insistent image of familial violence as providing the nexus for erotic passion.

In the field lunch that follows, with its effective repartee (partly local dialect), the positive richness of feeling of the rural family curiously sets off a negative image of a tramp. Toward the tramp the author directs a wrath quite disproportionate to the figure's minor role: he is slouching, ferrety, impudent, insolent, greedy, mean, parasitic, and debased. Geoffrey even steps out of dramatic role to think of the tramp as "the worst foe of the hyper-sensitive: insolence without sensibility, preying on sensibility." Such odd genteel righteousness disrupts Lawrence's style. But the tramp is the *bad* outcast; a few minutes later his wife, the *good* outcast, appears and provides the doubling love action of the story. "The young woman looked at Geoffrey, and he at her. There was a sort of kinship between them. Both were at odds with the world." Thus, Lawrence dramatizes the "opposition" or "polarity" principle of eros, not only in the archetypal familial violence, but in the foreignness of the love object. The need of the English farm youths for the strange and alien belongs with the rebellion aspect of the demonic. Perhaps the flight from incest lies behind the desirability of the unlike. In part, at least, the wise English youths have, like their author, some justifiable suspicions of Protestant Anglo-Saxons and so seek love outside of both the racial and the social norm. Whether it be a question of incest flight, superior sensibility, or social and moral rebellion, the search for passion in the alien and unconventional creates an eros that rejects the prescribed, the known, and the secure.

The remainder of *Love among the Haystacks* dramatizes the brothers' erotic completion with the two women that night at the haystack. Both men are deserving, a Lawrencean transvaluation of the moral imperative. Both also show themselves full of the crucial "wonder," which creates the enchantment of genuine desire. The sacramental heightening—Maurice dusting his body with flowers, Geoffrey warming the dirty feet of the rain-soaked wife of the tramp—exalts the simple lovers in a way to be sharply distinguished from Dickensian sentimentality or Flaubertian debasement. But while Lawrence does not treat simple love as emotionally simple, the novella does suffer from an idyllic flatness of conception. After the seduction, Paula is "openly engaged to Maurice," and "Geoffrey and Lydia kept faith one with the other." The actual perceptions of the preceding action, however, show the happy eroticism of the younger brother leading to a sharp conflict of wills with the foreign girl, and the more agonized eroticism of the Cain-like brother achieving fruition through humble adultery and a transcendent submission to his passional needs.

The agony of achieving the erotic becomes the basis of the ecstasy. In what was probably Lawrence's first story, the sentimental newspaper piece *A Prelude*,[19] a pair of childhood lovers are separated by social differences. With the aid of a Christmas mummery (the St. George story—dominated by the devil), true love easily wins out and rather simply illustrates the epigraph: "Sweet is pleasure after pain. . . ."

In a somewhat later story, *Second Best*,[20] both the symbolism and the theme become more elaborate. A girl, Frances, is talking to her sister Anne, who meanwhile captures a mole and then, in anger at its bite, kills it. To Frances, the dark, blind creature of underground life seemed "like a very ghost of *joie de vivre*." When the little sister holds up the dead mole, "one ruby drop of blood hung on the small snout, ready to fall. Anne shook it off on some harebells. Frances suddenly became calm; in that moment, grownup." Statements about the mole's death thus constitute statements about the loss of Frances' love: " 'I suppose they [moles] have to be killed,' she said, and a certain rather dreary indifference succeeded to her grief." This rather ponderously used device, exacting detail about a portentous object and sudden shifts to the inner emotion that the object represents, provides an illustration of the symbolist manner so prevalent in modern fiction.

Second Best develops the theme of the title: "If she could not have the best—Jimmy, whom she knew to be something of a snob—she would have the second-best, Tom." So Frances herself kills a mole and brings it to the second-best lover, Tom, in a "recklessness of desire." The doubling of the suffering of the unconscious, blind passion, represented by the mole, appears rather mechanical, and the theme of desire as blind fate reduces to a quick switch between two rather indistinct swains. But the symbolism of the dark unconscious, the ritualistic propitiation, the violation of social values (the second-best lover is socially lower than Frances), and the agony of final acceptance (" 'Yes,' she replied in a dead voice. But there was a thrill of pleasure in the death") become dominant elements in Lawrence's eros.

A more intense story, *Fanny and Annie*,[21] elaborates many of the same motifs around a woman's choice of a nongenteel second lover. Fanny, an attractive and well-dressed ladies' maid, with her bit of inherited money and her memories of finer things and larger hopes, has been disappointed in her more ambitious choice of a lover and now comes "back to marry her first love, a foundry worker." The "doom of home-coming" ("It is easy to bear up against the unusual, but the deadly familiarity of an old stale past!" [sic]) *appears* to center on the blow to her class pride. For Harry, a man with no money and "no sort of ambition," always defiantly chooses the "common." He doesn't wear a tie when he comes to meet Fanny at the station. This spoiled son of an obstinate and powerful lower-class mother rejects genteel manners and language, keeping up appearances, education, and even restricts his one talent as a tenor soloist to a small rural Congregational chapel because he refused to change his dialect pronunciation. "He just didn't care." Such insouciance creates passional strength.

The resolution of the conflict centers on the public denunciation of Harry by the mother of a "wild" former girl friend, Annie, now pregnant. The denunciation occurs during the Harvest Festival Sunday service in the chapel where Harry is soloist and Fanny is in the congregation. The scandal does not move Harry, or his family. Fanny submits to this—to the moral and social indifference of the working-class family and to a marriage based on passion rather than social pride.

Though Fanny's change of heart seems somewhat abrupt in Lawrence's treatment, the submission of gentility (and of female will) to the lower-class values goes beyond social class. For the social only provides a veneer to the erotic, just as the Christian provides a veneer to the pagan in the chapel's Harvest Festival. The more essential conflict in Fanny's mind turns about whether or not to accept the passional in its own nature. At the social level, Harry appears in Fanny's mind in negative terms, but from the opening appearance of his face as "flame-lurid," through her constant physical awareness of his winsomeness, warmth, fleshly sensitivity, and other marks of "defiant passion," there erupts the underlying positive physical image.

His amorality and his publicly denounced fornication with another woman, so unacceptable at the social level, re-enforce his attraction at the passional level. Indeed, the man's commonness, his rejection of gentility and ambition and moral anxiety, and his insouciance and individuality guarantee—as so often in Lawrence—his existential being. And *that* causes the real agony. In the central scene in the chapel Fanny is more overwhelmed with the man's physical being than with his social-moral violation. Even before the public scandal, she "knew her life would be unhappy," and that the "physical attraction which she really hated but could not escape" would be her "doom." This sense of doom reveals one of Lawrence's keys, for the agony of love inheres in the need to learn that the imperative of eros—physical and impersonal—contains a fatality that defeats all else.

Our emphasis here on one of Lawrence's most basic and profound insights should not, however, obscure an element of questionable focus in *Fanny and Annie* and in many of Lawrence's fictions: the identification of sexual virility with Harry is justified on individual and thematic grounds, but receives a stock overemphasis on the grounds of lower social class. No doubt the moralistic, genteel, ambitious middle class neutralizes being, sexually and generally, but only at the level of pure abstraction can the working class serve as an obverse reality. And Lawrence knows it, in spite of himself, for his heroic working-class figures, when fully developed (Harry is not) are declassed outsiders.

This shifty focus between the ostensible motif of class conflict and the actual theme of erotic doom can be seen fully in another early novella, the long *Daughters of the Vicar*.[22] Its materials recur often in Lawrence—the passional versus the cerebral sisters, the destructive Christian middle-class milieu, the moralistic and unmanly intellectual lover versus the rebellious and virile outsider, along with such subordinate motifs as the obscene love of the mother, the satire on moral benevolence, etc. *The Rainbow, Women in Love,* even *Lady Chatterley's Lover,* as well as many of the shorter fictions, return again and again to these materials; so does *The Virgin and the Gipsy*, Lawrence's last "English" novella, which will (in the concluding chapter) provide us with a final image of Lawrencean eros.

Those who approach Lawrence primarily as a social realist—partly perhaps because that is what the son of a coal miner is supposed to be, partly because of the belief that society is the only reality—find the fiction's perceptive images of the social order marred by the metapsychological idiosyncrasies of the author. This, however, means reading the fictions backward. The very ability to be incisive about the qualities and limits of typical social behavior derives from a suprasocial perspective. The social carping of "British" and imitation-British critics on morals, manners, and literary sociology always ends in affirming the social order, as is. But the genuine critic of society, recognizable by the insistence on the emotional life, religious depth, a declassed point of view, and a denial of the adequacy of any social form or force, intensifies certain qualities of life with an apocalyptic disregard for any ultimate social good or order. Lawrence, sometimes in spite of himself, repeatedly rediscovers this truth.

Let us examine *Daughters of the Vicar* in terms of its mixture of social and erotic drama. The first chapter illustrates social realism by its rather pat summary of how the High Church came to the mining community of Aldecross with its impoverished but snobbishly genteel Vicar. Of the Vicar we are told, with representative and external "realism," how he lacked "particular character, having always depended on his position in society." Separated by his class superiority from the richer emotional life of the miners, he raises children "unwarmed and rather rigid" from being woefully repressed into worship of the trinity of duty, ambition, and gentility. The second chapter gives a representative episode in the Vicar's daily life to display the social values at issue. He visits a coal-miner parishioner and answers the mother's laments for her son in the navy: "It will give him wholesome discipline and set before him some standard of duty. . . ." And so on. The character responds in a predictable way defined by his milieu and with a social consciousness that the author mockingly shows in all its grossness.

Other episodes show social-class consciousness as denying the reality of sentient being; but, in the third chapter, the competent though flat social realism submerges in Lawrence's favorite allegory of the passionate and frigid sisters and the intellectual villain. A monstrous clergyman, belonging to the lineage of George Eliot's Causabon, a "little abortion" of an Oxfordian with private means and a sinecure and a philosophical mind ("from which he lived"), represents both intellect and morality. With "no spontaneous exclamation, no violent assertion of expression of personal conviction," he appears as a decent and reasonable translation of virtue into "mathematical" kindness and "a calculated well-doing" that requires no awareness of immediate life. Such altruistic love reveals the longing of the impotent for "domination." With the malice of indignation that Lawrence usually displays for this type, the doctrinaire, Christian moralist-intellectual also has a malignant "internal trouble" that incapacitates him. The frigid sister decides the repellent but maritally eligible clergyman must be "really *good*." The passionate sister replies: "What right has *that* to be called goodness!"

The cold sister's marriage to the clergyman and "abstract goodness" becomes a spiritual crime masked as moral benevolence. She vows that "she *would* not feel, she *would* not feel." She "had sold herself," "murdering herself," and is filled with a "general destruction," which will be directed "towards charity and highminded living." Thus, in vehemently abstract terms, Lawrence insists upon the nihilism behind altruistic love.

Lawrence treats the two clergymen in the story with vindictive harshness, even in the smallest details: ". . . his [the clerical suitor's] feeble hand shook as he moved a Bible." When contrasted with George Eliot's sentimentalism about clergymen, we find that in both Eliot and Lawrence not realism but the view of eros controls the presentation. Despite anticlericalism, Eliot generally treats clergymen kindly because she sees love as quite close to Christian *caritas*—"affection and duty." [23] Much of sentimental realism's fictional basis derives from the secularization of Christian love; Lawrence's rejection of Christian love and of its secularized social and moral forms concurs with his violation of the conventions of realism.

The passionate sister rebels against morality in the name of love ("I *will* love—it is my birthright") and thus achieves "purpose" in life. While the act of love requires moral denial, the object of love requires social denial. Counterpoised to the Vicar's family is a coal miner's family; the son, Alfred, is a sensitively declassed workingman with literary and musical proclivities, like most of Lawrence's workingmen lovers. He, too, suffers from the Oedipal conflict and from the masturbatory erotic failure of self-consciousness, having "debauched" himself with the "idea of women" in the "indulgence" of "imagining sexual scenes" while fleeing actual women. The erotic failure to go "direct" to any satisfaction creates a pervasive "fear of living." To appear manly, the youth has achieved a persuasive semblance of manhood by a moralistic victory over himself; by the willed subordination to authority and to guilt and by "humiliation and self-hatred, he rose into a sort of inner freedom." In the Lawrencean view, the price of such moral-spiritual freedom demands more than a defeat of vitality; the character based on repression rather than fulfillment of the self collapses when the covert necessity disappears. In Alfred's case, the necessity is the mother: "Without knowing it, he had been centralized, polarized in his mother." (Polarized, as has been previously noted, is one of Lawrence's favorite terms for erotic relations.) As with Paul Morel in *Sons and Lovers*, the mother's death "carried him with her into an unformed, unknown chaos." Once again we are at the defining Lawrencean experience. Narcissistic, incestuous self-consciousness and false freedom of restraint collapse, and the young man's anguish and "almost insane" grief bring both a "great chaos" and a "wonderful" liberation. The nihilism within also gives him the cosmic sense of wonder, and he finds in the winter sky "a new night ringing about him."

He also finds love. The daughter of the Vicar comes to help out while the mother dies, though her egalitarian labor is hardly compatible with the Vicar's social pretensions. As she aids in the intimate ritual of a coal miner's back washing, she finds herself possessed by both a physical "tenderness," the personal quality of love, and by a "white, impersonal heat," the fateful quality of eros. This is Lawrence's real subject, and before it the social world pretty much disappears. The brief scenes that return to social realism are cursory. When the coal miner carries a message to the vicarage, Lawrence states rather than dramatizes the patronizing quality of class snobbishness. When Louise hopefully invites the coal miner to dinner at the vicarage, the scene, so obviously rich in possibilities to the social realist, receives a summary half page. In contrast is the long and elaborate development of the balancing visit of Louise to the coal miner's cottage, a scene not of social detail but of Lawrencean passion-prose: "lightning," "seared," "fiery anguish," "torment," "torture," "agony of chaos," "spell bound," "utter darkness," "glowing," "echo of pain," "agony," "cruelty," "hurting kisses wherein fear was transfused into desire"; and, of course, the "inscrutable," the "eternal," and the nihilistic swooning in passion "to a kind of death" and to "the blessed feeling of fatality" of the asocial and impersonal law of eros.

The Vicar's passionate daughter aggressively obtains the sensitive workingman for a lover-husband. The satiric conclusion to this frequently awkward narrative returns to the social scene with which the story opened; the Vicar's concern with prestige and his wife's concern with money are nastily exposed. However, this does not affect the lovers, whose passion consummates in a sharp break with the family and the restraining social order; they will emigrate to the colonies. Flight from the given society, as so often in Lawrence, provides the natural conclusion to passion. And, despite the irregular social realism of such fictions, the usual moral is that eros both negates and transcends the social.

III

Many of Lawrence's slight and poor fictions concern the same erotic perplexities that dominated these stories just discussed and his early novels. In *A Modern Lover*,[24] for instance, the struggle of courtship culminates in the dubious sexual denial of the heroine. The fearful woman wishes to keep love on an ideal, spiritual, and intellectual plane. (Miriam and Paul in *Sons and Lovers* are equivalent to Muriel and Cyril here.) Lawrence murkily implies that such sexual denial involves the total failure of personality. Without sex there can be no real passion between man and woman—Lawrence showed only contempt for the legendary Dante and Beatrice and the etherealized, rather than adulterous, side of courtly love. The overwritten *A Modern Lover* also draws upon the "second-best" motif of the manly and unintellectual lover as second choice—only explainable as an autobiographical obsession—and ends with the parting of the virginal man and woman. Obscure guilts and restraints have stopped the couple from carrying out the hero's (and the author's) credo: ". . . life is beautiful, so long as it is consuming you . . . rushing through you, destroying you . . . like a fire with a great draught, white hot to the last bit."

Lawrence never really departed from the view inherent in this central fire trope, although he played some variations upon it. Sometimes, as in the humorless sex-ritual scenes of *Lady Chatterley's Lover,* the author seems the victim of his own public role as master of eros. Such, too, would appear to be the explanation of a late story, *In Love*,[25] with its clichéd and brittle self-parody of the early love-agony materials. The dallying with Rudolf Valentino and with an extended conceit of an automobile for a girl (both fashionable things in the 'twenties, hated by Lawrence), and the female fear of sexuality (the girl climbs a tree to hide from her fiance before finally submitting) get badly marred by Lawrence's polemical sarcasm. Hester objects to "love": ". . . so doggy!" "Nothing can be so perfectly humiliating as a man making love to you." Her objection turns about her own fear of sex, and, contradictorily, about Lawrence's irritated disgust with modern ersatz sexuality—"spooning" and "the whole silly love-making game," which the youth did because expected of him. Unfortunately, Lawrence has not carefully utilized his apt distinction: the counterfeit of being *"in love"* in the modern juvenile sense stands sharply against the concluding "queer, quiet central desire" of someone who learns, through suffering and anger and need, the *"really"* deeper passion.

The point of many of the early love stories remains obscure, as does the erotic guilt in *The Trespasser* and the overexplained but not quite lucid erotic failure of Paul and Miriam in *Sons and Lovers*. In one of the pieces related to the latter, *Shades of Spring*,[26] a young man returns to his rural past. The lush spring scene and his former sweetheart represent his youth; it is less certain just what the shades obscuring this spring of life are. The young man recently married, and the girl took a lover—apparently of the second-best sort that Lawrence touches on in so many stories. The girl still wants the returned youth as an intellectual mate to balance the purely physical role of the gamekeeper. The hero rejects this, and leaves after he learns by eavesdropping that the girl and the gamekeeper are physical lovers. The story, probably for autobiographical reasons, does not resolve its own question of why "it had never been true, that which was between him and her."

That guilt may be stronger than love would also seem to be the point of many early fictions of Lawrence's, and even of a bad and slight genre piece like *Goose Fair*,[27] with its intellectual girl (reading Ruskin) who serves as the "conscience-keeper" of a factory owner's son. Though attracted by a simpler goose girl, he is caught up in the burning of his father's factory and ends in "bitter" submission to the "superior" girl. A contrasting tentative exploration of another sort of eros appears in Lawrence's early work *Once*,[28] an ostensibly military piece, which Lawrence linked with *The Prussian Officer* and *The Thorn in the Flesh*.[29] A demimonde lady tells her lover of the great sexual affair of her life. She had arranged for a handsome, aristocratic young officer, a complete stranger, to visit her; the exotic night included crushing rose petals between their bodies, binding her with a gold chain, etc. The point of this brittle, De Maupassant type of erotic fantasy—rather unusual in Lawrence—focuses on the role of pure "sensation." The woman tells the event to her current lover, busy fighting her sexual insatiability. Along with feminine mockery and some too-clever dialogue about the Edenic apple and the shortness of life, Lawrence seems to suggest that relentless sensual aggression results from earlier experiences of sexual degradation. The conclusion emphasizes that the woman has lost rather than won from her search for the perfect sensual moment and "sensation." Lawrence returns to this distinction frequently; as he put it in one of his essays: "Don Juanery, sex in the head, no real desire." [30]

The remaining "military" tale to be discussed, *The Thorn in the Flesh*,[31] turns about a more significant double episode— the breakdown of authority and the breakthrough of passion. The hero, Bachmann, a young army recruit of well-to-do peasant origins, feels "bound in a very dark enclosure of anxiety." With one of Lawrence's favorite devices, this inner torment contrasts with the natural order scenically presented in its "distant spaces of sky and fields all free with air and sunshine." The youth's anxiety takes shape in his overwhelming fear of heights, and his knowledge that because of that fear he cannot go through the practice scaling of fortifications like the other recruits. Lawrence vividly presents the alienation and shame that confront the youth waiting his turn to scale the wall. The scene of the scaling attempt emphasizes the drama of the youth's body. He nearly falls; then he finds in the crisis that his will cannot totally command his body; he suffers the ignominy of urinating and, finally, of being hauled to the top by the officer. Part of the revolt of the youth's body against his will is the revolt against brutal authority, the repulsion to being treated as a "mechanical thing." The total being of the youth is more sensitive than his mental processes, and he has revolted in spite of himself—in spite of his rational consciousness. The crux of the shame and rebellion comes when berated by his superior for his failure. From a response deeper than conscious choice, the youth "involuntarily" strikes the officer and knocks him into the moat below the wall. His "instinctive decision" is to leave the "military world, the shame," and he walks away "in a vision, free."

Now D. H. Lawrence is not in the usual sense an antiauthoritarian. He firmly and explicitly held to a doctrine of "natural" authority, to an ethic that he called "aristocratic," and, at least in part of his moralizings and fictions, to a demand for a heroic leader.[32] Temperamentally, Lawrence was repeatedly authoritarian. The revolt appearing in so many of Lawrence's fictions is not, then, revolt against all authority and society, but only against "mechanical" authority and society. (But Lawrence increasingly found less and less true authority in the modern world; hence the rebellion against authority in his final works becomes nearly absolute.) Lawrence, though no admitted pacifist, hated the military, and uses it to represent the worst form of authority. Appropriately, his hero in *The Thorn in the Flesh* does not revolt because of an idea of liberty but because of a revulsion to putting "flesh between the hands of authority." True authority draws its power from a deep physical response, never shames or violates the flesh, and results, in a favorite word of Lawrence's, in "tenderness." Thus the youth's rebellion as an unconscious physical response, and his flight toward erotic completion—the antithesis of false authority. Without conscious plan, the rebel flees to his sweetheart.

In revolting and in leaving the given order the youth moves toward extremity. The crucial adventure of alienation leaves him feeling that he has left "this land, this life." Now outside normal restraint, he makes love to his girl for the first time, and the "shame" of the body, which has so obsessed him, goes in a "furious flame of passion." For the girl, a simple and submissive orphan-servant to a good aristocrat, the love-making achieves an "intense anguish of bliss." Both the youth and the girl reach the new experience of being "one, complete." In new-found selfhood the young man feels "escaped, liberated, wondering, happy." He can now accept himself and his own limits, including his previous failure and shame: ". . . if I'm made like that, I shall have to abide by it. . . ." The intense sexual release of youth, of which Lawrence makes so much, is not simply desire for union but the initiation into unified being. Passion makes the man.

The outside world remains the enemy of passion. The sweetheart—a rather awkwardly handled "primitive," orphan, and gypsy, but also an obedient maid—accidentally reveals the youth's whereabouts and the military recaptures him. Once again an "object" rather than a person, he responds quietly to his capture. But "only the shell of his body was at attention," and he remains "true to himself," the self newly found through rebellion and eros. Ironically, the moment before his capture he has *ideas* of liberty, of "absolute, imperious freedom." The debacle is not quite complete since true authority, the Baron—a quite undeveloped figure in the story—responded in physical sympathy to the "deep nakedness" in the youth's look. He recognized the *"man"* within, and goes to do what he can for the youth.

The Thorn in the Flesh displays a powerful theme; an extended discussion of the story, however, as so often in criticism, tends to cover common-sense weaknesses. *The Thorn in the Flesh* should have been a better story than it is. The backgrounding of the characters is arbitrary and hasty, and the prose breaks down into frequent muddles: "Instinctively with an instinct of reverence and gratitude, her arms tightened in a little embrace upon him who held her thoroughly embraced." The companion story, the much harsher and loveless soldier tale of the same time and place, *The Prussian Officer,* achieves much more. As I have often noted, Lawrence's more destructive and loveless fictions show better, truer, art.

IV

Lawrence's profound insight into erotic subjectivity's pervasiveness and extremity takes more than one form. Most writers on Lawrence do not discuss his comic treatment of eros, and he is often charged with a complete lack of humor. However, a strong element of sardonic grotesque humor runs all through his work. Two comedies of common-life eroticism, *Monkey-Nuts* and *Tickets, Please,* and one witty love satire, *Jimmy and the Desperate Woman,* draw upon the humor of sexual warping and the absurdity arising from violating the absolute power of eros.

In *Monkey-Nuts*[33] the sexual triangle consists of two soldiers and a "land-girl" (World War I) at a commissary loading station in an English provincial town. Albert, the monkeyish forty-year-old corporal and wiseacre, shows the verbal aggression that characterizes the sexually ambivalent. His twenty-three-year-old helper, Joe, is an inchoate and tender youth just awakening sexually. The buxom, blonde land-girl banters with Albert, but her "silent forces" of the aggressive female aim at the confusedly reluctant Joe. Sexual arousal leaves him feeling "weak as if he had had a blow," and with the encouragement of Albert he avoids the girl and spends his time with "the boys." This dramatizes the traditional ambivalence of the young male between the masculine world and sexual initiation.

The actions of the characters depend on the principle that eroticism takes covert and not-quite-conscious forms in most people—Albert's sexual wisecracks, the girl's hypnotic concern with Joe, Joe's "uncouth rudeness." But erotic fatality overtakes them all. One night, returning from the circus, the reluctant Joe is trapped alone with the girl, who then embraces him. He "felt maddened, but helpless." The female's victory emphasizes the fearful threat of sexuality to the young male.

In the reversal of erotic opposition that follows, Joe takes on predatory sexual qualities—sulkiness, odd flashes of whimsey, a "handsome, slightly sinister look," and an antagonism to Albert. The libidinal shift of the youth from his friend to the girl makes Albert calculatingly jealous, and he persuades Joe to let him substitute for the younger man on a date with the girl. To the girl's distraught demands for Joe, Albert endlessly wisecracks: "He is not conducting the service tonight; he asked me if I would officiate." Albert brazenly offers himself as a sexual substitute. The girl flees. On returning home Albert assures Joe that the girl will not do for Joe. So once again the two men "slept in amity."

It will not do, I think, to slash the threads of emotional drama here and see this as simply homosexuality defeating hetero-sexuality. The bonds between the "pals" are not treated as directly sexual. The traditional unity of male companions, here shown in comic perspective, in part has to do with the authority of the elder, who plays the purposive leader and, by way of his wisecracks, the intellectual mentor. That the wise *senex* companion in arms is so emphatically an unacceptable lover leads to his assertion of authority and his attack on the sexual initiation of the youth.

In the final scene at the loading station, the girl earnestly calls Joe to come to her. Three times Albert detains the uncertain Joe with wisecracks. Finally, a "slow, jeering smile" gathers on Joe's face, and he mortally insults the girl by calling her "mon-key-nuts." The girl, shattered, leaves and returns no more. The two men are "reassured" and "relieved." In this simple but precise comedy of the covert erotic struggle, the masculinity of the soldier pals has won its revenge, not only on the female, but on their own sexual longings.

In another comic-grotesque story of a similar period and char-acter, the rhythm of the male-female "opposition" takes a reverse pattern. In *Tickets, Please* [34] the self-defeating loyalty of sexual camaraderie also provides the crux of the action. A group of "fearless young hussies" are the conductors on a wartime Midlands tram line. They feel that they ride the most "dangerous" trams in England, and to the girls the tram car steps create their "Thermopylae." The actions of the girls depend on the *esprit* that results from being "aboard this careening vessel of a tram car, forever rocking on the waves of a stormy land." The mock-heroic style prepares for the comedy of courtship as a sexual war between a super Don Juan and female Amazons.

The "certain wild romance aboard these cars" centers on the sexual prowess of the tram-car inspector, John Thomas. (His name comes from the same folkloristic personification that Lawrence uses in the sex-ritual scenes of *Lady Chatterley's Lover,* and it stands for the phallus.) The heroine is Annie, "something of a tartar," and apparently the only tram girl who has not yet walked out with John Thomas on a dark night. The apt, wise-cracking repartee, with which most of the action of the story develops, dramatizes a "subtle antagonism" between Annie and John Thomas, to the point where they are as "shrewd with one another as man and wife." It only requires a magical occasion for the slight turn from sexual aggression to sexual acquiescence.

The magical occasions in many of Lawrence's early stories are festivals—the Harvest Festival in *Fanny and Annie,* the old-fashioned circus in *Monkey-Nuts,* the Christmas Mummery in *A Prelude,* and the annual Statues Fair in *Tickets, Please.* These special times of gaiety and the voidance of moral restraint in common life were pagan in origin as well as in tone and meaning. The festivals, with their dancing, license, sensuality, and unpious holiday spirit, were maintained despite Christian prohibition until recent times. But what Christian morality couldn't do, modern mass-technological "entertainment" could do, and has done in the last four decades. Lawrence's work reflects the change that occurred in his own lifetime—the demolition of the "festival" by technological "entertainment"—and Lawrence's later works no longer depict festivals from actual life. Instead, the late Lawrence turns to the mythic effort to simulate primitive rituals, as in *The Woman Who Rode Away* and *The Plumed Serpent;* he nostalgically recreates the pagan forms in parabolic and private worlds in *Sun, The Man Who Died* and *Lady Chatterley's Lover.*

At the fair, lovely Annie meets John Thomas who rouses her to excitement, and takes her for a walk in the dark. The later development of the erotic relation inevitably transforms "excitement" into "intimacy." In time, Annie wants "to consider him a person" and have an "intelligent interest . . . and . . . response." But the seducer intends to remain a "nocturnal presence," rather than a "person," and veers away from what he sees as the "possessive female." Here we have a condensed history of the rhythm of usual love—predatory male and possessive female moving from attraction to excitement to intimacy to possession to resentment.

Thwarted by the seducer's ways, Annie's desires turn to revenge. She makes the rounds of the tram girls who have been John Thomas's "old flames" and organizes the female collectivity of "vindictive" desires. Seven former girl friends of John Thomas await him at the depot one night. Lawrence dwells on the subjective feelings involved in this scene, emphasizing the tension, "fear," "antagonism," "trance" state, "malice," and covert emotional anguish of the women. John Thomas is trapped in the station, and the girls demand that he "choose" one girl once and for all. He refuses and the girls assault him, tear his clothes, and beat him. Prostrate but "cunning," he "chooses" the vengeful ring leader, Annie. "I wouldn't touch him," she replies, but "her face quivered with a kind of agony." She turns away with a "bitter hopelessness," and "something was broken in her." The covert ambivalence between desire and hatred has defeated her, leaving an overwhelming sense of "torture." John Thomas is allowed to go as the seven mock-vestal females "uneasily, flushed, panting, tidying their hair and dress unconsciously," stand in uncertainty. The final image shows the "mute, stupefied faces" of the girls. The postcoital melancholy of this reverse rape concludes the collective female orgasm of love-hate. Defense of the sex has defeated sex.

In these two comic-grotesque studies of lower-class life, Lawrence's use of passional prose to describe the smallest acts aims at presenting the inner reality of inchoate characters. The disproportion between the subjective drama and the character's consciousness becomes comic, even though Lawrence displays uncommon insight into the complexity of "simple" people. But his emphasis upon the extremity of feelings and the perversity of the erotic is not confined to simple characters. For Lawrence, the sophisticated reveal themselves just as inchoate and extreme in their actual feelings as do the simple: self-consciousness provides a further warping of subjectivity, rather than a greater mastery of the emotions. Eros always borders the absurd, but becomes positively obscene in the sophisticated, and with them Lawrence's comic-grotesque tone moves from sympathetic bemusement to ideological satire.

In a late and generally well-done satiric comedy of courtship, *Jimmy and the Desperate Woman*,[35] Lawrence's hatred of the sophisticated professional littérateur sometimes falls into flat sarcasm. The protagonist, Jimmy, delivers a lecture entitled "Men in Books and Men in Life." The author's heavy hand adds, "naturally, men in books came first." But other elements of the characterization more aptly display Lawrence's contempt, for the literary Jimmy is the fashionable sexual anomaly. To his men friends Jimmy displays himself as the seducer of women, a "smooth skinned satyr," but to women Jimmy inevitably reveals himself as the helpless male who must "go and fall on some woman's bosom." Either way, however, he lacks real manhood since he cannot "stand alone for ten minutes." Similar anomalies apply to other aspects of Jimmy's life. This urban sophisticate with his private income thinks of himself as "a Martyred Saint Sebastian with the mind of a Plato."

As with Huxley's similar literary figure in *Point Counter Point*,[36] devoted to St. Francis and to erotic games in the bathtub, the highfaluting ideals provide the psychological corollary of corruption in tangible life.

Jimmy, part Lawrencean, longs for a "womanly woman," a traditionally submissive female who will fall on his bosom. And Jimmy, like the endlessly disenchanted Lawrence, always searches for "real" people; he hopes to find a true primitive, an "unspoilt, unsophisticated, wild-blooded woman," a "woman of the people." Jimmy goes to the "Lawrence country" in search of his primitive woman, the "demonish" region of the coal miners. Here lives a primitive poet, Mrs. Pinnegar, a bitter and dissatisfied ex-schoolteacher and miner's wife whose poems editor-Jimmy found "so splendidly desperate" that he published them. The urbane and parasitic little Jimmy shows a bit of confusion when he meets the tall, determined miner's wife with her "relentless, unyielding feminine will." The hostility, the "grimness," and the destructive tone of those who have "gone against" themselves, shocks him when he finally meets such "real" people. But the literary voyeur is also "excited" by it and takes a "gamble," though only one "in which he could not lose" since he had no deep feelings at stake. He immediately proposes marriage to this miner's harsh wife.

At this point Lawrence develops the theme of literary consciousness in a way that goes quite beyond the author's personal animosity to professional "culture." The story becomes a dramatic critique of the inability to see the world through other than literary-colored glasses. Even when Mrs. Pinnegar takes up Jimmy's strange proposal, which includes the adoption of the miner's child, it lacks actuality to Jimmy who sees it "as if it were all merely an interior problem of his own." He was "like a drunken man, his eyes turned inward, talking to himself. The woman was no more than a ghost moving inside his own consciousness, and he was addressing her there." As Jimmy persuades the desperate but doubting woman, he says, "Why it will

mean *life* to me," and he looked, "apparently, straight at her,"
for the first time. But "the curious cast was in his eye, and he
was looking only at himself, at shadows inside his own consciousness." And as the littérateur waits for his little drama to
unfold, he looks "like the death-mask of some sceptical philosopher, who could wait through the ages, and who could hardly
distinguish life from death at any time." This Lawrencean lover
has the whole burden of Western antiorganicism attached to
him—a Platonist who imagines himself a Christian martyr; a
member of the sophisticated leisure class with an aesthetic inability to confront the actual; and a critical mind imbued with
narcissistic and epistemological uncertainty about the tangible
world, which is part and parcel of our mechanistic order. Just
as men are things in books for the littérateur, and love is an
exalted idea, so all events are charades of consciousness, and no
real world exists for one who puts all experience into the mind
and the ego.

Jimmy reveals touches of the demon lover, with his desperate
insistence on *"life,"* his quest for the primitive-erotic partner,
his "sense of strong adventure," and his personal qualities of
"Pan" and "Mephistopheles"; but he is the false demon lover, a
"Mephistopheles blind and begging in the streets." However,
Jimmy wins a pyrrhic victory over a true lover, the woman's
husband. This small but muscular man, "alive with energy," has
the primitive's "barbaric wariness" covering the passion revealed
in his look: ". . . hot blue eyes stared vague and hot into the
red coals" of the fire. The miner also maintains the self-sufficiency and insouciance—"shutting the world out of his consciousness"—which characterize the Lawrencean hero. Such
men lack sweetness and light, and the miner is "jeering," "contemptuous," and "indomitable," in his treatment of Jimmy; but
he also despairs of the world, and of his wife.[37]

A brief argument between the urbane littérateur and the
primitive workingman poses the basic Lawrencean attitude.
When the miner defiantly says, "I'm a man, aren't I?" Jimmy

blindly questions it: "What do you *mean?*" And when the miner repeatedly asserts the corollary principle of manhood, that he "won't be made use of," Jimmy neatly replies that "it doesn't mean anything. We're all made use of. . . ." Logically, the littérateur may be correct in his skepticism about the miner's individualism, but he has missed, as he must, the whole point. The quality of manhood remains a final purpose and justification and its negation comes from accepting the status of an object, a thing "to be made use of," which limits the fullness of being that gives the only meaning to existence.

The embittered miner hates being made into an industrial object, a thing to be used, in the pit. This simple but pervasive point centers Lawrence's fundamental critique of industrial society.[38] The miner reveals the same bitterness about his wife, who makes use of him, and whose impersonal face appears to him "like a stone wall with holes in it." "At the house I'm made use of, and my wife sets the dinner on the table as if I were a customer in a shop." Impersonal service for an impersonal end results in acts of will rather than acts of love.

The husband, a hard man with unified being—"fixity of the male bones"—would rather be right than married and so gives his wife her "freedom." The soft lover, Jimmy, has won the desperately willful wife from the "hard" lover, and she is no "soft" beloved. In amazement, Jimmy says: "My God, however am I going to sleep with that woman!" His "will was ready, however, and he would manage somehow." It is, the author insists, a question of "will" rather than "love" in the mental gymnastics of pretending to be "really manly." For the comic-grotesque motive of the littérateur's courtship comes from the desire to be *the* man, and the closest he can come is to sleep with a man's cast-off wife. Jimmy realizes this when alone with the wife at the conclusion of the story: ". . . a perverse but intense desire for her came over him, making him almost helpless. He could feel, so strongly, the presence of that other man about her, and this went to his head like neat spirits. In some subtle, inexplicable way, he was actually bodily present, the husband. The woman moved in his aura." The littérateur married the consubstantial husband, the vicarious virility. By taking advantage of the desperate strife that lies between man and woman, he has approached reality as close as he can—the erotic perversity of secondhand experience. He remains, of course, as far from the true perversity of selfhood as ever, and, as several mocking comments in the conclusion indicate, the vicarious lover will inevitably submit to the desperately willful woman, and he will be even less a man.

These sardonically delineated reversals of passion, into resentment, repulsion, homosexuality, vicarious longing, and other forms of self-defeat, are not the effects of external causes. No doubt many things condition the erotic warpings, but finally, as most of the stories reveal, they belong to the very nature of the erotic. "Love pushed to extremes," wrote Lawrence in an early essay, "is a battle of wills between the lovers." [39] But love —high and low, simple and sophisticated—sooner or later by the very nature of the erotic imperative reaches the extreme. This is why the heart goes "hard with hate, in the midst of . . . love." Love, for Lawrence, contrary to those with easy religious or psychological nostrums, provides no palliative for hatred because *hatred exists as part of love,* as part of the very differences and limits and extremities of any actual lovers.

V

At this point, we may appropriately explore more fully Lawrence's stories of marriage. Passionate eros—as we have already noted and will yet develop more fully in terms of Lawrence's final fictions—exists and justifies itself without regard to anything else since the intensity of immediate existence becomes the ultimate end of life. But men will rarely accept any self-sufficient end without longing also to turn it into a means for other ends. Lawrence was no exception, and as a man and moralist he passionately advocated marriage. In a relatively early polemic he wrote: "The best thing I have known is the stillness of accomplished marriage. . . ." [40] And in his last long polemic, "*A propos Lady Chatterley's Lover*," Lawrence twisted Christianity back into its pagan sources in his defense of marriage as "the clue to human life." [41] But around and between such statements Lawrence dramatized marriages in which adultery was imperative and passion was exalted over domestic morality. The once again intellectually fashionable stance of sentimentalism about family life—what else to be hopeful about?—lacks relevance to Lawrence.

The personal inheritance of the author of *Sons and Lovers* was extreme marital discord, heightened probably by a considerable mixture of masculine and feminine identification and its inner conflict; his literary inheritance from *Middlemarch* and *Jude the Obscure* was the domestic struggle of wills; and his Blakean-demonic legacy was the dialectic of endless polarity, in which "it is the fight of opposites which is holy." [42] Instead of denying the traditional strife of marriage, Lawrence makes capital of it: ". . . when the opposition is complete on either side, then there is perfection." [43]

Even in an early marriage story of simple characters, such as *The White Stocking* [44]—a minor but successful fiction with a rich and complex sense of ordinary life—the focus rests on the harsh emotional extremity just below the surface of the commonplace. This better-than-ordinary marriage of a lower-middle-class couple is presented realistically, though with such symbolic touches as Valentine's Day—during which all the action, with a flashback in time, takes place. The day of love offerings reveals the chasm underlying a good marriage.

After two years of marriage, the gay, warm, loving Mrs. Whiston receives, for the second time, a Valentine from an old admirer and former employer (Sam Adams), which contains a white stocking and a pearl earring. She hides the gifts from her quiet, devoted, prudent husband, thus creating a dangerous opening in a marriage that otherwise appears to be "sure" and "permanent." The wife's "mischievous sense of liberty" carries her back to the time when the middle-aged-roué attentions of Adams had "both thrilled her and yet had nothing to do with her." Once dangerously aroused by his libidinous appeal at a party, she had recognized the attractions of predatory sexuality as a "perverse desire." When she reached for a decorous hand-kerchief—by a practical mistake analogous to the emotional mistake of her desires—she mistakenly came up with a white stocking, which Adams pocketed at the party. Whiston saw this, became angry without quite knowing why, took her away from the party, and, when in a mixture of fear and desire she refused to go back to work for Adams, married her. So within the "surety" of a good marriage arise the essential oppositions, which make for separate individuality and passions that never quite stay within any form of marital unity.

On Valentine's Day, therefore, an unconscious "irritation" and "uneasiness" surfaces. The wife's insistence on putting on the white stockings and showing them to her husband results in the domestic drama of you-will-I-won't (take them off) until the emotional "test" deepens. She becomes openly hostile and sexual, "jeering" at her husband's manhood; his pleasant and open face responds with a "curious little grin of hate," and he calls her a "stray-running little bitch!" She furthers the unconsciously desired confrontation by also admitting to her husband the hidden gift of the earrings from the roué, and so the decent and gentle husband strikes his wife, hard, in "his lust to see her bleed, to break and destroy her."

The wife capitulates to the male, which would seem to be what she wanted all along, and the earrings are returned. The cathartic conclusion repeats the scene that occurred at the party —tears, anguish, submission, and a tenderly inchoate embrace rising over the struggle between her bitchy hungerings and his lust of hatred. Both husband and wife are committed to their own extreme subjectivities and afraid of the destructiveness so basic to selfhood; in the crisis they do not find resolution by rational and moral means but by need, fear, release, and desire—ending in the ancient principle of female submission and male supremacy grounded in passionate need. These normal and trivial people are no breast-beating romantics, but they do learn "in anguish of spirit" of their own inner extremity and separateness within their relation. Such is the peace and unity of marriage.

For Lawrence, the polarity of true male and female, which makes for both the conflict and the significance of union, cannot be resolved in moral and rational terms but only in the marriage myth of a communion of the flesh.[45] The struggle for polar balance of male and female creates the crux even in Lawrence's early stories in which the mining milieu fixes the purpose and social order, so lacking in the later fictions. While such stories as *Strike-Pay, Her Turn, Samson and Delilah, Delilah and Mr. Bircumshaw, A Sick Collier,* and *A Miner at Home* are limited by their anecdotal slightness and, sometimes, by the money plot of realistic conventions when the theme is not significantly about money at all, they do show some Lawrencean grace of time and place and domestic perceptiveness.

Strike-Pay [46] follows a small group of miners through "payday" and then the "holiday" of jokes, a walk to a ball game, horse chasing, and rounds of beer and skittles. Only toward the end of this genre piece does Lawrence develop an abruptly pointed focus on one miner, Ephraim, a hard-luck figure who loses his strike pay. Ephraim also sees the accidental death of a navvy (summarily dragged into the story), and then goes "home vaguely impressed with the sense of death, and loss, and strife." Aware of the "greater" strife and harshness of life, he for once manages to survive the lesser "battle" of domesticity and asserts his manhood against his mother-in-law and wife. The story concludes with the resubmission of the wife to the Adamic authority in the microcosm of deathly struggle: "She attended to him. Not that she was really meek. But—he was *her* man. . . ."

In the sketch *The Miner at Home*,[47] Lawrence's precise and physical realism draws a harsh account of the husband and wife's bitter disagreement over his going on strike; the head-on domestic polarity, not the socioeconomic issue, inevitably controls Lawrence's treatment. The hard conflict of Eastwood domesticity informs—perhaps overinforms—Lawrence's perception of marriage through all milieus. He can, however, vary his tone and point; a more comic version of domestic strife in a mining family, *Her Turn*,[48] also turns upon a confrontation of male and female wills. Radford, a superior miner, an independent man, and even a bit of a poet, has married a proper wife, his equal. Again the man resists domestic duties and insists on spending the strike compensation for the pleasures of the masculine world—comradeship, drink, talk, independence. The husband justifies himself in this because his wife has saved a bit of money, and she can use the savings while he uses the strike compensation for his own pleasures. The wife counters by spending all the savings on new household goods to force the husband to share the strike pay. This brings the domestic strife to a head: "There was a certain smug satisfaction about her. A wave of anger came over him, blinding him." The husband raises his fist to her, but, recognizing his defeat, turns and goes out to the garden to play with a tortoise. (This animal metaphor contrasts with the wife's "cat-like look of satisfaction.") The next week the husband turns over the strike pay to his wife. It is the turn of the hard woman to restrict the freedom of the long-enduring male in the continuing marital bestiary.

In another wry anecdote of marriage, the neatly done *Samson and Delilah*,[49] female treachery also receives a comic resolution. A stranger, characterized as a true man by his "sense of mastery and power," comes to a Cornish mining-region inn. He has several drinks, and coolly waits until closing time to reveal himself as the landlady's husband who ran away to America sixteen years before. But the equally strong-charactered landlady will not submit and denies him, "clenched with the determination of death." The life-and-death struggle involved in any form of deep personal relations characteristically reverts to violence. The landlady claims the would-be husband an imposter, and, with the aid of some soldiers, subdues, ties, and evicts the struggling man. When the bruised stranger manages to get back to the inn, he finds, despite the woman's previous vehemence, the front door unlocked and the woman waiting for him in the kitchen. The violent purgation of marital union completed, the man enters, assures the woman he has come back with money, insinuates his hand between her breasts, and concludes that "a bit of a fight for a how-de-do pleases me, that it do. But that doesn't mean as you're going to deny as you're my Missis. . . ." As in his own life, amoral battle of strong characters provides the natural mode of marriage for Lawrence; in most of his fictions the female fights to make her point, but, unless she be a modern destructive woman, submits finally to male purpose.

If the man is not capable of dominant purpose, or if the female cannot or will not submit, Samson and the faith of marriage collapse. For example, in *Delilah and Mr. Bircumshaw*,[50] Mrs. Bircumshaw and a woman friend mock the husband for acting one of the three wisemen in a church play, clipping "this ignoble Samson, all unawares, from instinct." Mr. Bircumshaw, a modern, middle-class, weak man ("a bank clerk, with a quantity of unspent energy turning sour in his veins and a fair amount of barren leisure torturing his soul") lacks purpose: he "had a good deal of vague, sensuous, religious feeling, but he lacked a faith." "A man cannot respect himself unless he does something." The epiphany to this awkwardly done piece shows that the Delilah defeats herself when she defeated her husband, and their passion peters out in bed that night.

The failure of masculine purpose more precisely and poignantly orders a brief mining-milieu story, *A Sick Collier*.[51] The husband, Horsepool, a rather different man than the miners previously discussed, shows that Lawrence's working men, unlike those of sentimental realism (such as Dickens' Stephen

Blackpool or Joe Gargery) or of social allegory (such as the types of "proletarian literature"), are distinctly individualized. Manly, but "a bit simple," Horsepool combines traditional virtue (Protestant ethos of work, thrift, and abstention) with an unusual "physical brightness"—a characteristic Lawrencean metaphor for a being with potency and *joie de vivre*. In spite of his mental limitation, Horsepool makes a laconically tender marriage with a superior woman properly awed by his physical presence, leaving him "proud" in the masculine sufficiency of a properly "polarized" mate.[52] With a knowledge of Lawrence's related fictions (including the stories just discussed), we can recognize an unusual harmony in the marriage in *The Sick Collier; this* miner turns all of his strike pay over to his wife. But still the marriage unity depends on the husband's uniquely separate power, the physical authority of a being "compact with life." His manhood, and his side of the marital equation, is shattered by a painful mine accident to his bladder. The simple physical fellow then falls beyond his depth: ". . . this pain came from inside, and terrified him." Though finally able to be up, the incomprehensible pain continues. Against the background of the miners going on the holiday outing of strike-pay day, which represents the world of manly independence and assertion, the sick miner loses his last bit of self-control. He can't bear the loss of identification with the manly life and tries to join his mates. His wife restrains him. He shouts madly: "Kill 'er!" A neighbor woman rushes in to help, and he screams to her about his wife: "I tell yer it's 'er fault as the pain comes on— I tell yer it is! Kill 'er—kill 'er!"

No manhood is left after this agony, and the miner sinks down in sobbing self-pity. The story ends with the wife confiding to the neighbor woman her fears that the husband's sickness compensation may be stopped if it becomes known that he has gone out of his mind. The wife's concern with the home and the social establishment of the marriage relation reflects the end of the husband; without his manhood, the miner has no marriage, either physically or in the larger sense of authority. His marriage constituted the supreme achievement to him, and an unconscious anguish takes the form of murderous violence directed against his wife, a defensive reprisal for his being unmanned, sexually and socially.[53]

In sardonic contrast we may look at the desexualized upper-middle-class types that swarm through Lawrence's later fictions. Such is the eunuch Rawdon of Lawrence's mocking late little anecdote *Rawdon's Roof*.[54] A common line of Lawrencean perception, the subject of many of the late essays, shows in the tart narrator's statement: "You see the top of a sleek head through a window, and you say, 'By Jove, what a pretty girl's head!' And after all, when the individual comes out, it's in trousers." Actually, the Rawdon-it is married and writes most witty letters to his wife, who leads her own life; for her part, she wouldn't mind at all if Rawdon took up with an attentive neighbor's wife: "It would be a change for him [Rawdon], from loving himself." But Rawdon swore never to let a woman sleep under his roof, in a transparent case of "mystification" that shows his total lack of all the deeper, sexual, mystery of selfhood. When the neighbor's wife, Janet, distraughtly appears one evening ("Alec came home tonight in a bigger mess than ever, and wanted to make love to me to get it off his mind. . . . I'm in love with you"), Rawdon painfully and anxiously gets rid of her. In the meantime, the narrator amusingly discovers another woman under Rawdon's roof, in bed, belonging to Rawdon's "man." The cultivated amateur, Rawdon, has literally carried out the cerebral symbolist poet's injunction to let the servants live for him, thus denying the active polarity that makes life.

Marriage, then, for Lawrence, consists of a precarious balance of nonrational opposites. Hence his polemical insistence on "pure maleness in a man, pure femaleness in a woman." [55] (No doubt the author's own strong femininity provided an autobiographical imperative for this distinctive emphasis.) But it applies with dramatic truth only to those stories of unified and

simple characters with a purpose, and with maleness and femaleness defined by the milieu. In the more complex and rootless
characters of the novels Lawrence's own double nature, masculine and feminine, requires a double—or geometrical—marriage
of the opposites within. As a commentator on an earlier phase
of the contemporary decadence—effete males, masculinized females, and the various neutered ideal types so evident in clothing
fashions and popular entertainment—Lawrence's demand for
maleness and femaleness certainly fits. But heroic masculinity
and earth-goddess femininity play a very minor role in Lawrence's works. The anguished and self-assertive heroines, destructive antiheroines, willful matriarchs, sensitive sons, Christ
figures, poetical gamekeepers, schoolteachers, and consumptive
prophets—along with their pervasive sexual ambivalences—
need, but do not have, Lawrence's pure maleness and pure
femaleness. The true Adams of the earth to found marriages,
and the true Eves to receive them, provide the constant thematic
imperative, in contrast to the dramatized and perceived actuality.
Lawrence's art also belongs to this time and place; that is, it
turns about an essential decadence and malaise.

Only in primordial marriages of another time and place—the
nineteenth-century miners, the earlier generations in *The
Rainbow,* the unrealized future in *Women in Love, Lady Chatterley's Lover,* and *The Captain's Doll* (discussed below)—
does Lawrence show marriages that are not destructive failures
and in which anguish brings life rather than futility. Marriage
in its positive sense does not properly concern Lawrence—his
eros finally leads elsewhere. Since we have already discussed
many of the destructive pieces, we need but add, mostly in terms
of minor stories, a few additional perversities.

A badly overwritten early story, *The Overtone,*[56] makes a
characteristic point in Biblical and Congregational language.
The aging wife makes a "bitter psalm": ". . . my body was a
vineyard, my veins like vines . . . like a bowl of withered
leaves, but a kaleidoscope of broken beauties, but an empty

beehive. . . ." (Lawrence, like Blake and Melville and Whitman, can write badly indeed, especially when under the spell of the "Authorized Version" and the romantic-prophetic impulse to mythicize common experience.) [57] More pointedly, the wife feels that she was like "a stream, and he threw his waste in me." She hates sex; in a flashback episode, we see that she denied her husband's desire to make love in the moonlight early in their marriage. To him, it meant a "holy desire," born of a longing almost "religion" and "transfiguration," an approach to the "Burning Bush." But to the wife their intercourse seems "really his hate ravishing her." Another destructive woman has turned love into rape. The husband, who has become unconventional to desperately assert his defeated manhood, is but a "castrated bear." As Lawrence wrote in an essay, "marriage is no marriage that is not basically and permanently phallic." [58]

The castrating marriage in *The Overtone* also has a repeated Lawrencean irony; the frigid wife concerns herself with the Rights of Woman—liberal idealism covering personal inadequacy. [59] Another characteristic overtone appears in the relation between Philia and Eros; the sexually embittered pair are mockingly described as "good friends . . . the most friendly married couple in the county." Such a relation lacks both the conflict and the communion of true marriage.

In the also mawkishly overwritten *The Old Adam*, [60] Lawrence's exploration of marital polarity appears again within the irrelevant frame of social realism. At the start a housemaid is about to leave; at the end, the maid, "her fate disposed of by her 'betters,' passed out of their three lives." The *ménage à trois,* which provides the real subject of the story, includes a middle-class family and their young male boarder, a Georgian aesthete. The crux concerns the young man's "subconscious" battle with the husband—narcissistic aesthete versus burly businessman— ending in an actual fist fight, which the aesthete rather improbably wins. The dallying guilty wife turns back to her husband in "repentance" and "self-abnegation," giving up her sexu-

ally charged, intellectual conversations with the young boarder.
But the story reveals significantly that the erotic feelings of the
quasilover transfer to the husband after the fight. They became
"close friends, with a gentleness in their bearing, one towards
the other." The longing for a rather erotic masculine friendship
—a major motif in *Sons and Lovers, The White Peacock,
Aaron's Rod, Kangaroo, The Plumed Serpent, Women in Love,*
and some of the shorter fictions, as well as in Lawrence's life—
belongs with his insistence that men, like the husbands in the
mining stories, must achieve a deep camaraderie outside of marriage. While this closely conjoins with the recurrent homosexual
analysis in Lawrence's work, the insistence on a masculine
Philia to counterbalance heterosexual Eros may also be viewed
as recognition that marriage is not and cannot be the totality of
man's emotions. However, given the handling of *Old Adam,*
and similar episodes in the novels, the resolution would seem to
be a rather melodramatic and murky way of putting the basic
insight about marital threesomes: Who is seducing whom?

Here, as in so many of the stories with the "second-best"
motif, the woman chooses the lesser but more manly sensibility
—the *un*-Lawrencean male; simultaneously, some deeper communion between the feminine and masculine man arises. The
same choice but different consequences provide the material for
the atmospheric melodrama, *The Shadow in the Rose Garden*,[61] where the symbolic contrast between love and marriage
centers on a brutal honeymoon episode. The story starts by
focusing briefly on a small man viewing himself in a mirror—
"self-commiseration mingled with his appreciation of his own
physiognomy." He reveals himself as his wife's inferior in social
background and in sensibility. On this first day of marriage, the
wife, who has chosen the honeymoon place, insists on walking
alone to a rose garden adjacent to a house with "a sterile appearance, as if it were still used, but not inhabited." Such is the
nature of the past. For this scene of the woman's former passion, Lawrence's style rhetorically heightens. The "shadow" of

the title belongs to a man who comes over to the woman in the rose garden, her handsome former lover whom she believed dead, now speaking to her without recognition since he is only the shadow of a man—a lunatic. At first, she feels that the "whole world was deranged," and only gradually accepts the fact of the lover's madness. He is led away by his keeper.

Part of the significant effect of the story depends upon the rose garden of love. Upon entering the garden, the woman's "existence lapses" for a moment, and she becomes the allegorical figure, "a rose that could not come into blossom." Lawrence partly inverts the allegorical rose tradition; although elsewhere he holds to its "transcendence" with emotional satisfaction being a "rose of roses taking place." [62] An emotional antimorality provides the justification: "We know that the rose comes to blossom. It is our business to go as we are impelled, with faith and pure spontaneous morality [sic], knowing that the rose blossoms, and taking that knowledge for sufficient." [63] The physiological as well as the theological meaning of the rose appears in other fictions: in *The Man Who Died*, the act of coition and rebirth is achieved by "the piercing transcendence of desire" in "the interfolded warmth" of the priestess, "the woman, the heart of the rose! My mansion is the intricate warm rose, my joy is this blossom!" The female *belle chose*, the analogical form underlying the traditional rose symbolism of love, here becomes explicit.

In *The Shadow in the Rose Garden*, the negative identification of the unsatisfied honeymooning woman with the rose draws upon the same inversion of the rose as in William Blake's "A Sick Rose." [64] The woman's confrontation of her inadequate husband, after leaving the rose garden and her mad lover, turns upon the jealous hatred of thorny restraint. The wife admits that she has had a lover when her husband baits her: "You mean you . . . came to me to marry you when you'd done—"; "you mean to say you used to go—the whole hogger?" The sexual-social crudity of the husband expresses a horrified fascination with the tainting of sexual possession, a covert violence of jealousy so destructive but so basic to the traditions of marital fidelity.

When the wife adds that the former lover is now a lunatic, the husband asks "in a small voice" if the man recognized her. Once again, sexual consciousness—"sex-in-the-head"—provides the pain. His "small voice" of defeat—in contrast to his previous manner—shows recognition of the anguish of marriage. The story concludes: "At last he had learned the width of the breach between them. . . . It would be a violation to each of them to be brought into contact. . . . They were both shocked so much, they were impersonal, and no longer hated each other." It has been another of those cathartic moments highlighting the *gulf* of marriage. In *The Shadow in the Rose Garden,* love and marriage exist in antithetical separation. As a point of fact, this appears generally true of Lawrence's fictions. While true marriage may, at its best, be achieved by the sense of passionate fate that we call love, marriage itself is, at best, a dangerous equilibrium and convenience always threatening to break open and reveal the extremity of the eros that it never quite satisfies. The opposition, the abyss, between man and woman—often heightened by false morality and society, by lack of passion and warped desire—becomes the center of the human relation. Relatedness demands difference and polarity, and these differences are cosmic, ultimate. Conflict, then, appears as not incidental but essential: the transcendent effort at unity depends on more fully realizing the disparateness. The "ideal" unities of sentiment, reason, and goodness not only contradict the cosmic nature of existence but viciously destroy human relations. Recognition of authentic opposition, not the lessening of it, makes for more perfect union.[65]

But one suspects this makes for marriage in depth rather than marriage in time. For Lawrence, the erotic situation—most often, either agonized courtship or adulterous flight—focuses the nature of the lovers, and passion tests the quality of their being. Lawrence was aware of the limits of the erotic quest: "I think it is terrible to be young. The ecstasies and agonies of love, the agonies and ecstasies of fear and doubt and drop by drop fulfillment, realization." [66] But Lawrence's perceptions didn't really find a way out of this. Even if we leave aside all the fictions whose point is primarily negative, we will find but few fictions concerned with a creative continuity—raising children, completing a life work, growing old. Lawrence centers on the erotic moments, the extreme and passional eruptions, because, given his perspective, he can do nothing else. Eros, like death and surpassing moments of pain and joy, is worldless and timeless.

Love, as we see in the endings of Lawrence's longer and more affirmative fictions, remains problematic and indecisive when faced with the continuity of generation, work, and society. Lawrence refused to write complete love tragedies in which heroic passion leads to destruction and apotheosis; and he refused to write complete love comedies in which eros submerges in generation and social order. Instead, he wrote a kind of erotic melodrama—the violence, the shock effects, the frequent coincidences, the supernaturalism, the allegorically paired characters, the one-sided fate, the charged atmospheres, the world-sundering revelations. For, despite some perverse dialectics in which the negative becomes the positive, conflict becomes union, Lawrence's one subject resides in crucial moments of eros, fate, negation, awareness, selfhood, and aliveness.

VII

Yet Lawrence also persisted in writing profoundly equivocal courtship stories. *The Captain's Doll,* a courtship novella from his "middle" period, will allow us to examine the purpose, and the Lawrencean failure of purpose, defining Adamic maleness and the continuity of life. *The Captain's Doll,*[67] an abbreviated novel covering the courtship of a second wife in post-World War I Germany by the Scotch Captain Hepburn, uses a rather snobbish adaption of Lawrence's own character and marital arguments. It transforms the forty-one-year-old hero from a conventional husband to a self-defining man making a passionately purposeful marriage, though with surprisingly little emphasis on sexual passion.

The doll of the title, a portrait of the Captain—a graven image—was created by the impoverished Countess Hannele, the Captain's mistress in occupied Germany. Hannele's hold on Hepburn, despite her totemic command, totters with the arrival of Hepburn's wife, who imperiously demands the doll on the assumption that any image of her husband should be in her control. When Hannele learns that Hepburn really plays the adoring puppet for his wife, she sells the doll and departs. After the accidental death of his wife, Hepburn goes in search of Hannele and a new human connection. Pursuing the doll as a clue, he finally ends up with a grotesque image of himself, a modernist (apparently surrealistic) painting of the doll, and then with Hannele, who appears ready to make a rather decadent marriage to someone else. In the intermittent dialogue between Hepburn and Hannele on the significance of the doll, Hepburn comments: "The most loving and adoring woman today could any minute start and make a doll of her husband—as you made of me. . . . The doll would be her hero: and her hero would be no more than a doll." "And when she's got your doll, that's all she wants. And that's what love means. And so, I won't be loved. And I won't love." The primitive fear of the enemy controlling the totem is utilized in this novella to insist that marriage and manhood require something else than the feminine magic of love.[68] At the end, not only has the doll disappeared, but the modernist image denying selfhood and purpose (the scrambled painting) will be burned as a mark of submission by the woman.

Now, contrary to the muddy mystification of a good bit of contemporary aesthetic discussion, the doll of the novella simply provides a concrete instance of the theme; Lawrence never lets the symbol usurp the action, and the novella focuses on the man, not the doll. Lawrence's work, in contrast to some other forms of symbolic fiction (such as that of Poe and his modern followers in the "southern school"), does not use the symbol as the reality, nor even as the perception of reality, but simply as an analogy of the subjective problem of the hero. The actual world, not the symbolic world, is really real.

Before turning to what the hero substitutes for adoring love, we must examine his heroism, and see what leads to a unity and continuity beyond eros. With the exception of some trite early description ("an officer and a gentleman," etc.), Hepburn reveals the demonic-heroic qualities—a "queer one" with a black charm, dark magic, "strange dark vacancy," a "gargoyle smile"; a lack of social ambition, an obsession with the moon and the cold alien cosmos (rather awkwardly treated as astronomy); insouciance and self-sufficiency; and the repeated insistence on nihilism ("nullus," "not real," "unseeing," "vacant," "nothing," a fascinating "meaninglessness," denials of the "significance" of life, the insistence that "nothing in time or space matters . . ." that "there is nothing outside [immediate life] for human beings," and that "in great measure there is nothing"). Recognizing the indifference of the universe, Hepburn insists on "this minute" of life as all-important, for the "future is used up every day." This acceptance of the meaninglessness of the future and the total impersonality of the universe provides the heroic masculine stance. But while nihilism grounds the hero, his negation must be negated since he has turned the negative view of the universe into negative passional life. Thus he can casually inform his mistress that he will spend the week with his wife and, of course, make love to her; they had always been "such good friends" (thus such poor lovers), and she, "woman-like," expects love: "I like her to get what pleasure out of life she can." Eros as a neutral device for pleasuring someone else stands antithetical to all authentic passion and being.

The treatment here depends largely on comic devices—"our hero," "our dear Captain," the picaresque pursuit of the doll, the wry tone and scene, and the marriage resolution. Using, also, the traditional comic device of mistaken identities, Lawrence has the genteel and malicious Mrs. Hepburn—another nasty portrait of the upper-middle-class lady—reveal her husband's infidelity to another woman, except that the confidant turns out to be the mistress. Drawing upon his apt ear for speech, Lawrence shrewdly mocks the woman, but also displays, amidst the wife's bangles and malice and hypocrisy, a grotesque image of Hepburn when he on bended knee promised to make his wife happy. The only thing more fatuous than the pursuit of happiness is the pursuit of someone else's happiness.[69] And Hannele's recognition of Hepburn as the idealist lover of the grasping and nasty middle-class woman sadly and ironically disillusions her in her heroic lover: "Perhaps the long disillusion of life was falser than the brief moments of real illusion."

The comically detached author disposes of the wife, and his hero's weakness, with an artifice in direct contrast to the life-imitative irregularity of the later sections of the novella. (Moreover, after this point, Hepburn increasingly sounds like his author.) Mrs. Hepburn, as afraid of heights as of freedom, falls out of a hotel window. The hero reacts with the almost Swiftian misanthropy that recurs in Lawrence, an "instantaneous disgust, when anybody wanted to share his emotions with him," so that he "felt sick, even physically," at most human contact. But at this point the author intrudes the comic perspective to pull the nihilistic motif out of the downward path of wisdom:

All our troubles, says somebody wise, come upon us because we cannot be alone. And that is all very well. We must all be *able* to be alone, otherwise we are just victims. But when we are *able* to be alone, then we realize that the only thing to do is to start a new relationship with another—or even with the same human being. That people should all be stuck apart, like so many telegraph poles, is nonsense.

Hepburn wryly prepares to remarry. "The temptation this time was to be adored" instead of the adorer, and to marry an innocent young thing. But this, the hero recognizes, would still be the old fallacy of adoration-love—Lawrence's view of courtly, ideal-ized, feminized eros. And the true hero does not want sentiment but erotic fate, not a "rosy love" but a "hard destiny."

Hepburn's search in Europe for Hannele—via his pursuit of the doll, the graven image of false love—leads finally to the Austrian Tyrol. The novella becomes increasingly digressive and almost joins Lawrence's brilliant travel writings in the incisive "spirit of place" of the description of postwar Austria. Lawrence comments on the social types of decadence, good bread, the "wrong sort" of Jews (one of his sillier provincial bigotries), flowers, the sense of the lost past, the repulsive oddities of tour-ists, and the malice of those who must serve them; and, espe-cially, on the literal and metaphoric qualities of the mountain scene. Part of the special quality of Lawrence's descriptive pow-ers resides in a constant double awareness—"the place was beau-tiful, but the life wasn't"—in which he persuades the reader, in detail, of both responses. At the very moment of conveying the gaiety and expectation of a holiday outing, the author-hero be-comes aware that "the world is not made for man's everlasting holiday." And his description of the alien mountain scene makes this the essential part of the "pleasure" trip.

As with so many artists at least partly rooted in the romantic traditions, Lawrence's desire to imitate and comment upon the plenitude of life breaks out of the limits of the tale. Thus the metaphoric antithesis (once again) of the warm valley of life and the cold mountain of annihilation does not have a balanced treatment.[70] In a brief, vital scene, Hepburn crosses the lake in a small boat to Hannele's house; the boat glides through a group of vivacious and unself-conscious youths swimming in the warm water. Then "he saw her white shoulder, and her white legs below in the clear water. Round the boat fishes were suddenly jumping."

Immediately following this trope of sexual suggestion comes the reverse scene, Hannele and Hepburn's feast-day trip to the glacier in the mountains, which were "like a doom." The description of the ride and walk into the mountains evokes the Lawrencean hyper-sensitivity to harsh nature. The road runs through a "valley of the shadow of death." And, as in the later sections of *St. Mawr,* there arises a threatening sexual metaphor in the details of the animistic scene: a frightened mare runs frenziedly down the road, and Hepburn sees a "cleft . . . [a] secret, naked place of the earth." To find himself, the man must conquer this frightening female nature; he must outdo it by being fixed on something else "as if he were eternal, facing these upper facts."

The battle of the sexes on this glacial mountain side—Hannele and Hepburn act as if they had been long married—projects into the scene. The woman identifies with the cosmic scene; the man attempts to defy the cosmos. She attacks him for not submitting: "You can do nothing but find fault even with God's mountains." He translates her adoration of the mountains into an affirmation of the ideal, and vehemently attacks it: "I hate them. . . . I hate their uplift. I hate people prancing on mountain-tops and feeling exalted." " 'You must be a little mad,' she said superbly, 'to talk like that about the mountains. They are so much bigger than you.' " He denies this! Such demonic "black passion" and defiance of the cosmos appear to the woman as "megalomania." But she is also fascinated: "To what country did he belong—to what dark, different atmosphere?" Woman-like, her explanation reaches the conclusion that in some obscure way such a man must be expressing a demand for love. She admits that she loves Hepburn, but she also decides that she will not submit because she deserves the proper adoration and gestures of male submission. Lawrence's Hepburn, however, continues the author's assault on adoration love.

The couple reach the "grand beast," the "immense sky-bear" of the glacier, to which the man responds with "terror" and the woman with "ecstasy." Yet he finds the cold world demanding from him some sort of "ordeal or mystic battle" of self-definition. Unlike Lawrence's doomed heroes on the mountain of annihilation, Hepburn's trial with the destructive cosmos reduces to comic disproportion: he climbs the glacier uncertainly, clumsily has to go on all fours, scratches his fingers, and climbs back down. While hardly "mystic battle," his awareness of cosmic negation is there: "The wonder, the terror, and the bitterness of it. A world sufficient unto itself in lifelessness. . . ." Consequently, when he catches up with Hannele—despite her exaltation of the glacier, she has turned back—he makes his comic affirmation: "I prefer the world where cabbages will grow." This is Hepburn's statement of love.[71]

Comic battle dominates most of the remaining section of the novella, the trip back down the mountain to the warm valley. Hepburn, his manhood tested on the mountain, and his desire strong for the marital-cabbage world, proposes: ". . . if you were not going to marry [the other man], I should suggest that you marry me." Shocked by the unsentimental proposal, the woman insists marriage results only from adoring love. Coolly going on, "leaving aside the question of whether you love me or I love you—," he adds that love is a mistake. All love for a woman—for his mother, his first wife, and for Hannele—defeated him, turned him into a doll. "I don't want marriage on a basis of love." What then? He almost wants a "Patient Griselda"; most certainly he wants "honour and obedience: and the proper physical feelings." This, too, develops in a comic context: piqued by his unsentimental honesty, Hannele wishes to leave Hepburn, but there is only one seat for the trip down, next to him. Then she wishes to sit disdainfully apart, but the careening bus throws her against him. And so on.

Perhaps the true comic twist appears in a Lawrencean hero asking for almost quaintly old-fashioned marriage. In refusing the declaration of love, Lawrence's hero maintains the dark passion. The perverse courtship (and Lawrence really has no others) intentionally contrasts with the feminized, sentimental, rhetorical, and neutered courtliness that has long been, and still is, the dominant pattern of "love-making." Both verbally and physically, Lawrence eliminates masturbatory love-play; eros, even when put in the wry and metaphoric terms of *The Captain's Doll,* remains a form of individualized assault, however tender.

Love, honor, cherish, and obey—the traditional wedding order—provides the resolution, as with most love comedy. In this respect, *The Captain's Doll* shows the calm and orderly center of Lawrence's work with the hero envisioning something far different than romantic puppetry, yet a "desire" that goes "very much deeper than love" without being an annihilating "doom." But what is this destiny that transcends counterfeit-love, passion, and negation? While the rhetoric of traditional marriage provides the mythic resolution to the story, the tale concludes as just a prelude to marriage. The gulf of actual marriage, the agonized separateness so consistently at the center of Lawrence's images of eros, remains. Lawrence never did write the main movement, the story of modern destined marriage.

One reason for this goes beyond Lawrence's profound nihilism to the modern missing link—the faith in a genuinely purposive and continuing order of life. The sexual provides only part of this purpose. (Where "there is really sex there is the underlying passion for fidelity," [72] Lawrence optimistically wrote.) Lawrence also demands that a true union be based on a "sense of purpose," an awareness of greater activity and wholeness to be found in man's "wish to make the world new." [73] As Lawrence insists in *The Captain's Doll,* love itself cannot provide the Adamic purpose. "Unless," he wrote earlier, "a man believes in himself and his gods, *genuinely* . . . his woman will destroy him." [74] And even passion depends on this larger sense of individual value: ". . . there can be no successful sex union unless the greater hope of purposive, constructive activity fires the soul of the man all the time. . . ." [75] Thus, finally, Lawrence affirms a significant universe! But perhaps we should quote the rest of the sentence: ". . . or the hope of passionate, purposive *destructive* activity: the two amount religiously to the same thing, within the individual." [76] It is a typical Lawrencean perversity to see the destructive as equally valid as the constructive. Possibly, Lawrence overstates the demonic case. But perhaps not, since purposive destructive activity, within the individual, also creates a hard and genuine character.

Hepburn, in *The Captain's Doll,* clinches his marriage proposal by insisting that Hannele obey him because he will obey his larger purposes. This is akin to the Judaic wisdom that Adam loves God while Eve loves God by loving Adam. [77] But what is Hepburn's divine sanction, his larger purpose? He intends to write a book on the moon and to help develop a farm in primitive Africa. Since neither subject has dramatic presence in the novella, it is difficult to give them credence. But grant them for the moment; a second look will show that they, too, reveal but lightly disguised negations: the identification with the moon repeats the insistence on the cold and alien cosmos, the universal nihilism; [78] the farm in Africa represents, yet again, Lawrence's dream of the pastoral flight from modern civilization. Quite possibly, Lawrence's twentieth-century hero can do nothing else, despite his victories over his past, his solitude, his icy peak of annihilation, and counterfeit love. The authenticity remains in the effort at overcoming.

In *The Captain's Doll* the marital myth may provide the rounded conclusion of art to a somewhat irregular love comedy, but the creative purpose that gives the communion of man and woman a community remains uncertain. Purposive activity, except for negation, does not arise in other contemporary modern love fables, such as Conrad's *Victory,* Hemingway's *Farewell to Arms,* Fitzgerald's *Tender Is the Night,* and Faulkner's *The Wild Palms.* Most of these—consequently—attempt some version of the tragic resolution. Lawrence, who objected to moralistic Tolstoy killing off Anna Karenina, [79] never treats love, or the failure to translate love into marriage in a hostile world, as a tragedy, because he finds that eros has its own unique value, regardless of its outcome.

Marriage, for Lawrence, despite his harsh insights into both psychic separateness and the lack of worldly purpose, requires affirmation. Perversely: ". . . the sense of the eternality of marriage is essential to the inner peace, both of men and women. Even if it is a sense of doom. . . ." [80] For the very urgency of the opposition of man and woman, and the very hunger for a common purpose, require that united sense of fate beyond sentiment, morality, or even happiness. The negation and poignancy of marriage will not be tragic so long as it, too, can produce the Lawrencean absolute, "the good natural glow of life." [81]

Love (eros), though not to be simply equated with marriage, receives the same test, rather than that of any "moral good." Nor is it to be measured by the social stick. "While ever it lives, the fire of sex, which is the source of beauty and anger, burns in us beyond our understanding. Like actual fire . . . it will burn our fingers if we touch it carelessly. And so social man, who only wants to be 'safe,' hates the fire of sex." [82] Well he might, but, as the tales dramatize so fully, one cannot escape the flames of eros just by marriage, or by the warpings of covert erotic desire which are both more pervasive and more dangerous than desire itself. Yet the "fulfillment" and the "realization" of passion, and even of the anguish of polarity, provide both the understanding of actual life, and the sense of life itself. Thus eros is extreme, and final: ". . . only the flow matters, live and let live, love and let love. There is no point to love." [83]

CHAPTER V

Parables of Regeneration

The final aim is not to know, but to be.[1]

I

MUCH of Lawrence's work can only be understood as exercises in the religious life, as efforts indifferent to the niceties of art and the proprieties of reason—poems that are not, in their inexpressive anger, poems at all (much of the latter verse), and discussions that hysterically rage over everything (the half dozen volumes of polemic and large parts of the novels). Lawrence was a man with a message, a being, that is, impelled beyond any requirement of art or profit to confess and denounce and expose and demand. From his early self-identification as "a passionately religious man"[2] to his final self-chosen role as the heretical prophet in evil times—the last of God's angry men —he sought not art and knowledge, although contradictorily using the means of art and knowledge, but to renew the sense of actuality, to go beyond the knowable into extreme states of feeling, and to transform existence. His art and his arguments partly achieve uniqueness and partly falter because of these larger purposes, and, hence, without taking some account of his religious quest we fail to confront Lawrence's work. To treat of Lawrence's religion raises no discontinuity with the pervasive negative qualities we have been emphasizing. No idealism replaces the nihilism; no angels usurp the demons; no sweetness and light discolor the impassioned extremity. Only by and with

the perversities, not in spite of them, do we find Lawrencean
being.

Lawrence was religious as only, in the modern Western
world, the non-Christian can be. Indeed, much of his religiousness was rooted in ancient heretical traditions of anti-Christianity. His intellectual starting point, a widespread one in the
past century, assumed the collapse of Christianity: "The adventure is gone out of Christianity. We must start on a new adventure towards God." "I know the greatness of Christianity: it
is a past greatness." [3] The insistence on the death of God—
"the Almighty has vacated, abdicated, climbed down" [4]—provides a critical perspective to be sharply distinguished from
humanistic watering-down of religion and positivistic incompre-
hension. Such religious antireligion has manifold causes. Anti-
Puritanism provides one of the most obviously personal elements
in Lawrence's attack on Christianity. The emphatically pervasive
modern rejection of the traditional Christian view of immortality
—one felt even by many Christians—provides another element
and explains Lawrence's repeated insistence on this life. Lawrence's late-romantic exaltation of nature—from geraniums to
genitalia—raises yet another conflict with a Christianity that,
despite certain poetic and theological versions, has long been
predominantly antinature in its asceticism, other-worldliness,
and idealist metaphysic. Equally important, Lawrence's rejection of bourgeois society and standards, with which Protestant
Christianity finds almost a total identification, adds social indignation to his anti-Christianity. But the lack of vitality, the
puritan rigidity, the antinaturalness, the dead doctrine of immortality, and the *embourgeoisement* are only part of the
falsity of Christianity; Lawrence also has fundamental metaphysical criticisms. He repeatedly attacks the Judeo-Christian
"farce of cosmic unity" and its monotheistic "monomaniac." [5]
Lawrence hated "oneness" and its closed universe: he suggested
that metaphysical oneness denied vitality and change; social
oneness led to modern wars and mass society; and psychological

oneness never accords with the polarized spirit of man.[6] Cosmic, social, and moral unity is neither true nor desirable. "Equilibrium argues either a dualistic or a pluralistic universe. The Greeks, being sane, were pantheists and pluralists, and so am I." "We live in a pluralistic universe, full of gods and strange gods and unknown gods." [7] Lawrence's view of the good life as that of a small, pastoral, communal society also led to pagan rather than Christian tropes. His attitude toward priests, clergymen, and the larger established churches ranges from contempt to the incisive unmasking of spiritual malaise (in both early and late fictions). And for Lawrence, the Christ of Christianity, as we shall discuss later, does not represent salvation but symbolizes a pernicious morality. Anything left? Certainly: the prophetic, intensely individual, protesting, agonized exaltation of nonpietistic and noninstitutionalized Christianity remains an essential part of Lawrence's religious cast. His was a Protestant paganism.

The artist as religious heretic provides much of those traditions that moralists and academic hierarchs castigate as "irrationalism." For Lawrence, the rationalistic creates falsity at several levels. His own intellectual attack on intellectualism, in and out of the fictions, aims at mind-body, thought-feeling, and similar bifurcations of the wholeness of life for the individual. In sum, his major critique insists that the mind itself creates no real values—life is nonrational in its sources, powers, and qualities—and that the dominance of the abstract, divisive, and dehumanized result from the usurpation of the rational over prerational values. In historical terms, he sees both the money-class society of the nineteenth century and the technological mass society of the twentieth as showing the large-scale extension of such rationalization until categorical and mechanical attainments have resulted in a drastic loss of responsive life.[8] *"Non cogito, ergo sum."* [9]

Perhaps thus far only the positivist and the idealist, with their ostensibly contrary but actually similar redemptive beliefs in abstract mental constructs, would seriously disagree. But Law-rencean "irrationalism" goes further: "Life is a traveling to the edge of knowledge, then a leap taken." [10] The landing is an old one: "There must be a certain faith. And that means an ultimate reliance on that which is beyond our will, and not contained in our ego." [11] This state of being, which goes beyond knowledge, depends on the vital force that Lawrence variously called "the demon," the "sun within suns," "life," "the dark gods," "po-larity," "aliveness," "blood-consciousness," "the phallic power," "the elemental fire," "the godhead of energy," "the saviour," "the flame," "the flow of life," "the living flux," "the mystery," etc. The many tropes for the one force come from demonic perversity, salvational Christianity, Mediterranean forms of the fertility cult, and, with unconscious irony, from more modern forms of mysterious dynamism: the secret of life is "the contact, the spark of exchange. That which can never be fastened upon, forever gone, forever coming, never to be detained: the spark of contact." [12] As with all religious ultimates, paradox and parable, metaphor and incantation attempt to specify the "wonder" of sacredness that creates a pervasive quality rather than an objec-tive entity. Lawrence, of course, at times says some very silly things, and deduces some gross absurdities from the flux of energy and responsiveness that gives the meaning to life— though no more so than statements to be found in any other religious pronouncements.[13] His "religion of life" goes beyond any direct conceptualization, any social order, or any moral code.[14] When Lawrence attempts to describe (most often in novels) the "instinctual" or "intuitive" awareness necessary for recognizing the vital force, he usually writes an especially obtuse prose. Recognizing Lawrence's perverse dialectic of social and moral negation and of paradoxical emotional transforma-tion provides the clearest ingress into his religious vitalism.

But before looking at the perverse religious fictions, we must apply a bit of discrimination to the key trope of *desire*. Where the moralist believes in *goodness* which he achieves by *will*, and the Christian in *grace* which he achieves by some form of *abnegation,* the redeemed Lawrencean seeks *aliveness* which he achieves by *desire.* The vitalist, unlike the classical moralist and the Christian, neither commands nor submits but intensifies. Where the moralist and the Christian must reject the imperfect and the evil, which frequently derive from desires, the Lawrencean must accept his desires and reject the goodness, the will, and the codes of perfection and evil denying the desires. However, Lawrence does not aim at glorifying gratuitous or random impulses and pleasures. Neither selfish gratification nor hedonistic calculus is relevant. "Living consists in doing what you really, vitally want to do: what the *life* in you wants to do, not what your ego imagines you want to do. And to find out *how* the life in you wants to be lived, and to live it, is terribly difficult." [15] Contrary to traditional moralists, Lawrence insists that it is harder to act according to desire than according to ethical rule:

. . . all that really matters is that men and women should do what they *really* want to do. Though here, as everywhere, we must remember that man has a double set of desires, the shallow and the profound, the personal, superficial, temporary desires, and the inner, impersonal, great desires that are fulfilled in long periods of time. The desires of the moment are easy to recognize, but the others, the deeper ones, are difficult.[16]

The long and agonized effort to find out what one really desires, to reach the deepest needs that relate one to reality, to other individuals, and to the self, provides the cruxes of most of Lawrence's fictions. In the stories moral behavior is mechanical and easy, but passionate relatedness is long and arduous.

The reader hostile to the Lawrencean view may suspect that part of the easiness of moral restraint and the difficulty of passional release derives from the author's—and the culture's—excessively moral bias, so embedded in Christian and idealist sentiments. But to moralistically extend this criticism and hold up the sadist or rapist as a refutation of the value of desire misses the point. While the moralist may quite properly confess his own intimate dependence on violence and hatred, historical brutality and nastiness would seem to owe more to moral righteousness, religions of antilife, exalted ambitions, and claims for general welfare and justice, than to the fulfillment of individual desires.

As with the *arête* of the Greek hero, or the *satori* of the Zen Buddhist, fulfillment of the most complete desire carries one outside the ordinary ethos. The Lawrencean hero, too, must achieve a transcendent unity of self-acceptance and belief in himself, for "a thing you truly believe in cannot be wrong." [17] The deepest of feelings are autonomous and ultimate: ". . . desire in itself being beyond criticism and moral judgment." [18] If the desire *turns* to self-aggrandizement and utility, or to corruptive means for controlling some object of desire, then something else has willfully replaced the desire. Even destructiveness, uncorrupted to ideal proportions, commits at most the personal act of suicide. So long as desire remains an end in itself, it lies beyond good and evil.

Those momentous situations of self-revelation where rational and moral means lack relevance are the center of Lawrence's fictions. One of his better-known stories, *The Horse Dealer's Daughter*,[19] shows the characteristic pattern, in stark form, of the impersonal unfolding of desire. The piece opens with the description of the collapse of a way of life, the break-up of the late horse dealer's family, which provides the necessary chaos for liberating desire from the social order and for the moment of revelatory nakedness. The harsh and now bankrupt sons of Pervin, the horse dealer, have made their unawakened sister, Mabel, play Cinderella-drudge. Mabel's and her brothers' native vitality, revealed in the "curious, sullen animal pride that dominated each member of the family," has been soured by defeat. In Mabel's case, defeat also exudes from being tied to her dead mother. Brought by chaos into freedom, Mabel flees to her mother's grave, then somnambulistically ends the life of dreary compulsion by walking into the black, cold mire of a winter pond. In subordination to the image of her mother and the drudgery of her family, the "world of death" seems the greatest reality to her.

But the suicide attempt of one without desire is transformed by a fairy-tale coincidence. A young and inchoate doctor, Jack Fergusson, like the girl a despairing drudge, accidentally sees her go under the dank waters. He goes in to save her; and, although he cannot swim and goes over his head, he does save her. Originally entitled by Lawrence "The Miracle," [20] *The Horse Dealer's Daughter* may be viewed as one of a series of Lawrence's tales turning about a moment of regenerative baptism. The young man, "spell-bound," "mesmerized," by something deeper than his consciousness, "felt delivered from his own fretted, daily self." The courageous breakthrough at the moment of despair and death brings out the new agony of desire. The man sees the "terrible shining joy in her eyes, which really terrified him, and yet which he wanted to see, because he feared the look of doubt still more." The necessary faith in life takes the form of erotic confrontation. Having been carried home, undressed, and warmed back to life by the doctor, Mabel regains consciousness to find herself on the desperate edge between life and death, love and despair. Lawrence has carefully created a figure of profound naiveté, and so, naked before the man, she simply draws the conclusion of need: either he loves her, or she is dead. By the very nakedness of her self and her need, she forces him to recognize desire—"he had crossed the gulf over to her." The story ends with the man's agonized assent to desire: " 'No, I want you, I want you,' " was all he answered to her question of love, "blindly, with that terrible intonation which frightened her almost more than her horror lest he should not *want* her." Such elemental courtship is not only a choice of love over death but of love as itself a kind of death—the most characteristic mark of passion.

The insistence upon naiveté, partly created by placing the fable here in the focus of the ordinary and "realistic," illustrates a Lawrencean principle: ". . . the naive or innocent core of a man is always his vital core." [21] The choice of love, from the agonized awareness of desire, goes quite beyond any rational possibility. When innocence meets innocence at the Edenic moment of bared consciousness—death, nakedness, need—vital fulfillment and absolute irrational choice reach immanence. The deep desire then realized compounds fear and joy, for the principle of passion is not solely that of pleasure. Lawrence wrote, "happiness is not the whole of fulfillment" [22]—thus the sense of fatality and destiny, which overwhelms the ego with the deeper unitary need of the self to constitute the ultimate, religious moment of choice and awareness.

II

The regenerative moments, for Lawrence the paradigms of all creativity and meaning, consist of just such agonized efforts to realize the deepest of desires. But usually this enhancement of life requires emphatic negation of the triviality, the fixity, the ordinariness and, apparently, the guilt of usual life. Without a willingness to submit to the extremity of feeling, the watershed moments of desire would simply be the final stage of destruction, as with Lawrence's suicidal idealists. Or, to put the matter in other terms, rebirth requires a dying to much of life.

The regeneration may lead to, as well as require, destruction. Lawrence warns that the "blarney about pure constructive activity is all poppycock—nine-tenths at least must be smash-smash!—or else *all* your constructive activity turns out to be feebly destructive." [23] Despite his affirmative avowals of the "pure disinterested craving of the human male to make something wonderful out of his own head and his own self, and his own soul's faith and delight," because "the essentially religious or creative motive is the first motive of all human activity," [24] Lawrence's negations rarely achieve such purpose. Lawrencean creativity belongs to the romantic assertion of possibility and to the rebellion against what exists: "I know I exist, and I know I am I, because I feel the divine discontent. . . ." [25]

Now the aim of this rebellion cannot be any order of morality as such, since one seeks to break through all order, all goodness: "For what does goodness mean? It means in the end, being like everybody else, and not having a soul to call your own. You must be good and feel exactly what is expected of you, which is just what other people feel. Which means in the end you feel nothing at all. . . ." [26] The Lawrencean absolute remains solely individual: "To be," Lawrence writes, "means to be different." [27] Thus all certitudes other than the unique moments of individual subjectivity are pernicious; no political or social order, no ideal, rational, or cultural form, is fully self-justifying. The law, even the longing for the objective rule, destroys the subjective spirit. This insistence on his version of Protestant illumination in the midst of the endless flux holds central importance. "This is evil, this desire for constancy, for fixity in the temporal world. This is the denial of the absolute good, the revocation of the Kingdom of Heaven." [28]

Heaven, too, shows no fixed abode. Like an earlier vitalist, William Blake, Lawrence sees the religious image as the deification of human impulse: "What we have to remember is that the great religious images are only images of our own experience, or of our own state of mind and soul." [29] Because human reality contains the absolute, being must be physical, in its fully sexual sense. "Being is not ideal, as Plato would have it, nor spiritual. It is a transcendent form of existence, and as material as existence is." [30] Tangible existence, then, at its moments of intensity and regeneration, provides the religious absolute.

If we turn back to our earlier point about Lawrence's "irrationalism," we see it serving not simply as a critique of our hyperrationalized civilization, nor as simply demonic denial. Knowledge as self-consciousness, idea, or symbol, remains consistently antithetical to Lawrencean values. "No word, no Logos, no utterance. . . . It is the *Deed* of life we have now to learn." [31] Or again: "The goal is *not* ideal. The aim is *not* mental consciousness. We want *effectual* human beings, not conscious ones." [32] For Lawrence, and the religious view in general, the role of knowledge most clearly defines itself by its negative limits: ". . . in his adventure of self-consciousness a man must come to the limits of himself and become aware of something beyond him. A man must be self-conscious enough to know his own limits, and to be aware of that which surpasses him." So far, this could be construed as the traditional call to religion, but Lawrence goes on: "What surpasses me is the very urge of life that is within me, and this life urges me to forget myself and to yield to the stirring half-born impulse to smash up the vast lie of the world, and make a new world." [33] Negation— both of knowledge and of the world as is—remains the end of knowledge. And even the quality of true knowing depends not on logic and evidence but on the responsive individual: "Knowledge is always a matter of whole experience, what St. Paul calls knowing in full, never a matter of mental conception merely." [34] (This helps explain, in part, those characteristic avowals of Lawrence's that have so often been mocked as absurd, such as: "My great religion is the blood, the flesh, as being wiser than the intellect." [35]) With Lawrence, the point always comes back to tangible humans being given a cosmic significance. [36]

While Lawrence's insistence that, above all, "one wants to *be*" [37] provides no very exact prescription, that is partly because he wished to proscribe the mental and moral fixities of life. For, apparently by an act of faith, the regenerative wonders within man relate to the flux of the impersonal cosmos. Thus, after completing *Sons and Lovers*, a work partly within the nineteenth-century order of moral realism, Lawrence said that he would no longer write that way; now the "non-human, in humanity, is more interesting to me than the old fashioned human element—which causes one to conceive a character in a certain moral scheme and make him consistent. The certain moral scheme is what I object to." [38] His effort to present the primordial and impersonal being—the "it" instead of the "ego" —helps account for some of the peculiarities of his fictions, such as the poeticization, the magical elements (coincidences, fabulistic figures, ghosts), the metapsychological abstractions, the animal tropes, the emotional excesses, the cosmic incantations, etc. But is it possible to write major fiction concerned with the actual world yet staying outside of some version of the social and moral scheme that we call "realism"? Lawrence's aesthetic overreaching of fictional forms—religious purpose breaking out of realistic art, without finding an adequate form of its own—may account as much for the limits and uncertainties of his work as do his many personal idiosyncrasies.

Lawrence's heroes and heroines belong to odd and extreme types, marked by the author's strange compound of feminine sensitivity and compensatory masculine mania. His later self-made aristocrats appear at once delicate and harsh, withdrawn outsiders yet recreators of the world. The contradictory autobiographical elements frequently disturb the realization of character even in Lawrence's own terms. Yet these erotic messiahs also provide concrete extensions of Lawrence's religious views, implausible but theologically necessary heroes of the vital life. For if the human is divine, the dual order of religion—gods and men—returns by way of a double ethic; there must be some human figures at once actual in time and space and yet transcendent. Blake saw one law for the "lion" and another law for the "ox," and foundered in the attempt to give human form to his deified heroes in his narrative works. Nietzsche saw one law for the *öbermensch* and another for the herdman, and wrote wild fragments in attempting to find a dramatic way to show this quality. Lawrence saw subjective regeneration only for a brave few, and in his fictions those few often become implausible presences. Is such religious mythology beyond the adequate creation of any one man and artist?

We shall return to this point, but meanwhile some further preliminary comments on Lawrence's religious heroism. Lawrence warns that "when you start to teach individual self-realization to the great masses of people, who when all is said and done are only *fragmentary* beings, *incapable* of whole individuality, you end by making them all envious, grudging, spiteful creatures." [39] Lawrence's hatred of modern mass society repeatedly conjoins with his extreme individualism and becomes a dominant dogma: ". . . there are two great categories of meaning, forever separate. There is mob-meaning, and there is individual meaning." [40] His emotional assaults on mass meanings show a violent lack of compassion. However, they often result in insights: the special malaise of the mass—"the mass is more neurotic than the individual patient"; [41] the results of mass population and technology—"machine souls"; and mass education and entertainment—"masturbation." [42] In contrast to "the collective souls, terribly middling, who have no aristocratic singleness and aloneness," [43] are the heroic individualists who hold apart and to the vital mystery. For them, "virtue lies in the heroic response to the creative wonder, the utmost response." [44]

One of Lawrence's last novellas, *The Virgin and the Gipsy*,[45] presents a clear image of this strange and perverse heroism in ordinary life. The tale has the same drowning-and-desire pattern as *The Horse Dealer's Daughter*, the same harsh negation of Christian morality and middle-class gentility (and the same milieu and paired daughters) as in *Daughters of the Vicar*, the same outcast and virile dark hero as in the demon-lover tales, and the destructive matriarch who pervades so many of Lawrence's fictions. The intellectual villain, again, takes form as a clergyman, named Saywell. This hypocritical Vicar and writer fails as a man and a husband. Cynthia, his wife, ran away with another man because of an *"éclat* of revulsion, like a touch of madness," against the "atmosphere of cunning self-sanctification." Although a terrible blow to Saywell's "skulking self-love," he, like Tolstoy's Karenin, plays the role of tragical forgiveness. His failure as a man, Lawrence sardonically notes, helps his worldly success; the pathos aids the Vicar in becoming Rector. The wife does not appear directly in the story, but she provides the heritage of passional rebellion for her daughter, who refuses to

accept the father's idealized image of Cynthia as once "a snow
flower" of purity—idealism's denial of actuality—but instead has
the image of her mother as "a great glow, a flow of life, like a
swift and dangerous sun in the home. . . ." The mother had a
"dangerous sort of selfishness like lions and tigers." This Blakean
image of demonic force finally destroyed the marriage, leaving
the home "a complete stability, in which one could perish
safely," but leaving the daughters thinking of the mother as in a
"higher, if more dangerous and immoral world."

The family life in the early section of the novella is portrayed
with Lawrence's harshest mode of "realism." In the "dank air of
that degenerated middle-class comfort," with its mixture of odors
and tensions, gentility barely covers covert violence and physical
grossness. There is the old maid, "green-gray Aunt Cissie," with
her chocolates, her neatness, her family loyalty, her inevitable
operation; and, in several neat scenes, Lawrence presents her
outbursts of sick hatred. Lawrence does not overlook the covert
obscenities in the family order: Aunt Cissie sleeps with Granny
and hates it, and secretly hates her mother and herself. The
Mater herself is old, obese, almost blind, and cunning. A figure
with an "implacable will to power," she exercises authority
against her competitors—daughter, daughter-in-law, grand-
daughter. The good old lady, so active and so interested for one
of her age—so she appears to the visitors—is a bit physically
"unsavoury," and thus all the more the moral center of the
family. She holds to gentility, but has an odd greed in eating,
which expresses her "insatiable greed for life, other people's
life." Dozing in the overheated sitting room, an obese "fungoid"
creature when not looked at through loyal eyes, she seems "some
awful idol of old flesh." Her physical corruption at one with her
moral force, her avowals of decency based on her belief in
depravity, Lawrence dramatizes her in petty but encompassing
acts of will and deceit. This epitomization of the Lawrencean
destructive woman—an image of the author's maternal hatred—
is the deity of the middle-class familial order.

In summarizing the character of the Rector—weakened by being more statement than dramatization—Lawrence presents his essential analysis of the moralized middle-class sensibility. The clever father has denied his wife, both in physical fact and in memory, and has thus denied the living "connection" with another being that provides the test of life. In his wife's place he has put the grotesque matriarchal deity and the worship of his own stale comfort and fixity. A loving father to his two daughters, he betrays himself in two scenes with Yvette, his youngest and favorite. Once he mistakes the girl's generous carelessness as fraud and lying—it concerns money, of course. Another time he criticizes her for her friendship with a couple not legally married. (Despite his intellectual pretense he is "fanatically afraid of the unconventional.") His mental associations with the "illicit" and "immoral" run away with him. In "his mind he was thinking unspeakable depravities about his daughter"—just as he had about his passionate wife. (Lawrence fails to tell us what these obscene "horrors" are.) Saywell's extremity of feeling breaks out of his paternal moral pose; he says: "I will kill you before you shall go the way of your mother." The Rector fails to understand the amorphous and vague sexuality of a virginal mind, and his daughter is naturally shocked. He behaves with the pathology of repression and consequent self-hatred and violence. More broadly, the father expresses the "inferiority of a heart which has no core of warm belief in it, no pride in life." The violence of his morality-of-depravity matches his inability to assume or allow positive life in another. In contrast to his irresponsible wife, who had been a moral unbeliever, he is a "life-unbeliever." This simple distinction for dividing the sheep from the goats states one of Lawrence's most profound points: all moral and social criteria are paltry when it comes to the crucial touchstone of whether one has, or has not, a sense of the absolute significance of vital life.

Most dangerously, the intelligent Rector knows the need for "the *appearance* of love and belief and bright life." Senti-

mentalists are nasty people, especially so when their sophistication and cultivation allow them to undercut authentic feeling in
the name of love and goodness. It is less dangerous, Lawrence
dramatically shows, to be harsh or primitive. Yvette has thus
learned to distrust her father and to despise what he represents.
During the conflict with him the girl thinks of an exotic stranger,
the gypsy, and she "wanted to be confirmed by him against her
father. . . ." Rebellion and eros, as was previously noted, go
together.

While the negative emotions provide authentic imperatives,
the real problem is to go beyond them. You cannot just live on
insight and rebellion. The daughters of the Rector belong to
their father's milieu, and, as Lawrence comments on the girls, it
is "easier to shatter prison bars than to open undiscovered doors
to life." To recognize and to negate the Mater, the Rector, and
the Christian middle-class environment may be well enough,
but not enough. A void remains, and Yvette's recurrent lament:
"Why is nothing important?" What the heroine wants is "passionate belief." Lawrence puts the problems in religious terms,
but the affirmation must clearly be personal and romantic adventure for his young heroine. She needs something more than
repetition of the domestic and moral order in which she lives—
some larger and freer sense of destiny and life, even if only for a
moment. She wants, as she looks down the road from the bleak
rectorage, to see a wandering stranger singing "Tirra-lirra!"

Lawrence's odd combination of harsh realism and lyrical fairy
tale—there are some awkward changes in tone—turns about
another of his demon lovers, a gypsy man, a magical figure with
a "lordly air," the "pride of a pariah," and the "challenge of the
outcast." Naturally, he is dark, oddly dressed in a green jersey,
repeatedly described by images of fire. The image of romantic
salvation does not get sentimentalized by Lawrence. The gypsy
appears to be ignorant and crafty, although presented as a figure
of virility: he is expert with horses and has fathered five children upon his harsh wife.[46] The man's power resides not in his

goodness but in his violation of ordinary life, his enmity to what is. A "pagan" and satanic deity, one of an "old race" in its battle with "established society," he has "no conception of winning," only an occasional ability to "score" against the fixed world and its hostility to his "fire of life and a certain vagabond calm of fatalistic resignation." Lawrence, who brings romantic Satanism down to the level of ordinary life, unfortunately gives no inner dimension to his demon lover, only the "forever unyielding outsideness which gave him his lonely predative grace."

The romantic melodrama hardly appears as such in *The Virgin and the Gipsy*, since the action unfolds in terms of an almost cilchéd realism. Thus, Yvette first meets the gypsy when, for a lark, she and some friends visit the gypsy encampment and have their fortunes told. The secretive Yvette's fortune turns out to be the standard line, with a slightly Lawrencean twist of language: ". . . the dark man will blow the one spark up into fire again, good fire." Much later the gypsy tells the virgin of a second prophecy of his wife's: "Be brave in your heart, or you lose your game. Be braver in your body, or your luck will leave you." The dramatic context for these portentous utterances seems peculiar, for the bravery of heart and body includes the gypsy wife's aid in her husband's intended seduction of the girl, the killing off of the grandmother, and a brief passion that quite explicitly is not and cannot be usual love. Lawrence only plays the moralist as an immoralist.

One cold day Yvette drops in at the gypsy camp and warms herself at the fire. This symbolic act prepares her somnambulistic sexual submission to the gypsy, but they are interrupted by the chance arrival of a strange couple. This is a rich "bourgeoise Jewess" and the Nordic gentleman for whom she has left her clever husband. Not yet divorced, the rich, bohemian, and sensual woman lives with the major. The action, gratuitous to the literal story line, parallels the illicit passion of Yvette's mother, which starts the story. The Jewish woman—Mediterranean passion—and her Viking lover represent superior and self-contained enmity to "fake morality," and Lawrencean antagonism to the "abstract morality of the north." Lawrence at least partially identifies himself and his own point of view with the story within the story. The manly and unconventional former major, who knew this very same gypsy in the army (Lawrence's usual melodramatic coincidence of destiny), helps Yvette define her longings. The girl reflects aloud on her past desire for the gypsy. The woman objects, the primitive being aesthetically displeasing to such a cosmopolite. The girl replies that the gypsy is the only man who really *"desired"* her.

> "I wondered!" said Yvette. "Because it *was* rather wonderful really! And it *was* something quite different in life."
> "I think," said the major . . . "that desire is the most wonderful thing in life. Anybody who can really feel it is a king, and I envy nobody else."

When the woman complains that every "common low man" feels such desire, the man replies in true Lawrencean fashion, "that's merely appetite." He tells Yvette that she can only know for herself what desire is—the inversion of Protestant spirituality!—and the distinction between appetite and desire remains in the purely individual and subjective realm. The woman also objects that the girl couldn't possibly marry such a man, and the major agrees; her final objection is that a love affair of that kind would be degrading. The major does not directly answer; he simply raises the issue to a religious level: "That gypsy was the best man we had with horses. Nearly died of pneumonia. I thought he was dead. He's a resurrected man to me." This strange answer must mean that what may not be acceptable at a moral and social level may nonetheless be religiously true. The major goes on to further identify himself with the gypsy by adding that he (the major) is also a "resurrected" man. Like the gypsy, the virile man almost died, then miraculously returned to life. Men who have reached death and returned know the ultimate and pure value of desire, which supercedes all other values. The reborn man is ruled only by the royalty of his feelings.

This going beyond good and evil, to where existence only has meaning in terms of death and desire, illustrates Lawrence's religious center. But Yvette becomes no Lawrencean saint of sexuality. Despite her element of heroic perversity ("Yvette was always wayward, perverse"), she lives for the most part in the world of common sense. She usually sees, for example, the gypsy as he appears to the ordinary world: "She looked at him with her clear eyes. Man or woman is made up of many selves. With one self, she loved this gypsy man. With many selves she ignored or had a distaste for him." The point, surely, is well taken, and marks Lawrence's analytic intelligence, but why has he stated it so abstractly instead of showing it with the characters in action? Perhaps Lawrence's desire to mythicize the primitive figure in terms of his mysterious desirability works at loggerheads with his own intellectual perceptions; the mythic tendency controls the action of the story, although it never quite obscures the author's hard intelligence.

Yvette, we must note, does not love the gypsy in any usual meaning of the term. Every time the girl sees the gypsy she feels put in a "spell," a "sleep," a "somnambulistic" state, or some other obscure "deep" of her "secret female self." As with the earlier distinction between "appetite" and "desire," Lawrence uses a rhetoric of magic to partially obscure the amorality of the passional longing that he dramatically sanctions. The desire that Lawrence justifies used to be included within the moralist's category of lust. Lawrence attempts to show that authentic lust, not just love sentiment, has a validity outside the moralist's view.

An example of Lawrence's partial obscuring of the naked dramatic facts—and this may partly account for his abstractions and metaphors about levels of consciousness—can be seen in Yvette's thoughts about the gypsy. She asks herself if she has done something wrong in not being seduced by the gypsy, and she decides that it is "some hidden part of herself which she denied: that part which mysteriously and unconfessedly responded to him." Mysteriously? And what part can this be? Here we reach the obscurity of religious metaphor! Lawrence takes a favorite scene from the Bible, Peter's denial of Christ before the third cock crew, and by synecdoche uses the cock to represent the deepest of obligations. The virgin, like the disciple, defeats her own passions when she denies "the strange and lustrous black cock." This is not really obscure, of course, for we know that Lawrence and his heroine have a religious faith in the phallic prowess of the primitive dark gypsy: the metaphor of the Biblical "lustrous black cock" includes an erect dark penis.

Final acceptance of such rudiments of life has required an arduous purificatory negation for the questing virgin. Her rebellion against Christian restraint, family idolatry, and her father, plus her soul searching, her foray with her intellectual mentors, etc., result in a final transformation—disillusionment. Without "illusions," and now feeling herself an "outsider," she is ready for the simple gratifications, the pleasures that exist only for the moment. Yvette doesn't even have any illusion about her own future—"to expect a great deal out of life is puerile" editorializes the worldly, cynical Lawrence—and she consciously prepares to make an ordinary marriage to an ordinary man sometime in the future.

But first the regeneration, the return of the disillusioned to a sense of vital life amidst all negations and "ennui"—the moment of "destiny." The gypsy woman, along with her advice of bravery, gave Yvette a rather Freudian warning to watch for the water. The flood of passion and baptism comes when the reservoir that controls the river beside the rectory breaks: ". . . an ancient, perhaps even a Roman, mine tunnel, unsuspected, undreamed of, beneath the reservoir dam, had collapsed, undermining the whole dam." The description of the cause of the flood summarizes Lawrence's conviction that under Western Christian culture is the hidden but ever-present paganism that provides the true religion, the chaotic release into fulfillment.

By yet another parabolic coincidence, the gypsy has come to say good-by to the virgin at just the moment when the flood waters from the undermined dam reach the rector's home. He saves Yvette from the flood by pulling her to the top room of the house. They see the Mater clawing desperately in the flood waters at the bottom of the stairs, but they do not attempt to save her. Some deity must die for the new illumination; after the flood, the matriarch's body is appropriately found protruding from a pile of debris.

The cold and shocked virgin must literally be warmed back into life by the injured and bleeding gypsy. After the night of sexual consummation, the waters subside and the gypsy leaves. The family—all but Yvette and the Mater escaped the flood— return the next morning with help to rescue the girl from the nearly demolished house. She wakes in her bed: "Where was her gypsy of the world's-end night?" Instead of the demon lover she finds in her room the mundane daily authority, the antithesis of the night's rebel, a polite policeman. Immediately she knows that she will "keep the gypsy a secret."

Yvette, when afraid to go down the ladder the policeman has ascended, remembers the gypsy's advice: "Be braver in the body." A small but new heroism has been added to daily life by her regeneration in passion, and she descends the ladder to her loving family. As for the gypsy, she "was acquiescent in the fact of his disappearance. Her young soul knew the wisdom of it." The story concludes with her receiving an illiterate note from the now distant gypsy. He says that sometime he will see her again. There remains always the mythic possibility that the dark and alien dream-figure of direct passion may make a magical re- turn from his wonderings. As she finishes the letter, "she realized [only then] that he had a name." The regenerative eros has been impersonal, even inhuman. The otherwise ordinary ex-virgin has broken from authority and restraint and gained the secret arcanum of passion and extremity, and a new sense of bravery and self. That is all—no love, no marriage, no external power, not even any dogma, to this religious happy ending.

The Virgin and the Gipsy has some of Lawrence's usual fictional difficulties—occasional statement of feelings rather than dramatization, abstract disruptions of tone, and the uncertainty that comes from developing mythic elements (the demon lover and erotic regeneration) within an angrily observed social and psychological realism. Lawrence is hardly ever the perfect artist, coming closest to symmetry and tonal consistency only in his most sardonic and negative pieces. But *The Virgin and the Gipsy* provides one of his best parables of regeneration, without the muddled metaphors of social class used in *Lady Chatterley,* without the incantatory language and dogmatic avowals of some of the other late fictions, and without any messianic insistence that the religion of eros can transform all of the ordinary world.[47]

III

In contrast, we may perceive some of the more dubious aspects of Lawrence's religious impulse in another story of regeneration, the long tale *Glad Ghosts*.[48] This story of a week end at a country estate lacks the clean lines of *The Virgin and the Gipsy.* The narrator-protagonist—an only slightly disguised figure for the author—is another of the "outsiders" who "wander in uneasy and distant parts of the earth," an artist and prophet in a world that will "come to a violent and untimely end."

The *fin de siècle* material of unartistic artists, anemic aristocrats, and covert eroticism draws on a forced archness. The narrator explains that at "our famous but uninspired school of art . . . where I myself was diligently murdering my talent," was the beautiful and dilettante Lady Carlotta ("she could feel that I was It"); and he goes on to insist, without dramatization, that the point of the forthcoming story lies in "some passionate vision" of "the unborn body of life hidden within the body of this half-death which we call life." But, as in the quite similar *The Ladybird* (written a few years earlier), adultery with the stock heroine of the "snow white skin," rather than the regenerative vision, dominates.

The Lady does not marry the outsider but one of the "living dead," the passé aristocratic ghost, Lord Lathkill. This sexually poor marriage ("the two of them seemed vague, as if they never got anywhere"), is cursed by the husband's war wounds, the death of their children, and a pervasive melancholy. The cursory plotting settles into the main episode when Mark Moirer, the artist-narrator, returns from abroad and visits the Lathkill's Derbyshire home, a portentously "underworld" estate of gloom, which suffers from "fixity" and the "obscene triumph of dead matter." More concretely, we find the fatal matriarch, the dowager Lady with the coldness, shrewdness, "pin point blue eyes," and "icily white stare" of the "modern witch" and vicious northern moral will—that "cold air about her, of being good, and containing a secret of goodness." With heavy hand, Lawrence has made her a vegetarian, prohibitionist, puritan, and degraded idealist—a spiritualist.

Another guest, Colonel Hale, is also an "unmanned" figure; his first marriage to a clever, willful, mothering, and repressive witch has been continued beyond death by the dowager's spiritualistic communications with the jealous wife's ghost. The dowager and the ghost have persuaded Hale not to sexually consummate his second marriage in order to remain pure for his next incarnation where he will solely "serve Woman." Pagan religious metaphors provide, for Lawrence, the proper antagonist to Orientalistic theosophy, and at dinner the narrator demands the presence of the true gods, Bacchus and Eros. But by a dramatically incoherent switch, Lord Lathkill suddenly becomes the antagonist of his mother's religion, shedding his "nothingness" and the "dead smell" of morality. Bacchus, with whom Lawrence lacks a really familiar footing, disappears in the remounting of the gods, but Eros grows in a scene of desultory dancing, rhetorical conversations about the flesh, and near surrealistic images such as the narrator's obsession with unseen "intermittent black hairs" on the thighs of the virginal Mrs. Hale.

For awhile it looks like simply a question of organization as to whether the narrator or Lord Lathkill will deflower the Colonel's wife; however, the narrator feels that Lady Carlotta's "small breasts seemed to speak" to him while dancing, and a situation of double adultery develops. The dowager tries to intervene with some spiritualist hysterics; the "life-flow" moves up and down in preseduction uncertainties; and the drawing room conversation improbably develops some of Lawrence's favorite motifs of sexual metaphysics, such as Lathkill's speech about replacing Jesus' *"Noli me tangere"* with "touch me *alive!"* Lathkill argues Hale out of his spiritualism and his dead wife with a disquisition on worshipping the body as a sacrament; he also asks the narrator to "help" his, Lord Lathkill's, wife. His neo-Biblical speeches about incarnate flesh, crocuses, thighs, plum blossoms, bellies, torrents of spring, etc., as well as his invitations to the narrator to seduce his wife, may be out of character, but they succeed with Hale, who rejects matriarchal spiritualism and takes to "pondering with his body." His regeneration into youth, however, has the drawback that the "youngness that was on him was not for her," his virginal wife. After this rhetorical success, Lathkill goes to bed—whether or not with the Colonel's wife remains unclear.

The narrator, after listening to his host's sermon and eyeing his host's wife, beds down in the mansion's "ghost room," haunt of a benign female spirit whose rare appearance "inevitably restores the family fortune." Apparently, the ghost represents the sexual desire of Carlotta, still alive in the spirit but not in the "living body." As Moirer falls into sleep, Lawrence falls into several pages of prose poetry, which indicate that the sexual sacrament requires certain tricks of consciousness: not the man but his ghost will achieve "intangible meetings and unknown fulfillments of desire," for the ghost state frees one from "circumstances" and "mufflings of consciousness"—and conscience?

—reaching finally "beyond the strata of images and words, beyond the iron veins of memory . . . to sink in the final dark like a fish, dumb, soundless, and imageless, yet alive and swimming." Thus reaching the primordial flux of life, one finds nihilistic vitality "at the heart of oblivion, which is also the heart of life."

Here also "deep answers deep"; or, more concretely, "she came." In the morning the narrator is uncertain whether his "mating" was with a ghost, a dream, or Lady Carlotta. The prose poem about the "profundity of darkness," the "new-awakened God," the fish and the sea, and the feelings of a "whale that has sounded to the bottomless seas" suggests some superlative adulterous orgasm kept outside direct memory and guilt. Evidence for whether or not the *roman à clef* aspect of the story concerns an actual seduction by Lawrence of one of his friends, or merely a fantasy of one, is not available; but in the fiction the seduction carries over into the daylight world. As the narrator concludes his visit he sees his host's wife as if she "were the ghost again" and he were "down the depths of consciousness." In a concluding letter, Lord Lathkill announces to the narrator the fruits of the resurrection of the flesh, a son, Gabriel, "by the grace of our ghost," "ghost-begotten." Mrs. Hale has also given birth to a female Gabriel, and the now hearty Hale looks Lathkill in the eye, and "we understand." Thus all achieve regeneration in a collapsing world.

Lawrence's religiosity has carried him over the edge in *Glad Ghosts* to a forced and rhetorical story as well as an obscene insistence on the smoothly working products of double adultery, adorned with sacramental flourishes, but without suffering in either the actual world or the inner feelings. But adultery that requires acquiescent husbands, the fictional trickery of the supernatural tale, and the obfuscation of religious rhetoric seems not so easy after all. The guilty elaborateness and good-time-all-around ending go even beyond *The Ladybird*. Part of the muddiness relates to Lawrence's ambiguity toward the vestigial upper class, which he clearly perceives to be at a dead end but yet treats with a mixture of repulsion and identification. Whatever the personal motives may be that encourage the bad art, it is Lawrence at his poorest. It is not just an awkward tale; a religious principle—*"with my body I thee worship!"*—has been turned to sexual titillation and easy week-end therapy.

IV

Lawrence's bland, rhetorical, and untragic versions of tragic romance, such as *Glad Ghosts* and *The Ladybird* and *The Border Line* (the best of them), are not his only religious mythology. The stories of initiation into desire, such as *The Virgin and the Gipsy, The Horse Dealer's Daughter, Love among the Haystacks,* and in part at least many of the other courtship stories depend on essential differences from his tricks with decaying aristocrats.

We have already examined a third pattern of religious tale— the harsh antilove fable of the sacrificial transformation of consciousness, such as *The Woman Who Rode Away* and *St. Mawr.* The ritualized cosmos in these later religious fictions makes its malign demands. But, as we find in the romantic poets, the malign-benign turns ambiguously one, and the destructive can readily become the affirmative.[49] The regenerative cosmic rituals in Lawrence's work match the destructive rituals. The rebellious lovers assert their distinctive individual being by defying the universe, but they also weary of their individuality and, by defining their rebellion with the cosmos, come to identify themselves with it.

So with the Lawrence who wrote: "I am weary even of my own individuality."[50] He seeks, especially in his final prophetic works like *Apocalypse,* to identify with the cosmos and to find, like William Blake, that rebellion itself is finally the assertion that "everything that lives is Holy."

What man most passionately wants is his living wholeness and his living unison, not his own isolate salvation of his "soul." Man wants his physical fulfillment first and foremost, since now, once and once only, he is in the flesh and potent. For man, the vast marvel is to be alive. For man, as for flower and beast and bird, the supreme triumph is to be most vividly, most perfectly alive. Whatever the unborn and the dead may know, they cannot know the beauty, the marvel of being alive in the flesh. The dead may look after the afterwards. But the magnificent here and now of life in the flesh is ours, and ours alone, and ours only for a time. We ought to dance with rapture that we should be alive and in the flesh, and part of the living incarnate cosmos. I am part of the sun as my eye is part of me. That I am part of the earth my feet know perfectly, and my blood is part of the sea. My soul knows that I am part of the human race, my soul is an organic part of the great human soul, as my spirit is part of my nation. In my very self I am part of my family. There is nothing of me that is alone and absolute except my mind, and we shall find that the mind has no existence by itself, it is only the glitter of the sun on the surface of the waters.

So that my individualism is really an illusion. I am a part of the great whole, and I can never escape. But I can deny my connections, break them, and become a fragment. Then I am wretched.

What we want is to destroy our false, inorganic connections, especially those related to money, and re-establish the living organic connections, with the cosmos, the sun and the earth, with mankind and nation and family. Start with the sun, and the rest will slowly, slowly happen.[51]

The above passage, I think, reasonably represents Lawrence's affirmations. Typically, his own definitions of belief require the denial of Christian dualism (both "the afterwards" bifurcation of existence and the "soul" as distinct from the "flesh"), the denial of rationalism ("the mind has no existence by itself" and it destroys organic life), and the denial of the bourgeois mode ("money"). Using the fictions as the touchstone of what Lawrence most authentically means, we find the denial of Christian, rational, and bourgeois values self-consciously present in most of them. However, I do not find that the belief in race, family, nation, and world soul significantly appears—"only the glitter of the sun." Lawrence does start with the sun and the sense of desperately intense aliveness, and it leads him into certain organic connections; but it should also be noted that he moves away from, rather than toward, the large collective values. His

sun worship brings the weary and alien individual back into a
relation with the vital energies, within and without, but the
sense of cosmic power still leads to the denial of all lesser
authorities, fixities, and pieties.

The sources of Lawrence's sun worship appear several and
various. The personal intensity of the sun experience very likely
was increased by Lawrence's slow death from consumption;
even more, sun-worship goes with the alienation that drove him
in a world-wandering pursuit of the sun and some sense of
organic relatedness to place. The sun also provides a salvational
art-image. To the faulty and doomed lovers of *The Trespassers*
the sun produces a malign end to love; to the good lovers of
Women in Love, Aaron's Rod, and *The Lost Girl,* regeneration
leads to the rejection of the moral cold of the North as they follow the benign sun to the pagan South. In the theocratic Mexican fictions—*The Woman Who Rode Away* and *The Plumed
Serpent*—the sun is literally an object of cult worship in Lawrence's adaption of Aztec ritual. In his collaborative Australian
novel, *The Boy in the Bush,* it is "The Great God . . . of the
yellow sun" who gives the frontier hero his virile strength to
conquer the "white-demon" of the moon-feminine and thus have
two wives! [52] The heroine's solar love in *Sun* leads to regeneration; the antiheroine in *The Lovely Lady,* who also "voluptu-
ously" used the sun as a secret "lover," turns malign. And in
novellas like *The Virgin and the Gipsy* and *The Man Who
Died,* the sun provides an important trope of passion and, finally,
of a "sun beyond suns" of final revelation. Probably, only such
an image, which expresses both good and evil, can properly be
designated a religious symbol.

By the time the sun worship becomes elaborately self-conscious in Lawrence, during his American period, it has taken on
the mythological traditions of past sun cults: ". . . the sun is
always *sun beyond sun beyond sun.* The sun is every sun that
has ever been, Helios or Mithas, the sun of China or Brahma, or
of Peru or of Mexico: great gorgeous suns, beside which our

puny 'envelope of incandescent gas' is a smoky candle-wick." [53]
As with William Blake's famous insistence that he saw a chorus
of angels singing when he looked at the sun, a religious subjectivity and its attempt to give sacred responsiveness to the
cosmos involve a denial of the adequacy of rational and scientific
categories of perception. Thus, in his early metapsychological
polemic, *Fantasia of the Unconscious,* Lawrence attempted to re-
furbish an ancient and heroic cosmic duality with "two sheer
dynamic principles in our universe, the sun-principle and the
moon-principle." [54] While the sun-moon tropes inform a few of
the fictions, particularly those of unresolved sexual conflict, in
the late work such as *Sun* the two-suns trope dominates:

> The sun has a great blazing consciousness, and I have a little blazing
> consciousness. When I can strip myself of the trash of personal feelings
> and ideas, and get down to my naked sun-self, then the sun and I can
> commune by the hour, the blazing interchange, and he gives me life, sun
> life, and I send him a little new brightness from the world of the blood.[55]

The relationship with the cosmic force, not the objective nature
of the sun, creates the Lawrencean crux. Sometimes, indeed,
with the typical esotericism of the heterodox traditions, he denies
the independence of the religious symbol from man: "Instead of
life being drawn from the sun, it [the sun] is the emanation
from life itself." [56] Previously, Lawrence demanded the heroic
individualism of the "sun-self" and its social manifestation in an
"aristocracy of the sun." [57] He uses the point many times, writing casual verses to "Sun-Men" and "Sun-Women" and to the
"Aristocracy of the Sun." [58] In a piece of verse-jotting, he writes:
"I feel aristocratic, noble, when I feel a pulse go through me
from the wild heart of space, that I call the sun of suns." [59] The
responsiveness to natural wonder, the "gaiety" of physical aliveness, do not work for everyone; the malign sun exists for the
false sun worshippers: "The great sun, like an angry dragon,
hater of the nervous and personal consciousness in us, as all
these modern sunbathers must realize, for they become dis-

integrated by the very sun that bronzes them. . . ." [60] Thus, the double ethic turns on sacramental feeling, and the negation of the sun worship which Lawrence shrewdly called "anti-thought," [61] cuts both ways, depending on the worshipper.

The revival of the sun cult in Lawrence, as in Blake, undoubtedly belongs to the general usages of heterodox thought going back to repressed Mediterranean cults and the sun as a symbol of fertility, passion, and the golden life. Neither moral asceticism nor scientific rationalism quite succeeded in suppressing the Golden Age mythology—partly, no doubt, because both rationalism and Christianity have repeatedly absorbed and drawn upon Golden Age imagery of idyllic social order and personal fulfillment in the recurrent pastoral ideal of the natural and simple life. The recrudescence of sun worship in the twentieth century can be found in the self-conscious Mithraism of Henri de Montherlant and in the more generalized Mediterranean sun paganism of Kazantzakis, Giono, and Camus. At more popular levels, as Lawrence was one of the first to note, there appeared the phenomenal vogue for sun-bathing, which still increases. Spreading after World War I, and reaching its most elaborate form of religiosity in organized nudism, sun-bathing is usually rationalized in hygienic and athletic terms, but much of it is clearly ritualistic and therapeutic. Lawrence, drawing on personal experience and need, on the sorts of comparative mythology sparking so much modern literature, and on the impetus of heterodox sources—including his early Protestantism and the memory of his favorite hymn which includes the line, "Sun of my soul, thou saviour dear" [62]—plus a modern war-world despair with "civilized" forms, carried out one of his own prescribed roles: "To man, the very sun goes stale, becomes a habit. Comes a saviour, a seer, and the very sun dances new in heaven." [63]

More than an artistic device, but less than a formalized religion, Lawrence's sun sacramentalism receives elaborate development in the story *Sun*.[64] This shows the common bifurcations of Lawrence's later works, with its double scene (urban New York and primitive Sicily), its split development (psychological realism and mythic regeneration), and its dual attitude toward its own sacramental process (fervent yet finally ironic). Lawrence was no primitive animist, and his efforts to be "part of the sun as my eye is part of me," necessarily involve some straining at a posture, which shows up in the artistic dualisms.

The modern romantic heroine, Juliet, wife of a cursorily typed businessman, sinks into illness from her "helpless enmity" to urban and marital life; she also suffers from "love-anguish" and her "incapacity to feel anything real." Though "skeptical of the sun," she flees in a quasimystical pilgrimage through "chaos" and the "dark" to primitive Italian isolation in the sun. ("Italy," Lawrence wrote of his first trip there, "is so non-moral." [65]) Here, in a scene laid with Lawrence's usual intense description, the "mystery" (rite) will be developed. A rather consistent sort of phallicized description aids the theme. For example: ". . . out of this blue-grey knoll of cactus rose one cypress tree, with a pallid, thick trunk, and a tip that leaned over, flexible, up in the blue." As Lawrence wrote in one of his essays: "Look at the strong fertile silence of the thrusting tree. God is in the bush like a clenched dark fist, or a thrust phallus." [66]

The heroine develops a "secret" yearning to see a transcendent reality, "the naked sun," which would dissolve her anxious consciousness in a new sense of "wonder." With devotional discipline, she systematically lies naked to the sun until, "sun-blinded" and "sun-dazed," she achieves a unitary "connection" with the cosmos—with "the sun in his splendour, and her mating with him. Her whole life was now a ritual." Her orgasm with the sun—"in the cosmic carnal sense"—is not the end of the affair. The sacramentalism of the scene, the masculine personification of the sun, the woman's ritual-sexual responses, and the incantatory repetition of the prose reach their apogee in cult absorption. Juliet now "belongs to the sun"; her beauty is not only from but "for" the sun; her total "consciousness" directs her to the sun; it is the sun whom she dare not "offend"; she brings her child in dedication to the sun; and her sun ecstasy has filled her with "something greater than herself," something that gives her the brave strength (even a courage of the body to overcome her fear of snakes) for "a new way of life."

Emphasizing some of the typical details and their obvious parallelism with traditional religious patterns, in the midsection of the story, seems necessary in view of the many critical moralistic discussions of the work in terms of sunbathing. *Sun* is a religious tale, with *cultus* patterns and consequences. One is the double ethic, the special conduct appropriate to the initiate. Juliet now belongs to a separate order from the "unelemental," "unsunned," unregenerate "graveyard worms." And from this follows the amorality that provides the dramatic crux of Lawrence's religious pieces. Thus Juliet's "good" but "grey" businessman husband comes to take her back to New York; she refuses to go and, with the power of her naked sunned flesh, gets him to agree that she may do what she wishes to gratify her new sun needs. This is to include her desire for another communicant in sun sacramentalism, an anonymous and virile married peasant who, like the sun, has sent a "flame" over her body and would be a "procreative sun-bath to her." She seeks not the anxiety of love, but pure existential desire: "Why not meet him for an hour," says the heroine to herself, "as long as the desire lasts, and no more?" Again, adultery as impersonal eros receives the Lawrencean sanction. But Lawrence's tough intelligence reappears in the conclusion of the story. The good-gray husband, acting not from sacramental strength but from a "desperate kind of courage of his desire," wants his bit of the divine. And because of the power of the ordinary, the woman will conceive with the futile husband rather than with the virile peasant. In the usual edition, this is due to the "fatal chain of continuity." In the unexpurgated, "Black Sun," edition, the conclusion is that she "would feel her husband's futile little penis inside her once again." [67] Either ending, one supposes, is prepared for by the author's earlier comments on "the vast cold apparatus of civilization," which is "so difficult to evade."

The religiousness that provides the controlling purpose of *Sun* by no means allows that the story be taken as a *roman à clef* that got out of hand, or as a metaphoric "sport." In an important sense the story may be viewed as a tour de force against moral and humanistic perspectives. That husbands—American businessmen or not—have difficulty competing with the sexual cosmos and virile peasants takes subordinate place to the simpler truth that an anxious and sexually defeated woman finds the direction of her womanly nature by sexual-sacramental regeneration. The only relevance of the good-gray moral order derives from its importance in showing the discrepancy between the continuities of life and the needs of the basic self. Within its terms, the incantation and amorality of *Sun* succeed. The drastic limitations of what Lawrence treats as religious experience and meaning, and the peculiarly obsessive prose, were not always evident to Lawrence. In a previously quoted passage from his last polemic, Lawrence said: "Start with the sun, and. . . ." And what? In *Sun, The Virgin and the Gipsy,* and the other authentic religious fables, personal regeneration and its self-knowledge—physical bravery, greater self-sufficiency, freedom from compulsive anxiety, and relation to the natural—are achieved; but this does not redo the relations of "mankind and nation and family." Lawrence, too, intermittently falls into the trap of most religious writers and tries to turn his beyond-good-and-evil insights and experiences into universal dogmas and pieties.

V

The Lawrencean attitude, as we have repeatedly noted, depends on the perversities of inversion and antithesis. By nature impatient and dogmatic, and by assertion reductive and anti-intellectual, Lawrence does not always acknowledge the degree to which he depends on reversals and counterstatements and demonic dialectics. His view ends as fundamentally and permanently heterodox. But when the argument is made that with the change of orthodoxies the Lawrencean view belongs to the past—a recurrent point with literary journalists—the point has been missed. The repression and falsification that Lawrencean sexuality and responsiveness oppose, and the sophistication and decadence that Lawrencean primitivism and provincialism attack, will disappear at the millennium, though their forms and emphasis may vary in the meantime. The Christianity that Lawrence's vitalism inverts will probably not last, but its moral fixity, dualism, and universal ethic may well be larger than the historical religion. And although Lawrence draws upon pagan and primitive pre-Christian materials in his antithesis to Christianity, the view seems essentially post-Christian.

In one of his last works Lawrence writes: "The very oldest ideas of man are *purely* religious, and there is no notion of any sort of god or gods. God and gods enter when man has fallen into a sense of separateness and loneliness." [68] Perhaps the very newest religiousness also shows the same characteristics. Anyway, the myth of the Golden Age, upon which Lawrence draws, seeks a relatedness to the alienated cosmos, his repeated ideal of being "one living *continuum* with all the universe." [69] After the fall into lonely, despairing, dualistic, and self-conscious separation from the vital sources of life, something more than innocence is needed for regeneration—some god or gods, some heroic and absolute transformation. The savior-hero who acts out this change in awareness takes various forms in Lawrence's work—the theocratic figures of the "leadership" novels (*Aaron's Rod, Kangaroo, The Plumed Serpent*); the individualistic, amoralistic demon lovers as saviors; and the final symbolic figures of regeneration. Lawrence usually avoids the modern and egotistical heresy of making the artist a seer and savior, though his reborn heroes do take on manic similarities to Lawrence.

The Christ figure fits much of the Lawrencean pattern of the reborn hero; but because he provides the vehicle for Christian morality Lawrence obsessively attacks and inverts him. "Remember," he writes to a correspondent, "I think Christ was profoundly, disastrously wrong." [70] The best he can say for Christ is given to a young girl in the rhetorical story *The Overtone*.[71] She rhapsodizes on her desire for a heroic man: "Pan and Christ, Christ and Pan." (Pan, as in other stories of Lawrence's, is also identified with Dionysus.) The two gods have different functions: "Pan will give me my man, and Christ my husband." Pan rules the night, joy and desire; Christ rules the day, justice and morality. "And night shall never be day, and day shall never be night." That Christ exists in the "pale light" for honesty, fair-dealing, and brotherhood means that he cannot reach some of the essentials of life. But, unfortunately, as we learn elsewhere in Lawrence, the great god Pan is dead; Christ killed him.[72]

This amoralized Manichaean division of the world into dark and light, vital and moral values—a distinction running through Lawrence's work—reaches as close as Lawrence ever does to a reconciliation with Christianity. And this mostly appears in stories the mawkishness of which suggests the inauthenticity of the reconciliation. Lawrence's faith in the passional dark looms too large to allow him to divide life with Christianity, anymore than he can make a *rapprochement* with modern, urban, technological mass society. But the incomplete power of the dark hero—the gypsy, the demon lovers, the theocratic leaders, the intense outsiders—forces him into flight from the world of day; otherwise he would become, like Christ, a public savior instead of a regenerated individualist. In other words, the hero would become a sacred success, and "every saint becomes evil the moment he touches the collective soul of man." [73]

Lawrence's final novella, *The Man Who Died* [74] (originally titled "The Escaped Cock"), denies any division of the world between Christ and Pan by turning Christ into Pan. The crucial metaphor, of course, is sexual. In a late essay, *The Risen Lord*, Lawrence insists upon the "joy" of resurrection into life as far more important than the "agony" of crucifixion into salvation.[75]

In this reversal of the tragic rhythm, pleasure rather than pain and ecstasy rather than suffering become the final desideratum of the true hero.

The rebirth motif dominates Lawrence's late work—as a trope in stories like *The Virgin and the Gipsy, Sun,* and *Lady Chatterley's Lover;* as a subject for essays and verses; and as an unresolvable answer to Lawrence's old obsession with death and oblivion in several fictional fragments. "The Flying Fish," [76] for example, describes a partly autobiographical Englishman named Day and his near approach to death: ". . . the ordinary day . . . loses its reality. . . . It has cracked like some great bubble, and to his uneasiness and terror, he had seemed to see through the fissures into the deeper blue of that other Great Day. . . ." The extreme linkages (the "day of demons" and "wonder, wonder"), the violent antipathy to humanity, and the fascination with the scenic infinite (mountains and sea) belong to the usual Lawrence. But the lifting of the Cain curse of wandering, the hero's return home, the dualism of the "greater day" of the reborn and the "lesser day" of ordinary mankind, with its suggestion of some dualistic eternal realm, belong to a necessarily fragmentary effort to circumvent his own basic attitude. The trope of the "days" carries over into *The Man Who Died,* but there the wandering, the denial of the fixity of life (home), and the rejection of dualistic eternal life show a significant difference of direction. For the same reasons, another fragment, "The Undying Man," [77] is necessarily incomplete. Here Lawrence's death obsession seeks a way out in a fantasy of an eternal life "force," embodied in an immortal artificial man created by a Jewish philosopher. In this parody of Genesis, the Jewish philosopher suddenly realizes that to be eternal and yet a living man on earth "would be better even than being God!"

But Lawrence knew that "immortality is in the vividness of life," and that fantasies of a separate eternity of consciousness or of a denial of mortal aliveness would not provide his final image of meaning. Truer was the heresy of the Protestant–anti-

Protestant: "Christ risen, and risen in the whole of his flesh, not with some left out." Especially not with the "genitals of a man" left out.[78] Ironically, the means for this sharp inversion of traditional piety, as with so many other modern religious myths, was provided by the rationalistic scholarship of Frazer's *The Golden Bough* and the Cambridge, and related, schools of anthropology. The Osiris-Isis myth, an essential basis of the novella, returns the Christ figure to his ritualistic and primitive sources. Lawrence, unlike the rationalistic scholars, is not interested in a reductive and more or less naturalistic explanation of the myth; for him the myth has become demoralized but not demythicized, and so he affirms the new form of the myth but not its new rationalization. It is myth, not reason, "which reaches the deep emotional centres every time." [79]

It is also true that Lawrence's anti-Christianity presupposes, if not Christian belief, a considerable residual sensitivity to the traditional Christ myth, with the novella serving as a reverse epilogue. Lawrence, like George Moore in *The Brook Kerith,* and Lermontov and O'Neil in their Lazarus parables, starts in the tomb after the Crucifixion. Lawrence then carries his Christ through an alternately wry and righteous rejection of his past, elaborates upon Christ's ritualistic love affair with a pagan priestess, and leaves him finally as a defiant and seasonal wanderer *in* the world. *The Man Who Died* is almost a satyr play to resolve the Crucifixion tragedy.

The story starts with its sexual pun, the proudly defiant gamecock that belongs to a grubby peasant. The bird breaks its tether and escapes. "At the same time, at the same hour before dawn . . . a man woke from a long sleep in which he was tied up." The cock and Christ parallelism finally merges in the newly found defiance and virility of the hero. (The sexual symbol of the bird is probably connected with the Christ in Lawrence's mind through Peter's denial before the third cock crew, a metaphor explicitly used by Lawrence in *The Virgin and the Gipsy.*) The gamecock, no ordinary bird ("good for twenty hens," a "ringing defiance" in his crow), has romantic longings for the infinite in his "listening to the challenge of far-off unseen cocks in the unknown world." While the man-who-died (the only name Lawrence gives the impersonally archetypal hero) lies recuperating in the sun, he watches the cock "cry out the triumph of life." This calls forth from Lawrence a representative passage of expressionist prose; its visual elements have the feverish distortion of a Van Gogh painting:

> The man who had died stood and watched the cock who had escaped ruffling himself up, rising forward on his toes, throwing up his head, and parting his beak in another challenge from life to death. The brave sounds rang out, and though they were diminished by the cord round the bird's leg, they were not cut off. The man who had died looked nakedly on life, and saw a vast resoluteness everywhere flinging itself up in stormy or subtle wave-crests, foam-tips emerging out of the blue invisible, a black and orange cock or the green flame-tongues out of the extremes of the fig-tree. They came forth, these things and creatures of spring, glowing with desire and with assertion. They came like crests of foam, out of the blue flood of the invisible desire, out of the vast invisible sea of strength, and they came coloured and tangible, evanescent, yet deathless in their coming. The man who had died looked on the great swing into existence of things that had not died, but he saw no longer their tremulous desire to exist and be. He heard instead their ringing, ringing, defiant challenge to all other existing things.

This passage—like much of Lawrence's writing—progresses from natural description through an expressionistic intensification (primary colors and swirling forms) to abstract metaphor, culminating in a reversal of senses (sight to sound) in which the essence of the visual becomes auditory. At the literal level, the man who had died is simply opening his eyes wider at the cock crow, but this provides the metaphoric experience for the penultimate Lawrencean affirmation of life—the naked vision of the assertive elemental flux that defies all-encompassing destruction.

In the above passage the function of the gamecock is to provide a starting point for a central metaphor that moves into abstraction. The literal gamecock slips out of the story in the middle, his symbolic functions transferred to the hero just as the other creatures in Lawrence's vitalistic bestiary (the fox in *The Fox*, the stallion in *St. Mawr*) drop out of their fictions. The symbolic object has no independent existence, no sacramental significance in and of itself.

The gamecock leads the man arisen from the tomb to the peasant who hides him; the bird then becomes the hero's totem when he first leaves the peasant and goes wandering in the world. When the Christ meets some former disciples, he explains that he is a "healer." The suspicious disciples ask: "You are not a believer?" The Christ replies: "Yea! I believe the bird is full of life and virtue." The new Christ puts his faith in his living cock, not in his abstract message. The final scene with the bird, however, relegates the literal cock to ordinary life. The gamecock kills a "common cock" in an inn yard and is left to take care of the widowed hens. "Thy aloneness," says the Christ, "can take on splendour, polished by the lure of the hens."

Is the hero to follow the same pattern of the return to virile command of ordinary life? Lawrence several times seems to flirt with that resolution, but in the end does not follow it. While the hero, like the cock, has broken "the cord of circumstance," his way appears more equivocal than that of the bird. The Christ has his Christian past, society, and death to overcome. First, the death longing: "Who would want to come back from the dead?" To this strangely world-weary question, Lawrence has early given an incantation of agony, which supplements his naturalistic explanation of the resurrection: "They took me down too soon." Waking in the tomb, he feels "numb" and "cold" and "full of hurt"; and "full of hurt" and "numb" and "cold" and "full of hurt." And we get tiresome verbal repetition of this state. Although this incantatory verbosity has little merit as prose, it does indicate the obsessive quality of Lawrence's concern with the coldness and nullity of death. The anguish of dying repeats both the language and the emotions of sexual arousal. The two agonies provide Lawrence's dialectic of the emotions, and only by emphasizing the dominance and extremity of both can we see, like Lawrence's Christ as he watches the copulating birds, that "the destiny of life seemed more fierce and compulsive to him even than the destiny of death."

Between these polar similitudes little else can have deep significance. The negation of society, or, in Lawrence's terms in the novella, the "disgust" with "humanity"—"especially humanity in authority"—includes the "nausea" of social "disillusion" and violent disgust for the "compulsion," the "mania of cities," the "fear," and the "necessity," which constitute social life. Lawrence's list of abstract social vices later includes "jealousy" and "property" and "smallness" and the iron rule of "circumstance." It must be admitted that Lawrence's abstract negation of the social world and his equally abstract affirmation of the "phenomenal world" and "life" show a weakness of style, in which, ironically, the contrary assertions are undifferentiated from their objects and thus lack living immediacy. Several dramatic episodes—one major one in each of the two sections of the novella—make concrete the social negations of the regenerated hero. The first concerns the peasant and his wife, the owners of the escaped cock, who shelter the Christ. Lawrence does not sentimentalize these primitives. The peasant acts only as a sulky and cowardly antianimal, laughing at the struggles of the brave gamecock to escape his tether. The peasant hides the Christ figure out of servile fear of a "master," and perhaps out of the hope of profit—his wife later greedily accepts money from the Christ. The man-who-died saw the peasants "as they were: limited, meagre in their life, without any splendour of gesture and of courage." The virtues of such ordinary people, such as their charity to the hero, result from fear or selfishness. The people have no vital "fire," no "nobility," and no possibility of greater awareness or action. But at their best, apparently, ordinary people, as viewed through the vitalist's double ethic, must be peasants—"slow inevitable parts of the natural world."

The man-who-died, separated from a simple union with the

natural world by his awareness of death, finds the available sexual body of the peasant woman unacceptable—lacking in "tenderness" (sensitivity). The Christ's resolution in this scene provides that ordinary humans, or at least those leading simple and organic lives, should be treated with compassion, and left as they are. Says the former messiah, "Let the earth remain earthy, and hold its own against the sky. It was wrong to seek to lift him up." Thus the Christ figure rejects the egalitarian, universal ethic of Gospel Christianity.

He next stops at a small colony of refugee Romans—Roman is practically a word of abuse in Lawrence's view of history [80]— ruled by a wealthy widow. The Roman matriarch stands for hostile and willful authority, the vicious guardian of morals-and-property, thus dramatizing another variation of Lawrence's image of the destructive woman. The Roman colony, mostly slaves, strikes repulsion in the hero and, using the "day" metaphor from the fragment "The Flying Fish," he insists that the "common world" is uniformly hostile to those with an enlarged sense of life. As one of the heaven-defying "reborn," the hero was "in the other life, the greater day of the human consciousness"; thus he had the "irrevocable *noli me tangere* which separates the reborn from the vulgar."

The hostility between the once-born and the twice-born returns repeatedly in the novella—the slaves see the Christ as a malefactor and at the end attempt to trap him on the matriarch's orders. But in one passage the hero insists that the twain shall meet, that the "life of the little day" must be encompassed by the "greater day" vision of the reborn, "else all is disaster." However, this notion of religion as a social institution functions inconsistently with the dramatic pattern and point of the story. Lawrence and his Christ have fallen back into their confessed sin of "excessive salvation."

The Lawrencean antagonism to "humanity" partly comes from his negation of the Christian view, at least in its traditions of moral, social, and ideal universality. In a conversation with the Magdalen a few days after rising from the tomb, the Christ refuses to promulgate the messianic victory: "My triumph . . . is that I am not dead." He insists, however, that he died to his past life and mission and has a new view of salvation. "The teacher and the saviour are dead in me; now I can go . . . into my own single life." Briefly but insistently, Lawrence has his Christ reject most of the other key Christian tropes. He wronged Judas; he was the victim of his own "excessive salvation"; he overemphasized the significance of the Word. He now recognizes that "virginity is a form of greed," and that the individual negation that leads to the abstract love of Christianity is false: "I would embrace multitudes, I who have never truly embraced anyone." Willed benevolence turns destructive; it serves not the release of love but the "compulsion of love." Clearly, the "Messiah had not risen." Instead appears a post-Christian individual man who vows "to be alone"—"pure aloneness which is one sort of immortality." As an autonomous individual, now free of the falsities of duty and restraint, he has lost "care," "fret," the "striving self," and found his "own limits." The whole point of regeneration is the return to individual selfhood with the escape from anxiety.

Despite the denial of restraint and duty, much of this, surely, restates Protestantism in its extreme emphasis on purely individual salvation. Consistent with this is the strong note of ironic self-disparagement ("what have I done to save?") and the flight from guilt of a Christ who entirely repudiates all of his own past; there rises something harshly inhuman in the denial of all continuing human relations and all certitudes but that of the solitary pilgrimage-flight. There are painful touches of Lawrencean misanthropic pathos in the novella's hero—not the traditional thirty-three-year-old naive Jesus but a "middleaged and disillusioned" man. This is a rather misleading bit of self-pathos for a Lawrence who was practically born disillusioned, and who had all the indignation and violence of a man longing for the return to a primal innocence, unity, and enchantment that he has never quite had or believed in.

The quest for the magic sense of aliveness has Lawrence turn his Christ (at the end of the first half of the novella) into a "vagabond," a solitary romantic wanderer who can defiantly say: I "inherit the earth, since I lay no claim to it." In a world he never made, and in a society to which his only obligation rests on his own stark individuality, his alienation provides the basis for his more intense existence. This leads to committment to the primary Lawrencean value: "The goal of life is the coming to perfection of each single individual." [81]

From the tomb the Christ had "risen without desire," and thus he is not truly resurrected into full life. Since the hero is the superior man, however, his desires must be impersonal and non-egotistic, and separate from social circumstance and necessity. In his purificatory wanderings—in the "pure brightness" of the sun beside the "immaculate loneliness of the sea"—the hero comes to a pagan sanctuary (adjacent to the despised Roman Matriarchy) where a virgin woman (daughter of the matriarch) tends a temple dedicated to "Isis in search." Lawrence's favored Mediterranean scene of sea and sun, hill and pagan worship, calls forth the usual graphic description. The virgin, waiting for the "reborn man," wants no husband but a religious hero. So, "wrapped in her dream" of the pre-Christ sacrificial hero, she awaits Osiris.

The vagabond Christ and the Lady of Isis come into their first contact by a scene they jointly witness. A slave girl kills a pigeon and is interrupted by a slave boy who first beats her and then, in a natural reversal of emotion, puts his "hand between her thighs" and covers her with his body on the open rocks in "the blind frightened frenzy of a boy's first passion. . . ." Oddly enough, this scene of vivid natural sexuality does not, apparently, achieve real passion in the eyes of the watching unresponsive Christ and the disdainful priestess. The intercourse of the two children serves as a contrast to the agonized and ritualized coitus, soon to take place, between the religious figures. Despite some of Lawrence's polemics to the contrary, the dramatic ordering and the metaphoric language of the fictions seem to indicate Lawrence's lack of interest in simple and natural sex.

As one expects in romantic fictions, the contact between the Christ and the priestess—once she sees that he has the Crucifixion scars—becomes magically quick, and the result of the usual "mysterious fire." That is, this passion is not the result of nature but, in Lawrence's words, a "destiny" of "splendour." In part a metaphysical intercourse as well as a literal one, the sexually aggressive priestess, who has "the courage of life," and the sexually passive Christ, who has "the courage of death," engage in a peculiar reversal of what are considered usual sexual roles. The woman anoints the man's wounds, and then massages his entire body. In the process of this ritual action, the priestess takes on symbolic import for the Christ, and, though it is night (in contrast to the natural sexuality of the children in the sunlight), she becomes "sun beyond suns," and to "touch her was like touching the sun." The Christ now feels "The other inward sun that streams its rays from the loins." [82]

The woman is not simply a sexual but a sacramental object to the man, a "golden" and glowing thing of "rapture" and "mystery" and mystic "tenderness," a "mansion" for the Biblical longings of the Christ. Her buttocks seem to him the "soft white rock of life." Perhaps the culminating image of the woman appears in the sexual "blossom": ". . . like the heart of a rose, like the core of a flame." Much, too much, of this story takes on the rhetoric of the traditional and worn heresy of the religion of eros.

The man-who-died achieves his desires and real resurrection in terms that are a malicious inversion of Christianity. When the Christ feels "his power rise in his loins," Lawrence continues the sexual punning that started with the image of the escaped cock: "I am risen!" As the Christ makes sexual entry, he says, "Lo!

. . . this is beyond prayer." Early in the story the Christ had an ironic explanation of why he could not bear to be touched—"I am not yet risen to the father"—but now that he has had the sexual touch, and is "risen" in a more literal sense, his only relation to the authoritarian deity is an accusation: "Father! . . . why did you hide this from me?"

It would not, I think, be incorrect for the more or less orthodox Christian to see this defiant and ritualistic sexual orgasm of the Christ and the pagan priestess on the altar as a Black Mass. Lawrence cannot resist repeated attacks on cold Anglo-Saxon religious attitudes; for example, his Christ says as he leaves the Lady of Isis, "Great gods are warm-hearted, and have tender goddesses."

The religiosexual consummation—"the many petalled darkness"—that the hero has achieved, however, reveals some of Lawrence's usual ambiguous qualities. The Christ has obtained the priestess by a kind of fraud, by intentionally letting the Lady of Isis take him for Osiris, which he does not believe he is. What exists between the man and the woman cannot be designated love in any usual sense: she is realizing her religious "dream," and he is realizing his religious quest for the escape from the pall of death. It also becomes essential, apparently, that the experience be kept impersonal in order to maintain its extreme intensity, as in each of the fictions we have discussed in this chapter. The Christ says to himself: "I will ask her nothing, not even her name. . . ." And the Lady of Isis says, "He is Osiris, I wish to know no more." The nameless, mysterious, extreme, and sacramental relation follows the form of a sexual fantasy, or the dream-ridden act of drunken or half-asleep love, in which erotic heightening is achieved by slyly avoiding obligation and guilt, by the impersonality of the passion.

We should not, then, sentimentalize Lawrencean eros; its transvaluation of the ordinary requires a dehumanizing extremity, as Lawrence emphasizes by juxtaposing and describing the passion in terms of death, "another sort of death: but full of magnificence." The magnificence results not only in the sense of self-completion but in the new sense of the "circumambient universe" and its vividness.[83] "How full it is, and great beyond all gods," says the Christ of his sensations of the world as he leaves the priestess and the temple. For Lawrence, like the more demonic late-romantics such as Rimbaud, any derangement of the ordinary world or the senses justifies itself if it will lead to a divinely vibrant sense of physical sensation. (But Lawrence becomes truly remarkable in his ability to achieve this by natural means—no orgies, mutilations, or hashish.) The Christ has achieved "being in touch," and aliveness is self-justifying: ". . . the sea and the rain, the wet narcissus and the woman I wait for, the invisible Isis and the unseen sun are all in touch, and at one." Apparently, by contact with the literal woman he has reached the invisible union of the world. The "joy of being in touch" becomes a religious state characterized by its subjective transformation of everything: "All changed, the blossom of the universe changed its petals and swung around to look another way. The spring was fulfilled, a contact was established, the man and the woman were fulfilled of one another, and departure was in the air."

That "departure" provides the shocker. The subjective transformation of the world does not change actuality. Still a hostile world, a social order opposed to the "destinies of splendour" of the religion of life, the religious hero's destiny must be to go alone, always fleeing the fixity of life. The matriarch jealously plots; the resentful populace (the slaves) are ready to trap him. By the time he does leave, the priestess is pregnant and wants to establish a home, but all of the characterizing qualities of the romantic-religious figure run contrary to this: "I am a man, and the world is open." Or, as he said when he first came to the sanctuary: "I go west as the road goes"; and as his deity, the sun, goes: ". . . invisible suns would go with me." He is, as the

Christ-Osiris mythology indicates, a ritual figure; and Lawrence's dissolvement of his ritual drama uses the seasonal rhythm: "I shall come again, sure as Spring."

The Christ flees in the night. His true ending simply identifies with the flux of life, the daily resurrection: "So let the boat carry me. Tomorrow is another day." [84] But just before that last line another of those crucial demonic images occurs: ". . . the gold and flowing serpent is coiling up again, to sleep at the root of my tree." As Lawrence wrote in *Apocalypse:* "The great problem in the past was the conquest of the *inimical* serpent and the liberation within the self of the gleaming bright serpent of gold, golden fluid life within the body, the rousing of the splendid divine dragon within a man. . . ." [85] The final power of life and regeneration comes in a demonic image. The moralist may be forgiven for not seeing the difference between the inimical and the bright serpent in the tale itself, for there is only one serpent in the story, simultaneously inimical and bright.

This tour de force of a novella seeks to answer what Lawrence calls the modern question of the Sphinx—"the riddle of dead-alive man." [86] The answer is not to provide yet another version of that typically Western solution, "the good life"—a social system, a moral order, or, finally, the escape from sociomoral failures into ideal transcendental realms. Lawrence, as has been noted in the discussion of his "organic" utopianism, intermittently and irritably attacks much of modern society from his vision of a pretechnological and communal society—really the traditional social view of the sage—but this solution, as Lawrence clearly saw, stands so far apart from modern historical reality that it is but a touchstone of our sadness. (Even in the stories discussed in this chapter, though they little concern themselves with a social program as such, there always appears an image of this "good life"—the gypsy caravan, the country estate, the primitive Italian peasantry, the ancient Mediterranean paganism.) So, as Lawrence dramatizes his affirmations, they must take the form of an immanent religious myth for individual regeneration. Thus, the dark gods of life's vitalities must be brought back into the active day of the sun, but in making the dark gods supreme they must not be turned into the deities of the ordinary day.

The result is a strange combination of salvational parable and exotic romance unlike his fictions of more ordinary life, though all have the same elements, whether it be the attack on Christianity, the glorification of the outcast hero, the destructive image of society, or the crucial experiences of annihilation and eros. *The Man Who Died* provides a final desperate statement of these elements. But there is a peculiarity that points to a considerable failure. The form of stories like *The Man Who Died* and *The Virgin and the Gipsy* belongs to that of the romantic quest, the tale of adventure that leaves ordinary life and ascends into the remarkable. Most of Lawrence's stories tend to this form, even the negative fictions; *The Man Who Loved Islands, The Princess,* and *The Rocking-Horse Winner* are simply inverted romances with a satiric edge. The legendary and heroic adventure provides a leap out of inevitable social and moral commitments, a break with dulling common sense, and a suspension of natural weariness and weakness, so that the paltry daily order and known world do not command the totality of life. And if one but had the courage, the magic, and the destiny, then he would find heroic aloneness and passion and freedom. No matter that most men dare not, cannot, and even should not follow the sun; still, the world is wide and life is open.

But, I suspect, no one, including D. H. Lawrence, has quite been able to believe this in the twentieth century; the imagination, like the world we live in, is all too well filled, ordered, and closed. The leap into the unknown, the wild romance, the solitary adventure, the high deeds past all men's believing? No. (Whether anyone in the past could have made such a choice, or whether such a choice was made at considerable price, provides no issue, only that men have believed in legendary heroes, adventure into an unknown and open world, and visions of absolute freedom. Even those who believe that the world increases in progress and comfort do not believe it increases in freedom and wonder.) Lawrence's romances are archaic in material—rural youth, gypsies, the pagan past—and often arbitrary in tone and point. Lawrence, one may have noted, fought and re-did a way of life and a religion that he himself believed already defeated and dead. Myths and legends are not the product of one man and artist. Whether the forced tone and the blurred mixture of argument and romance is the failure of the times or the man, Lawrence partly makes up a religious adventure rather than lives it.

The problem may be put another way. *The Man Who Died* is a provocative but violently idiosyncratic fable. The most irritating weakness—besides the inappropriate similarity of the Christ to his author—appears in the style. Much else besides the death agony (quoted earlier) depends on a tediously incantatory and hallucinatory repetition. While there are many passages of graphic expressionistic description and some hard aphorisms, there is too much of Lawrence's poeticized rhetoric and insufficient dramatization. These weaknesses spread wide through Lawrence's work, for he intermittently falls back on a dubious rhetorical mode in the temptation, and perhaps the necessity, to turn religious insight into religious piety.

Religious adventure and insight may be art, but religious preaching and piety rarely can be. When Lawrence insists too much and uses his abstract rhetoric, incantations, and repetitions, and when his angry demands override all humor and compassion, the reader feels the demand for affirmation rather than truth. The failure is not unique with Lawrence; parallel weaknesses have often been noted in the late Hemingway and Faulkner, and might be profitably extended to, say, the late Blake and Shakespeare. Not a matter of youth versus age—Milton and Dickens suffer from such vitiation in almost all their work—it is a question of the peculiar tension and flow that makes art, and the piety that does not: insistent sacramentalism, like remorse and self-deprecation and universal benevolence, is both dubious and dull. Perhaps the religious mode creates the most dangerous temptations of all human activities. "There is only life and anti-life," [87] writes Lawrence. But too much religion of life reverses into antilife, though with Lawrence never so far as to entirely submerge the qualities and the perverse insights of vivid being.

Afterword

. . . a perfection by perversity
for the self-consuming self—
a fire to answer the fire—
for only the soul opposed
to all its own goods
so brightly burns to synthesis.[1]

PERHAPS the sixty-odd stories, sketches, and novellas discussed here do not give the complete Lawrence; or, at least, they may emphasize a Lawrence more harsh, peculiar, and perverse than might first appear to either the casual or the academic reader. Whether or not the focus on the nihilism, demonism, and extremity present *the* Lawrence, I believe they present a large part of Lawrence's artistic and intellectual process. Obsession, violence, misogyny, rebellion, inversion, alienation, and heresy are so pervasive and powerful in Lawrence's work, and so intimately related to his person, role, and qualities of being, that the onus of misreading lies upon those who fail to reckon fully with the perversity. Lawrence's negations, I have repeatedly argued, provide the affirmations and protect them. Thus his basic nihilism shows forth as one of his more fortunate characteristics. It takes a deep nihilist to be so excruciatingly aware of, and resistant to, surrounding ordinary nihilism, which is so much more nasty because counterfeited and unacknowledged. And for Lawrence, as for the angry Jewish God, the art of being is to create a world out of nothingness.

In his essay on Poe, Lawrence brilliantly criticized those who search for the "prismatic ecstasy of heightened consciousness" and so end in destruction.[2] Lawrence, himself, searched for an intense ecstasy of heightened unconsciousness, by way of destruction. But within the forms of art and intelligence, he inevitably belongs within the traditions of destructively "heightened consciousness." He follows the intensification of nature, love, death, marriage, alienation, and flight until they reach destruction—and the affirmation that lies beyond it. But Lawrence, we should also note, enlarges the scope of the extreme exploration of consciousness by not limiting it to the extreme sensibilities. Years after the essay on Poe, Lawrence wrote: "It is only in supreme crises that man reaches the supreme pitch of annihilation. The difference, however, is only a difference in degree, not in kind. The bank clerk performs in a mild degree what Poe performed intensely and deathly."[3] All of us are perverse.

Lawrence's domestication of extremity, I fear, has misled some into reading it simply as domestication; at the risk of reading it just as extremity, we must emphasize Lawrence's insistence that our consciousness turns about an annihilating waywardness, and so necessarily longs for both destruction and regeneration, though few have the candor and courage of their own inner experience. Much of the discussion here affirms what others have variously called the "Dostoyevskian," the demonic, the radical, the nihilistic, or the "crisis" view of man's nature. Lawrence had it, hated it, insisted upon it, sought to transcend it, and never lost it. Thus, look back over the fictions and note again that every appeal to life evolves from a death longing, every image of a good world arises in denunciation of a bad one, every communion belongs to an assertion of isolate separateness, every commitment is part of a flight, every love prepares itself in torment, and every regenerative moment predicates itself on the power of nothingness.

Lawrence's perversity kept him from ever fully achieving the pieties he pursued, such as the mergence in love, utopian community, and a new religious order. But his longing to transcend his negations by faith in the simple, organic, immediate, and messianic kept him from cynical stasis and acquiescent debilitation. If his "polarity" was not the informing spirit of his works, he might have been a tyrant or a saint, but he would not have written his perceptive and agonized testament. He testified to the heritage of the permanent prodigal.

The general point here is not new; Lawrence belongs to the more volatile Western sensibility in its critical energy, its self-against-self, its dialectical, overreaching, protesting, world-embracing-and-defying perverseness. We may, like Lawrence, be unhappy about this perverse bent, and long to reaffirm a simple and immediate order of life. We may even, in weak moments, like Lawrence at his flabbiest, pretend to no longer share in the unique Western sensibility. Usually, however, a polarity such as Lawrence's provides its own agonized answer, a heroic self-demand in which the intelligent, sensitive, and moral must attempt the passionate, sensual, and religious. For the individualistic intellectual to become a hero of life, he must invert his own nature until the delicate one becomes the adventurer, the too-civilized becomes the primitivist, the intellectual casuist becomes a vital irrationalist, and the limited mortal achieves moments of oneness with the flux of the universe while yet remaining outside all the fixities of life. Always outside, even of his own aspirations and nature, he thus becomes the true individual.

Characteristically intellectual, Lawrence sometimes dallied with ways back in—moral reform, mysticism, theocratic power— but his works show, with remarkable insistence and intermittently powerful art, that he succeeded in staying with one of the few strategies the Western intellectual has for authentic transcendence—the very perversity that he flees, utilizes, and, at his best, makes into vital being. The perverse view, which may well be an inadequately acknowledged part of our common sensibility, uses angry intelligence and sophisticated art to achieve relations to reality that, apparently, certain primitives and mystics attain by less tortuous means. But if one can read or write "mod-

ern" literature in any sort of relevant way, he is really no vital
naïf. Once aware of the superrationalisms by which most of us
now inevitably live, the return to enchantment can only come
by way of disenchantment. Fuzzy-mindedness provides no escape for the intelligent; sentimentality provides no way in for the
perceptive. Denial and defiance must precede affirmation and
faith, and, more important, must remain part of them.

Lawrence's particular perverse way was to follow out the
denials and defiances beyond all rational and formal ends to the
absolute and noncontingent qualities of existence. The immanence of annihilation, the passions in their own right, the re-
volts against society, the gulfs of human relations, and the moments of regeneration make total demands of consciousness and
even violations of the self. But as long as the sense of direct
reality remains present, recognizable in that there "is always
excess, a brimming over," [4] we should, and in fact will, engage
that impious, irrational, immoral, and really impossible Lawrencean imperative: "I shall accept all my desires, and repudiate
none." [5]

In one of his profound and characteristic jottings, Lawrence
noted: "Sexless people transmit nothing." [6] The living quality of
transmission, not what is transmitted, provides the crux here.
Regardless of Lawrence's mixture of shrewd, nostalgic, and ex-
acerbated ways for reinvigorating the ordinary world (there is no
other), which constantly threatens to become fixed, alien, and
meaningless, the intense qualities of life must remain primary.
The world and its ways seem less important, even less civilized,
than the "exquisite courage of brave men" [7] seeking to realize
"life and anti-life." [8] Passion, rather than sentiment or precept,
provides the strongest affirmation. When it comes to the crucial
feelings, blandness is far worse than barbarism. And when it
comes to knowledge, people without perversity know nothing.

Lawrence knew a great deal, because of his intimate sense of
the fusion of life and antilife in human being, society, and the
cosmos. Thus, while his work often descends into the arbitrary

and synthetic, it is rarely trifling or dull. All art fails, and the most important fails most of all in its presumptuous efforts to go beyond the usual limits. Although excess may lead to wisdom, it remains excess, and even the wisdom may be hard to take. Should we sometimes be unable to admire the results of the quest for the limits of experience, we can still have sympathy and awe for the qualities of intense being it requires. "Life! More vivid life!" [9] cries Lawrence. Given things as they are, some strange and annihilating extremes become necessary to achieve that wonderful and agonized fullness. Such perversity is a true art.

Bibliographical Notes

FOREWORD

1. *The Letters of D. H. Lawrence,* ed. Aldous Huxley (London: William Heinemann, 1934), p. 695.

2. The most convenient list of other studies may be found in Maurice Beebe and Anthony Tommasi, "Criticism of D. H. Lawrence: A Selected Checklist with an Index to Studies of Separate Works," *Modern Fiction Studies,* Vol. V (Spring, 1959). About half the stories are discussed, in ways generally antithetical to my approach, by F. R. Leavis, *D. H. Lawrence, Novelist* (New York: Alfred A. Knopf, 1956).

3. D. H. Lawrence, *Fantasia of the Unconscious* (London: Martin Secker, 1933), p. 15.

4. *Phoenix: The Posthumous Papers of D. H. Lawrence,* ed. Edward D. McDonald (London: William Heinemann, 1936), p. 330.

5. *Studies in Classic American Literature* (New York: Doubleday Anchor, 1953), p. 13.

6. For biographical background, I have drawn primarily on Lawrence's own writings, then on the two studies by Harry T. Moore, *The Life and Works of D. H. Lawrence* (New York: Twayne Publishers, 1951), and *The Intelligent Heart: The Story of D. H. Lawrence* (London: William Heinemann, 1955), and, to a lesser degree, on the various other biographies and memoirs. Some of the latter appear in *D. H. Lawrence: A Composite Biography,* ed. Edward Nehls (3 vols.; Madison, Wis.: University of Wisconsin Press, 1957-59). Useful discussions and examples of Lawrence criticism may be found in *The Achievement of D. H. Lawrence,* ed. Harry T. Moore and Fredrick J. Hoffman (Norman, Okla.: University of Oklahoma Press, 1953), and *A D. H. Lawrence Miscellany,* ed. Harry T. Moore (Carbondale, Ill.: University of Southern Illinois Press, 1959).

7. Examples of my views of more recent Lawrence scholarship and criticism may be found in the notes to several of my articles, cited above, and in my reviews of two rather unsatisfactory books—Armin Arnold, *D. H. Lawrence and America* (New York: Philosophical Library, 1959), and Eliseo Vivas, *D. H. Lawrence: The Triumph and the Failure of Art* (Evanston, Ill.: Northwestern University Press, 1960)—in the *Journal of Aesthetics and Art Criticism*, XIX (Spring, 1961), 356–57. Some representative critical statements on Lawrence and some documents on his censorship problems appear in *Literary Censorship*, ed. Kingsley and Eleanor Widmer (San Francisco: Wadsworth Publishing Co., 1961). I briefly discuss several other aspects of Lawrence in a forthcoming book on Henry Miller (Twayne's United States Authors Series) and in a volume in preparation on the "literary rebel" for the University of Southern Illinois Press's Cross-currents/Modern Critiques series.

CHAPTER I

1. *Fantasia of the Unconscious* (London: Martin Secker, 1933), p. 64.

2. *Phoenix: The Posthumous Papers of D. H. Lawrence,* ed. Edward D. McDonald (London: William Heinemann, 1936), p. 373.

3. *Ibid.,* p. 324.

4. *Ibid.,* p. 755.

5. *Ibid.,* pp. 686–87.

6. *Reflections on the Death of a Porcupine and Other Essays* (London: Martin Secker, 1934), p. 26.

7. "Let me derive from life or direct from death, according to the impulse that is in me." *Phoenix*, p. 687. The incantatory obsession with death becomes overwhelming in the later fictions, such as *The Man Who Died* (discussed in Chapter 5), but the preoccupation can be traced all through Lawrence's work. The most emphatic statements of the death ecstasy are found in such late poems as "Gladness of Death," "Oblivion," "Ship of Death," "The End, the Beginning," and "Target." *The Complete Poems of D. H. Lawrence* (London: William Heinemann, 1957), Vol. III.

8. *Phoenix,* p. 682.

9. *Ibid.,* p. 653.

10. *The Complete Short Stories of D. H. Lawrence* (London: William Heinemann, 1955), I, 95–116—hereafter cited as *Stories*. Because of the numerous brief quotations, inclusive page numbers are cited at the start of the discussion of each story, and not again, unless quotations from other stories intervene. A slightly different version of this section appeared as "D. H. Lawrence and the Art of Nihilism," *Kenyon Review*, XX (Autumn, 1958), 604–16. A letter, which has several times been cited as illustrating the sexual-military motif of the story, notes that "Cruelty is a form of perverted sex." Lawrence adds: "Priests in their celibacy get their sex lustful, then perverted, then insane, hence Inquisitions. . . . And soldiers get their surplus sex and their frustration and dissatisfaction into their blood and *love* cruelty." *The Letters of D. H. Lawrence*, ed. Aldous Huxley (London: William Heinemann, 1934), p. 74. The evidence for Lawrence's preoccupation with homosexuality is cumulative, and the motif will be repeatedly indicated below.

11. *Twilight in Italy* (London: William Heinemann, 1950), p. 280. For a passage giving the icy mountain as representing life denial, see *Women in Love* (New York: Modern Library, 1922), p. 467. See also the discussion of *The Captain's Doll* in Chapter 4.

12. It would be possible for those with a taste for allegorical readings to develop one here, using Lawrence's statement: "The soul of a man is a dark forest with wild life in it." *Studies in Classic American Literature* (New York: Anchor Books, 1953), p. 21.

13. *Stories*, III, 722–46. This story, along with a number of others to be examined later, makes nonsense of the literary rationalist's contention that Lawrence could not write in logical form. But Lawrence's use of rational form perversely mocks rational benevolence and idealism. Lawrence writes: ". . . it is one of the terrible qualities of the reason that it has no life of its own." He adds: "Make any people mainly rational in their life, and their inner activity will be . . . destruction." *Phoenix*, p. 254. An incompleted story of Lawrence's about closely related materials and themes is *The Man Who Was Through with the World*, ed. John R. Elliott, Jr., *Essays in Criticism*, IX (July, 1959), 213–21. Since this has more positive elements than the story discussed above, Lawrence's conflicting attitudes toward intellectual withdrawal, which run all through his life, may partly account for the incompletion of the piece. For a detailed argu-

ment about another nihilistic parable, see Kingsley Widmer, "The Negative Affirmation: Herman Melville's 'Bartleby,'" *Modern Fiction Studies,* Vol. VIII (Autumn, 1962).

14. For a characteristic attack on the will, and especially willed love and goodness, see "Nobody Loves Me," *Phoenix,* pp. 204–11. "Insist on loving humanity, and sure as fate you'll come to hate everybody." Lawrence's vitalism naturally opposes sentimentalism and mysticism—other forms of the idealist fallacy.

15. For the "mystery" and "quiescence" of love (including times of chastity for those who are well mated), see "We Need One Another," *Phoenix,* p. 193; see also "Sex *versus* Loveliness," *Assorted Articles* (New York: Alfred A. Knopf, 1930), pp. 19–30.

16. Lawrence perceptively viewed suburbia as synonymous with social matriarchy and as the great enemy of passionate life. Suburbia even threatens authentic lovers, whose passion can bear almost anything but a "suburban villa" in the *First Lady Chatterley.* Lawrence also insists that one of the most crucial modern problems is the "societal" defeat of the emotions; he adds that one must somehow "prevent suburbia spreading over Eden (too late! it's done). . . ." However, the answer to middle-class pseudocivilization cannot be barbarism since there is also the problem of "how to prevent Eden running to a great wild wilderness. . . ." *Letters,* p. 688.

17. The phrase "counter-romanticism" ("inevitably the off-spring of romanticism") comes from T. S. Eliot's note on Baudelaire, *Selected Prose,* ed. John Hayward (London: Penguin Books, 1953), p. 190. For a discussion of some counterromantic motifs and an example of it in its self-defeating form, see Kingsley Widmer, "Conrad's Pyrrhic *Victory*," *Twentieth Century Literature,* V (Autumn, 1959), 123–30.

18. For sex, see note 15, above; for the critique of modern society, see the material cited in Chapter 3; for flowers, see *Sons and Lovers,* throughout, and almost any biography of Lawrence; for utopianism, see *Letters,* pp. 214, 219, 336, 426, 572, and also *D. H. Lawrence's Letters to Bertrand Russell,* ed. Harry T. Moore (New York: Gotham Book Mart, 1948), throughout.

19. Moralizing many years later as a sort of elder statesman of rebellion, Lawrence put the point in another form: "The danger for the young is that they will question everything out of existence, so that

nothing is left. But that is no reason to stop questioning. The old lies must be questioned out of existence, even at a certain loss of things worth having. . . . then the real fun will begin putting the right things back. But nothing is any good until the old lies are got rid of." *Articles,* p. 10.

20. *Stories,* II, 303–33. Contrary to popular and academic prejudices about Lawrence, he is here dealing with his "primary" society, not primitives, miners, or aristocrats, but bohemians.

21. The "Anna Victrix" section of *The Rainbow* (London: William Heinemann, 1950), pp. 140–93, rather murkily explores the same victory of the maternal wife over the sensitive husband. The reverse emphasis shows the woman's self-defeat as an individual when she "relinquished the adventure to the unknown" for the family. This novel, incidentally, seems to have been falsely sentimentalized into what it is not by a number of clever critics.

22. As with so many other writers, Lawrence's response to the Great War appears to be the watershed moment for his rejection of England, modern mass society, and traditional "civilization." See his letters of the war period and the autobiographical "The Nightmare," *Kangaroo* (London: William Heinemann, 1950), pp. 235–86.

23. *Sex, Literature and Censorship,* ed. Harry T. Moore (New York: Twayne Publishers, 1953), p. 115.

24. *Stories,* II, 283–302. Some of the material of this story was also used by Lawrence in a play, *The Widowing of Mrs. Holroyd.* A further discussion of similar material and Lawrence's treatment of marriage will be found in Chapter 4.

25. Essentially, Lawrence reaches the same point with Paul Morel after the death of his mother. In the concluding scene, the now rootless and despairing hero makes a final rejection of childhood sweetheart, his home, and his past. It is a near total negation, and not an affirmation of anything else—his art has been abandoned; his later love has, with a peculiar sexual twist, been disposed of; and he has no other purpose. He is thinking to himself that he must "stop all this restlessness and beating against death," but he cannot, and "in the vastness and terror of the immense night . . . which will remain at last eternal," the hero finds himself "at core a nothingness." *Sons and Lovers* (New York: Modern Library, 1922), pp. 489–90. While he resists the childish longing to take a shortcut to death and follow his

mother, he concludes by staying isolated, rootless, purposeless, and unfulfilled. The turn in the night toward "the faintly humming, glowing town" (p. 491) is a negative image to Lawrence, who hated cities and towns from start to finish. The most that can be said for the hero is that, good Lawrencean, he will continue to beat restlessly against the annihilating limits. He aptly stated the theme earlier in the book: "Some sort of perversity in our souls . . . makes us not want, get away from, the very thing we want" (p. 332).

26. *Stories*, II, 427–40. The closest Lawrence got to a sensualist type was the generally well-done portrait of Constance's father in *Lady Chatterley's Lover*.

27. *Stories*, I, 274–82. The more metaphoric baptisms will be discussed with Lawrence's religious views in Chapter 5. The concluding quotation comes from *Articles*, p. 252.

28. *Stories*, II, 546–81. Discussion of related heroines will be found in Chapter 3.

29. For fuller discussion of this distinction, and of the misapplication of traditional concepts of primitivism, see Kingsley Widmer, "The Primitivistic Aesthetic: D. H. Lawrence," *Journal of Aesthetics and Art Criticism*, XVII (March, 1959), 344–53.

30. (London: William Heinemann, 1950), p. 41.

31. *Porcupine*, p. 194.

32. *Phoenix*, p. 194.

33. *American Literature*, pp. 148–49.

34. *Phoenix*, p. 99.

35. *Mornings in Mexico* (London: William Heinemann, 1950), p. 87.

36. *Porcupine*, p. 59.

37. Many similar examples, of dubious honesty, could be cited for comparison, such as Graham Greene's *The End of the Affair* and William Faulkner's *Requiem for a Nun*.

38. "Preface," *Touch and Go: A Play in Three Acts* (London: C. W. Daniel, 1920), p. 12.

39. *Letters*, p. 64.

40. *Phoenix*, p. 540.

41. *The Portrait of M. M.* is the title appropriately provided by the editor in a rare reprinting of this little-known piece. *Woollcott's Second Reader*, ed. Alexander Woollcott (New York: Viking Press,

1937), pp. 153–226. Originally, it appeared as the "Introduction," to M. M., *Memoirs of the Foreign Legion* (New York: Alfred A. Knopf, 1924). Lawrence thought it was some of his best writing, as reported by J. Middleton Murry, *Son of Woman* (London: Jonathan Cape, 1934), p. 133. I have discussed, for economy, just this one representative example of Lawrence's imaginative sketches. Only pedantic dogmatists would demand their primary separation from the stories so-called; other similar pieces might well be discussed here, such as *A Chapel among the Mountains* and *Hay Hut among the Mountains,* both posthumously published in *Love among the Haystacks* (London: William Heinemann, 1930), and some of the fine imaginative prose pieces in *Phoenix, Twilight in Italy,* and *Mornings in Mexico.*

42. (New York: New American Library, 1956.) It is important to recognize that the *Portrait of M. M.* is not just an oddity of experience and literary form but a significant type of both. For an examination of Henry Miller's piece, see my forthcoming volume on Miller (Twayne's United States Authors Series).

43. *American Literature,* p. 74.

44. *Phoenix,* p. 520. "This is our true bondage. This is the agony of human existence, that we can only feel things in conventional feeling patterns" (p. 753).

CHAPTER II

1. *Phoenix: The Posthumous Papers of D. H. Lawrence,* ed. Edward D. McDonald (London: William Heinemann, 1936), p. 90. In context, the statement refers to "the black demon of savage America." Lawrence—to add to our discussion of the primitivistic in the previous chapter—is equating the primitive and the demonic. For additional comments on this, and on the material below, see Kingsley Widmer, "Our Demonic Heritage: D. H. Lawrence," *A D. H. Lawrence Miscellany,* ed. Harry T. Moore (Carbondale, Ill.: University of Southern Illinois Press, 1959), pp. 13–27.

2. While there are a number of studies of the devil in terms of demonology, dogmatics, iconography, literary history, and pathology, most of them lack relevance to the demonic traditions in modern literature. A useful historical compilation is M. J. Rudwin, *The Devil in Legend and Literature* (Chicago: Open Court Publishing Co.,

1931). Less naive and less useful is Mario Praz, *The Romantic Agony* (New York: Meridian Books, 1955), an erudite technical study of pathological demonic motifs severed from the works. A catalogue of some of the works in which the devil takes a major role is Watson Kirkconnell, *The Celestial Cycle: The Theme of Paradise Lost in World Literature* . . . (Toronto: University of Toronto Press, 1952). Other academic compilations dealing with the Gothic background, artistic iconology, etc., could be cited, but few of them seem to get to the point. More important for understanding the devil as patron muse of the literature of revolt would be individual attention to such notable practitioners of the demonic arts as Blake, Rimbaud, and Melville. Similar problems in slightly more modern dress are touched upon in Claude Mauriac, *The New Literature*, trans. S. I. Stone (New York: George Braziller, 1959). American "Hip" or "Beat" writing and cultism—with its sexual extremity, intensification of alienated subjectivity, nihilistic affirmations, derangement of the senses, and moral inversions and flight—would be relevant as but another aspect of traditions of the Black Mass, the feast of fools, and the demonic-cult forms. As with Lawrence, such strategies *aim* to use excess and perversity to embrace the religious absolute. See Kingsley Widmer, "Literary Rebel," *Centennial Review*, Vol. VI (Spring, 1962).

3. *Studies in Classic American Literature* (New York: Anchor Books, 1953), p. 93. Lawrence frequently practices this method.

4. Lawrence reveals other characteristics of the romantic-demonics; as with Blake and Baudelaire, he holds that "Satan was the hero of *Paradise Lost.*" *Phoenix*, p. 559. For a reapplication of this view to Milton, see Kingsley Widmer, "Milton's Iconography of Renunciation," *ELH*, XXV (December, 1958), 258–69. Lawrence's poems also show the characteristic tropes—for example, the "orthodox" angels are "dull" and "tarnished with centuries of conventionality," and so fail to see the devil's brightness. "Lucifer," *The Complete Poems of D. H. Lawrence* (London: William Heinemann, 1957), III, 42. In the preceding poem, "Old Archangels," it is Lucifer who becomes the "morning star" of rebirth. Similar praise appears in "Lucifer," *Poems*, III, 140.

5. Lawrence constantly and emphatically rejected moral imperatives. As a youth he said: "With *should* and *ought* I have nothing to

do." Quoted by Helen Corke, *D. H. Lawrence's "Princess": A Memory of Jesse Chambers* (Thames Ditton, Surrey: Merle Press, 1951), p. 41. Many years later he is still at it when he approvingly quotes the nihilistic Rozanov's "profound" aphorism: "I am not such a scoundrel yet as to think about morals." *Phoenix*, p. 368. The few times Lawrence uses the word "morality" in a positive sense—as in "Art and Morality" and "Morality and the Novel," *Phoenix*, pp. 521–32, or in such phrases as "pure spontaneous morality," *Phoenix*, p. 156—the context shows it to be a synonym for "vital." From the commentaries on Lawrence, one could make a lengthy catalogue of critics who have willfully missed this obvious point.

Incidentally, there are marked similarities between the notions of Rozanov, the decadent Russian intellectual, and Lawrence, which do not seem to have been noted. Two of Rozanov's books were translated by a close friend of Lawrence, S. S. Koteliansky, and Lawrence reviewed the translations. *Phoenix*, pp. 367–71 and 388–92. In *Solitaria* (London: Hogarth Press, 1927), Rozanov, like Lawrence, talks of sex as the way to God (p. 37), of the sun as "greater than Christ" (p. 30), of "passion" as the true force of life (p. 93), and of phallicism in connection with Dionysus and the apocalypse (pp. 76 ff.). In *Fallen Leaves* (London: Hogarth Press, 1929), Rozanov, too, puts life over literature (p. 6) and paganism over Christianity (p. 40)—unless Christianity becomes "phallic" (p. 56)—since "pseudo-compassion" is destroying our civilization (p. 116). Rozanov attacks the "onanism" of the middle classes (p. 145); insists that *"sex is power"* (p. 56); and so on. Although he is apparently a considerably duller writer than Lawrence, we can find much that appears in Lawrence's later works. See also Lawrence's much earlier "Foreword" to Leo Shestov, *All Things Are Possible*, trans. S. S. Koteliansky (London: Martin Secker, 1920), pp. 7–12. Shestov, like Lawrence, attacks "moral people" (p. 55); insists on "chaos" and "ceaseless change" as the ground of true existence (p. 90); praises the knowledge to be learned from "savages" (p. 123); and constantly reiterates his hatred of idealism (pp. 138 ff.). Here is not so much a question of "influence," though some of that is highly probable, as that these alienated, defiant, and extreme intellectuals frequently tell us more about the basic Lawrencean perspective and traditions than the usual discussions of the English novel and English social life.

6. *The Complete Short Stories of D. H. Lawrence* (London: William Heinemann, 1955), II, 347–65—hereafter cited as *Stories*. Because of the many short quotations, inclusive pages are cited once at the start of the discussion.

7. Or as Lawrence typically writes: "The darkness, this has nourished us." *Reflections on the Death of a Porcupine and Other Essays* (London: Martin Secker, 1934), p. 69. The tropes of death-darkness-sex have various permutations, as we shall note, in Lawrence's work. Lawrence is quite self-conscious about the principle behind the dark-light imagery: "The mind, that is the Light; the senses, they are the Darkness." *Twilight in Italy* (London: William Heinemann, 1950), p. 59.

8. Insouciance is one of the major positive qualities of the Lawrencean hero, or at least something he agonizingly strives to achieve—the escape from anxiety perhaps being the twentieth-century state of grace: "There is much more life in a deep insouciance, which really is the clue to faith, than in this frenzied, keyed-up care, which is characteristic of our civilization, but which is at its worst, or at least at its intensest, in America." *Phoenix,* p. 156. See also one of Lawrence's best familiar essays, "Insouciance," *Assorted Articles* (New York: Alfred A. Knopf, 1930), pp. 31–37.

9. "All we have to do is accept the true chaos that we are. . . ." *Phoenix,* p. 262.

10. This much-anthologized story has frequently been given weirdly "positive" interpretations, but see Lawrence's own comment: "I've done *The Blind Man*—the end queer and ironical." *The Letters of D. H. Lawrence,* ed. Aldous Huxley (London: William Heinemann, 1934), p. 459.

11. *The Short Novels of D. H. Lawrence* (London: William Heinemann, 1956), I, 3–69—the second work in the volume (the pagination is not continuous). Lawrence thought of this novella as a venture into new realms. See *Letters,* p. 459. Some insight into the story can be gained by comparing it with an earlier version, "The Thimble," *The Seven Arts,* No. 5 (March, 1917), pp. 435–48. In the rather murky and inconclusive earlier story, the accidental discovery of a decorated thimble (one is inclined to suspect some uncertain Freudian symbolism relating to the armored castrating female) brings to a head a marital conflict with a willful woman. In *The Ladybird*

Lawrence has "poeticized" the materials by adding the emphatic erotic triangle and the demonic motifs.

12. *Fantasia of the Unconscious* (London: Martin Secker, 1933), p. 175.

13. In addition to some of the short fictions, which will be discussed below, three of Lawrence's novels are particularly concerned with "leadership": *Aaron's Rod*—a weak novel because of its casual refusal to develop its picaresque characters and scenes as such, but frequently insightful in its arguments about love and individuality; *Kangaroo*—a few graphic autobiographical scenes, but the rebel has confused his defiance with politics, and gets silly; and *The Plumed Serpent*—with the exception of the "realistic" scenes, which belong with Lawrence's fine travel sketches, a sick diabolist fantasy. Lawrence also emphasized his version of political authoritarianism in many of the essays, such as "Blessed Are the Powerful," *Porcupine*, pp. 145–60; "Aristocracy," *Porcupine*, pp. 222–40; and "Democracy," *Phoenix*, pp. 699–718. He also attacks the counterfeit values under democratic labels in many of his violent "Pansies" and "Nettles" (satiric verses), *Poems*, Vols. II and III. The basic value, at all periods of his work, is that "brave men are forever born, and nothing else is worth having." *Phoenix*, p. 122. But the brave man's role varies in Lawrence's work from rebellion, through phases of utopianism, to the inevitable authoritarianism of political revolution, to his final cosmic rebellion. Rebellion, however, remains more basic than authority in Lawrence: "I long to get into some sort of free, lawless life. . . . I *hate* and *abhor* being stuck on to any form of society." *Letters*, p. 434.

14. "We have made a covenant with death, and with hell are we at agreement. . . ." Isa. 28:15.

"I can become one with God, consumated into the utter darkness of power, till I am at one with the darkness of initial power, beyond knowledge of any opposite." *Porcupine*, p. 25. The darkness of death, sex, and the demonic provides the annihilation of duality, Lawrence's way out of an insistent division and "polarity." At his most extreme, Lawrence writes: "Don't tell me there is no Devil; there is a Prince of Darkness. Sometimes I wish I could let go and be really wicked—kill and murder. . . . It is this black desire that I have become conscious of." *Letters*, p. 237. Lawrence was rarely a man who could let go, and outside of periods of hysterical illness (World War I and Mexico), he did not wish to turn amorality into evil. He is, of course, one of a number of symptomatic modern figures in his recognition that evil, but not goodness, transcends the ordinary human condition.

15. *Stories,* I, 187–96. The story was one of Lawrence's very earliest, though perhaps originally in a somewhat different form. See P. B. Wadsworth, "Foreword," D. H. Lawrence, *A Prelude* (Thames Ditton, Surrey: Merle Press, 1949), pp. 14–15. The point is of some importance in indicating the early and central role of the demonic in Lawrence's work.

16. *Stories,* III, 587–604.

17. *Ibid.,* 630–46. The brief *Smile* does not merit further discussion.

18. *Stories,* II, 394–410.

19. Perhaps the word "demon" is quite incidental in the description of Hadrian; generally, however, "demon" is not incidental in its regular appearance in Lawrence's work at moments of the sharply aroused erotic. The sensual, at least in northern whites, Lawrence equates with the demonic: at certain crucial times there comes forth the "primary or bodily self—appearing often like a black demon, out of the fair creature." *Articles,* p. 233. Lawrence's erethisia, which provides the main trope in this story, appears in much of his writing.

20. *Short Novels,* I, 3–69 (the third work in the volume). Lawrence may not have consciously intended the demonic emphasis in the stories of provincial life, at least not to the degree that becomes evident in some of the other fictions. That Lawrence knew his more "English" writings were about the past is clear in a number of comments. "*The Fox* belongs more to the old world." *Letters,* p. 569.

21. The linkage between the demonic and the fox also appeared in the early *A Fragment of Stained Glass,* as we noted above. The fox, like the stallion in *St. Mawr* (discussed below), represents the passions, partly because he is predatory, wild, magical, and gold-red in color. "Gold-red" is the symbolic color for potency, Lawrence notes in *Apocalypse* (New York: Viking Press, 1932), p. 99.

22. Rev. 16:2.

23. Perhaps it should be emphasized that Lawrence is not alone in the demonic insight about the anguish, amorality, and excess necessary for the crucial commitments of life. W. B. Yeats, for one example, touches a similar chord: "Even the wisest man grows tense/

With some sort of violence/ Before he can accomplish fate,/ Know his work or choose his mate." "Under Ben Bulben," *Collected Poems* (New York: Macmillan Co., 1951), p. 342.

24. But see also Lawrence's ironic sketch, *Man Is a Hunter*, *Phoenix*, pp. 34–44. The hero as a hunter, as with Lawrence's gamekeepers in his first and last novels, suggests command of the natural order and of a predatory outlaw power.

25. Lawrence indicated that he had to cut the length of *The Fox* for publication, which may partly explain the disjunction; see *Letters*, p. 481. But that is not a sufficient explanation of the novella's weaknesses.

26. The "blue flower," a major symbol of aspiration in Novalis, suggests that those interested in "sources" might find many in German romanticism for Lawrence's Gothic effects.

27. *Letters*, p. 688.

28. See "The Duende," Appendix V, Federico García Lorca, *Poet in New York*, trans. Ben Belitt (New York: Grove Press, 1955). This, of course, is a parallel, not an "influence." It is widely recognized that the major themes, gestures, forms and attitudes of the major modern literary figures are rarely understandable within national or linguistic boundaries. Like Lawrence, they were spiritual refugees before they became physical refugees.

29. "Love," *Phoenix*, p. 136.

30. *Short Novels*, II, 3–147 (the first work in the volume).

31. Lawrence praises "the Great God Pan" as a pagan-primitive image of virility who is "more demon than God," in "Pan in America," *Phoenix*, pp. 22–31. He argues that "civilization" lessened Pan's power until he "died, and turned into the devil of the Christians" (p. 23). Pan, like other images of the demonic, repeatedly appears as a trope in Lawrence's work. Knut Hamsun, Michael Arlene, and others, were also resurrecting Pan during this period.

32. Lawrence discusses the horse symbol at length in *Apocalypse*, pp. 97–99. He writes that the horse was the "dominant symbol" in pagan times of virility and the "dark soul." Also: "The red horse is choler; not mere anger but natural fierceness, what we call passion." He makes the same point in *Letters*: "In modern symbolism, the horse is supposed to stand for the passions" (p. 592). Cico, the passionate Italian who elopes with the heroine in Lawrence's *The Lost*

Girl, has a magical relation to horses; Ursula, at the end of *The Rainbow,* is nightmarishly overwhelmed by surrounding horses who indicate her sexual failure. Constance, in *Lady Chatterley's Lover,* thinks of the white and dark horses of the soul.

33. The destructive woman—one of Lawrence's major preoccupations—will be discussed at greater length in the following chapter.

34. Modern civilized people "are bored because they experience nothing. And they experience nothing because the wonder has gone out of them." *Articles,* p. 186. "Our cosmos is a great engine, and we die of *ennui.*" *Mornings in Mexico* (London: William Heinemann, 1950), p. 129.

35. Lawrence plays upon fire imagery here: cosmically, it is lightning; vegetably, it is the scarlet columbine and the "pure-fire red" of herb honeysuckle; animally, it is blood. All are given demonic twists, and even the life red of the roses is "set among spines the devil himself must have conceived of in a moment of sheer ecstasy." This is not to deny the aptness of Lawrence's literal description, but merely to note that the description has distinctive directions.

36. Lawrence, we must remember, grew up in the world of Darwinism and social Darwinism (he read Spencer). He says, later: "I don't believe in evolution. . . ." *Mornings in Mexico,* p. 8. But this does not negate completely Lawrence's intellectual inheritance of "the struggle for survival," though given an antipositivistic and antiprogressive twist. See his harsh title essay on the competition for existence in *Porcupine,* pp. 192–222. Life is justified by the survival of the higher forms, but: "What do we mean by higher? strictly, we mean more alive. More vividly alive" (p. 207). In such works as *St. Mawr* there seems implicit a pagan cyclic view of history, and the more vividly alive are waiting for the new hero, the new god.

CHAPTER III

1. *Reflections on the Death of a Porcupine and Other Essays* (London: Martin Secker, 1934), p. 17. The meaning of the statement is discussed later in the chapter. A somewhat different version of the material in the first two sections of this chapter appeared as "Lawrence and the Fall of Modern Woman," *Modern Fiction Studies,* V (Spring, 1959), 47–56.

2. *Fantasia of the Unconscious* (New York: Thomas Seltzer, 1933), p. 128.

3. *Studies in Classic American Literature* (New York: Anchor Books, 1953), pp. 102–3. Lawrence argues that "unless a woman is held, by man, safe within the bounds of belief, she becomes inevitably a destructive force." And: "Unless a man believes in himself and his gods, *genuinely;* unless he fiercely obeys his own Holy Ghost, his woman will destroy him. Woman is the nemesis of doubting man. She can't help it." Further more: ". . . if a woman doesn't believe in a *man*, she believes, essentially, in nothing" (p. 104).

4. *Assorted Articles* (New York: Alfred A. Knopf, 1930), p. 236.

5. *Ibid.*, p. 38. A very large part of Lawrence's later discursive writing is devoted to these aspects of the nature of man and woman.

6. *Fantasia*, p. 76.

7. *Ibid.*, p. 77.

8. *Ibid.*, pp. 77–78.

9. Many of the following stories draw upon figures recognizable in Lawrence's letters, and discussed in the biographies. But because there has already been so much discussion of the fictions in biographical terms, they will be ignored here. The biography, of course, insists on Lawrence's mixed attitudes toward the *haute bourgeoise* ladies, or imitations, whom he treated with both flattery and malice. Most of the stories can stand by themselves.

10. *The Complete Short Stories of D. H. Lawrence* (London: William Heinemann, 1955), III, 701–21—hereafter cited as *Stories.* All otherwise unidentified quotations are from the inclusive pages of the last story cited.

11. *Phoenix: The Posthumous Papers of D. H. Lawrence,* ed. Edward D. McDonald (London: William Heinemann, 1936), p. 711.

12. It is not incidental that many of Lawrence's harshest stories of destructive women draw upon Americans with their outraged idealism. In flight from the traditional Anglo-Saxon culture, which he felt to be dying, Lawrence found the American counterfeit characterized by an even more certain "doom." However, we should not forget that Lawrence was undoubtedly the most American—the most alienated, restless, violent, declassed, sexual, extreme, and un-English—of English authors.

13. *Stories,* II, 473–512.

14. *Psychoanalysis and the Unconscious* (New York: Thomas Seltzer, 1921), p. 100.

15. *Articles*, p. 36. Anxious moral concern with the world is a failure of insouciance and individuality. "Is love of humanity the same as real, warm, individual love? Nonsense." *Phoenix*, p. 712.

16. The reversals of passion—the perverse law of human nature—are major and recurrent points in most of Lawrence's fictions, and provide much of the characteristic form. See, for a statement of the issue, *American Literature*, p. 90.

17. The Poe and Hawthorne essays are particularly suggestive, throughout, on what Lawrence himself is doing. *American Literature*, pp. 73–121.

18. *Phoenix*, p. 245.

19. For the negation of ownership, see *Articles*, pp. 61 ff., as well as statements cited below; for the attack on money, see *Apocalypse* (New York: Viking Press, 1932), especially the concluding section, and also many of the late verses; for the rejection of the longing for security, see *Phoenix*, p. 20; for the fullest expressions of Lawrence's views on industrialism, see *Lady Chatterley's Lover*, throughout, and the late verses.

20. *Twilight in Italy* (London: William Heinemann, 1950), pp. 235 ff.

21. *The Collected Letters of D. H. Lawrence*, ed. Aldous Huxley (London: William Heinemann, 1934), p. 118.

22. *Ibid.*, p. 548.

23. *Ibid.*, p. 552. This may also be part of the point of Lawrence's allegorical sketch, *Mercury*, in which a thunderbolt kills two men on a tourist peak in front of a statue of the god. Certainly, Lawrence is making much of the vitally awesome and destructive cosmos and its gods, all of which are not comprehended by the modern crowd. *Phoenix*, pp. 35–39.

24. *Articles*, p. 74.

25. *Ibid.*, p. 61.

26. *Letters*, p. 835.

27. *Articles*, p. 180.

28. *Phoenix*, p. 559.

29. *Porcupine*, p. 60. In a later comment, which may be applied to the middle-class emotions, Lawrence writes: "Sentimentality is a sure

sign of pornography." *Pornography and Obscenity* (New York: Alfred A. Knopf, 1930), p. 25.

30. *Articles*, p. 180.

31. *Stories*, III, 844–53.

32. *Phoenix*, p. 711.

33. *Letters*, p. 638.

34. *Apocalypse*, p. 150. This view may readily be linked with antiobjective existence theologies, such as that of Nicolas Berdyaev, *Slavery and Freedom* (New York: Charles Scribners Sons, 1944).

35. *Stories*, III, 790–804.

36. *Letters*, p. 638.

37. Lawrence often comments negatively on the Flaubertean tradition. See, for example, his remarks in a review of Thomas Mann, *Phoenix*, pp. 308–13. A rebuttal of the canons of the "well-made novel," as applied to his own works, appears in a personal piece in *Phoenix*, pp. 795–805.

38. *Stories*, III, 761–68.

39. *Sons and Lovers*, chap. vi.

40. "Monuments, museums, permanencies, and ponderosities are all anathema." And he adds a shrewd comment: "Material simplicity is after all the highest sign of civilization." *Phoenix*, p. 122.

41. "The Novel," *Porcupine*, pp. 108–9.

42. *Stories*, III, 805–26.

43. For some of Lawrence's statements on the necessity for masculine purpose—one of his most obsessive points—see *Porcupine*, p. 149; *Psychoanalysis*, pp. 94 ff.; *American Literature*, pp. 102 ff.; *Fantasia*, pp. 14, 90, 93, 97, 107, 169 ff.; and the discussion in Chapter 4, where it is argued that Lawrence never quite realizes masculine purpose in his fictions.

44. "There is hardly a woman on earth who can live cheerfully without some intimate relationship to a man; unless she substitutes some other woman for the man." The same point is applied by Lawrence to men as well. *Phoenix*, p. 188. A popular academic writer on Lawrence informs me this is now recognized by everyone, which seems doubtful. Lawrence, and the popularization in America of some of his notions, by John Steinbeck, Tennessee Williams, Sherwood Anderson, and others, may have broadened the currency of such awareness. For Lawrence, the erotic is an absolute force, which

can be given perverse and varied forms but cannot be ignored or eliminated.

45. Other examples of the destructive woman will be discussed in later chapters. It should also be noted that they appear in each of the novels—Mrs. Morel in *Sons and Lovers*; the wife and the Marchioness in *Aaron's Rod*; Gudrun and Hermione in *Women in Love*; Winifred in *The Rainbow*; Kate in *The Plumed Serpent*; Constance's sister in *Lady Chatterley's Lover*; and similar figures in the other novels. They are all intellectual, or would-be intellectual, women. Those who achieve feminine grace by submitting to male purpose (and consequently reject the modern world), include Ursula in *Women in Love*, Alvina in *The Lost Girl*, Constance in *Lady Chatterley's Lover*, and similar figures. But, because of Lawrence's pyrrhic intelligence and his emphasis on life as an open process, all conclude on a note of uncertainty.

46. *Stories*, I, 71–94. This story was first published posthumously (1934).

47. This story digresses, irrelevantly, to let Lawrence bring in a minor artist figure illustrating his usual negative view of the literary life; the poetic young man "had never come into touch with life, save through literature, and for him, since he was a rather fine-hearted young man, with a human need to live, this was a tragedy."

48. There is considerable ambiguity about Lawrence's metaphors for the deeper "consciousness" (variously qualified as cosmic, impersonal, phallic, blood, dark, etc.); it generally appears to be "unconscious" in good part, nonegotistical, primordial, closely related to death and sexual urges, but broader than sex in the usual sense. Some of his definitions are rather odd: "Phallic consciousness is the thing we mean, in the best sense, by common sense." *Letters*, p. 716. But he also writes that "the phallus is only the great old symbol of godly vitality in a man, and of immediate contact." *Sex, Literature and Censorship*, ed. Harry T. Moore (New York: Twayne Publishers, 1953), p. 114. See also the well-known statement on religion of the blood, *Letters*, p. 94. Since Lawrence repeatedly notes that he is speaking symbolically ("Phallus itself is but a symbol," *Porcupine*, p. 184) any definition and interpretation must depend on the context.

49. *Stories*, I, 54–70.

50. *Stories*, III, 827–43.

51. *Stories,* II, 513–27.

52. "I do think a woman must yield some sort of precedence to a man, and he must take this precedence. . . . Consequently, the woman must follow as it were unquestioningly." *Letters,* p. 458. But Lawrence has, particularly at his best, a more basic and exalted principle: "Neither man nor woman should sacrifice individuality to love, nor love to individuality." *Porcupine,* p. 177. We can generally find in Lawrence the desire, finally, to make each value nonexchangeable, incommensurable, unique.

53. This, at least on the conscious level, is a justification of the attack on intellectual women: they despise men. "It is not familiarity that breeds contempt: it is the assumption of knowledge." *Articles,* p. 186.

54. Contrast this with Lawrence's "Surgery for the Novel—Or a Bomb," and "Why the Novel Matters," *Phoenix,* pp. 517 ff. and 533 ff. See also "The Novel," *Porcupine,* pp. 103 ff.

55. Lawrence used the blue tits in the earlier "Anna Victrix" section of *The Rainbow* (London: William Heinemann, 1950), p. 191. The wife watches the birds after having defeated her husband; she impersonally orders them to stop fighting but is thrilled by their domestic strife "as if she belonged to the bird's world, were identified with the race of birds." Verbal and metaphoric repetition were basic to Lawrence's hostile insistence and cosmic impatience. The more general pattern of the bird imagery will be suggested in the next section of this chapter.

56. *Letters,* p. 756. This is on his friend Aldous Huxley. Lawrence has many similar comments on "self-conscious" modern literature that is not "quick" with life, though Lawrence, as much as any modern, suffers from that which he condemns: ". . . the accursed perversity of the spirit, the self-aware-of-itself." *Phoenix,* p. 766.

57. *Stories,* II, 379–93.

58. *The White Peacock* (London: William Heinemann, 1950), p. 198.

59. Both of these will be discussed in the concluding chapter. Another version of this section appeared as "D. H. Lawrence: Birds of Passion and Birds of Marriage," *University of Kansas City Review,* XXV (October, 1958), 73–79.

60. *Aaron's Rod* (London: William Heinemann, 1950), p. 178—

probably from Walt Whitman's poem "Dalliance of the Eagles."
   61. *Psychoanalysis*, p. 112.
   62. *Articles*, p. 50. Lawrence repeatedly makes the point in the essays in this volume.
   63. *Ibid.*, p. 50.
   64. *Sex, Literature and Censorship*, p. 96.
   65. "There is only one sin in life, and that is the sin against life, the sin of causing inner emptiness. . . ." *Phoenix*, p. 745.
   66. *Porcupine*, p. 60.
   67. *Phoenix*, p. 345.

CHAPTER IV

   1. *Phoenix: The Posthumous Papers of D. H. Lawrence*, ed. Edward D. McDonald (London: William Heinemann, 1936), p. 153.
   2. The harshly exalted demand Lawrence makes can be seen in a personal remark: "If ——— wasn't such a frightened masturbator, he'd know that sex contact with another individual meant a whole meeting, a contact between two alien natures, a grim *rencontre*, half battle and half delight always, and a sense of renewal and deeper being afterwards." *The Letters of D. H. Lawrence*, ed. Aldous Huxley (London: William Heinemann, 1934), p. 557.
   3. *Studies in Classic American Literature* (New York: Anchor Books, 1953), p. 74.
   4. *Apocalypse* (New York: Viking Press, 1932), p. 196.
   5. *Psychoanalysis and the Unconscious* (New York: Thomas Seltzer, 1921), p. 101.
   6. *Ibid.*, p. 95.
   7. *Reflections on the Death of a Porcupine and Other Essays* (London: Martin Secker, 1934), p. 176.
   8. "Love," *Sex, Literature and Censorship*, ed. Harry T. Moore (New York: Twayne Publishers, 1954), p. 176.
   9. *Psychoanalysis*, p. 100.
   10. *Fantasia of the Unconscious* (New York: Thomas Seltzer, 1933), p. 128.
   11. *Phoenix*, p. 156. Blake, again, has a similar view: "General good is the plea of the scoundrel, hypocrite and flatterer." This radical assault on ethical universals would seem to be a distinguishing mark

of the vitalist tradition. Nietzsche makes similar criticisms of morality as "deception," "fabrication," artistic "fiction," and even as "outrageous imposture," when defending his beyond-good-and-evil pessimism and "perversity of stance." See *The Genealogy of Morals*, trans. Francis Golffing (New York: Anchor Books, 1956), p. 10 (Nietzsche's "Preface" of 1886).

Since Lawrence's relation to Nietzsche has often, quite properly, been mentioned by critics, we might note several specific points that do not seem to have been cited. In Lawrence's early and autobiographical story, *A Modern Lover*, Nietzsche is cited as one of the final "points" in the sophisticated young man's education. *The Complete Short Stories of D. H. Lawrence* (London: William Heinemann, 1955), I, 6—hereafter cited as *Stories*. This, and the use of Nietzschean phrases in *England, My England* (cited in Chapter 1, above) may also be paralleled in some of Lawrence's expository writings, as when he praises Nietzsche for "demolishing" the "Christian religion as it stood." *Phoenix*, p. 304. More relevant to the discussion here, Lawrence summarized the Nietzschean view of love: "Passion . . . the female ministers to him . . . he walks the earth like a Lord. And it is to this state Nietzsche aspires in his *Wille zur Macht*." But he also attacks Nietzsche's views, despite a certain similarity to his own, as "spurious feeling." *Phoenix*, pp. 490–92. Later references to Nietzsche are usually negative, as with the expression of distaste of the hero of *The Border Line*. *Stories*, III, 589. Lawrence's repeated criticism of "will"—it is both a major negative characteristic of the destructive women and of industrial mass civilization—may derive some of its force and pertinence as a critique of Nietzsche's "will to power." This seems to be the implicit context for Lawrence's statement: "We have a confused idea that *will* and power are somehow identical. We think we can have a will to power." Since Lawrence finds power primarily in unwilled sexual charisma, he condemns will to power as "just bullying." *Porcupine*, p. 145. Lawrence's praise of aristocracy, his eye for the covertly sexual, his insistence on the regenerative cycle, his amoralism, his Dionysiac paganism and anti-Christianity, his positive nihilism and search for direct transcendence—all have strong similarities to Nietzsche's views. But their equally emphatic differences on power, will, science, reason, egoism, etc., may be just as important.

12. For further details, see Lawrence's characteristically harsh portrayals of the Christian clergyman in *Daughters of the Vicar* and *The Virgin and the Gipsy*. Lawrence once admonished a correspondent: ". . . it seems to me a *blasphemy* to say that the Holy Spirit is love." *Letters,* p. 26. (For Lawrence's own theology of the "Holy Spirit" see the intermittent discussion in *Twilight in Italy* [London: William Heinemann, 1950].) For how can Christianity, which Lawrence sees as denying desire, have anything to do with the Eros that is its demon? See *Letters,* p. 361.

Altruistic and passionate love should be distinguished, and not simply in moralistic terms. Unfortunately, very little adequate discrimination about the varieties of love appears in literary studies, though it is a major subject of our literature. Denis de Rougement's discussion of modern love literature is one of the few, but it is both ill-informed and irrelevant. His polemic against Lawrence, for example, links him with Erskine Caldwell and with "National Socialism, Fascism or Communism"—solely, it would seem, on the basis of one work—*Porcupine. Passion and Society,* trans. M. Belgion (London: Faber and Faber, 1956), 236–37; this is the revised edition of *Love in the Western World.* Another quasiliterary study of the modes of love is the bland popular essay of M. C. D'Arcy, *The Mind and Heart of Love* (London: Faber and Faber, 1954). D'Arcy's urbane neo-Thomism slides over most of the incompatibilities of various modes of love; this is made easier by either ignoring or misquoting the more problematic literary works (see the misquotation and misuse of William Blake's "The Clod and the Pebble," p. 228). A more accurate Catholic view, within its narrow limits, is that of A. J. Denomy, *The Heresy of Courtly Love* (New York: Declan X. McMullen, 1958), who recognizes fundamental antagonisms between pagan-courtly-romantic love and Christian-moral love. The usual academic literary studies, such as C. S. Lewis, *The Allegory of Love* (New York: Oxford University Press, 1936), and Maurice Valency, *In Praise of Love* (New York: Macmillan Co., 1958), assume the compatibility of Christian and courtly-romantic modes of love. Valency, apparently unacquainted with the works of St. Paul in his field, finds no incompatibility between predominant Christian views and sexual love. Some full-scale distinctions, such as those made for the classical-patristic period by Anders Nygren, *Eros and Agape* (London:

S. P. C. K., 1953), seem to be essential. The Lawrencean passionate eros, incidentally, must be distinguished from the egotistical theories of love—as well as from the Christian, the classical, and the moral—such as the tradition of Stendhal's *De l'amour*. It is to this tradition that Jose Ortega y Gasset's *On Love: Aspects of a Single Theme* (New York: Beacon Press, 1957) belongs, despite his criticisms of Stendhal. An antithetical approach to love, much closer to Lawrence, might be represented by V. Solovyev, *The Meaning of Love* (New York: International Universities Press, 1945). This forerunner of existentialism insisted that "sex-love" was an "independent good" (p. 16), with its meaning uniquely separate from procreation and the race. Also, like Lawrence, he points to the literal meaning of the resurrection in the flesh (p. 78), the intimacy of love and death (p. 22), the superiority of sexual love to ideal love (p. 29), etc. However, Solovyev's fusion of eros with the Russian God, via the immortality of sexual desire, is a quite different metaphoric leap than Lawrence's emphasis that "the way to immortality is the fulfillment of desire." *Phoenix*, p. 369. For practical reasons, we must leave aside here the problem of Lawrence and Freud and the odd crossings of the religious-passionate and the rationalist-therapeutic views of eros; part of this has been discussed by Fredrick Hoffmann, *Freudianism and the Literary Mind* (Baton Rouge, La.: Louisiana State University Press, 1948). I cannot see the least appropriateness to Lawrence of the synthetic views of eros of Carl Jung or Erich Fromm—approaches sometimes suggested by writers on Lawrence.

13. *Letters*, p. 88.

14. *Porcupine*, p. 176.

15. *Ibid.*, p. 77. Lawrence repeatedly makes clear that "fulfillment of desire" is not to be equated with marriage. See *Letters*, p. 361. Yet the form of most of his novels moves awkwardly within the love-to-marriage pattern of the nineteenth-century English novel. This discrepancy may account for some of the blurred writing and development.

16. *Phoenix*, p. 156.

17. *Ibid.*, p. 153. I refrain here from discussing in detail the sexuality upon which Lawrence insists, including his demands for various forms of sexual enrichment or "deviation." Lawrencean sexuality has been badly treated by the moralistic writers. Aldous Huxley, for

example, despite sometimes penetrating remarks about Lawrence, characteristically distorts him. See his appalling "Appendix" to "Love, Sex and Physical Beauty," *Collected Essays* (New York: Harper and Brothers, 1959), pp. 82–89. He interprets a passage from *The Plumed Serpent* as an illustration of the Huxleyean doctrine favoring "male continence" (incomplete sexual intercourse). Other readers of the passage in context may find that Lawrence attacks clitoral orgasm and sexually aggressive women. Certainly, male continence is generally anathema to Lawrence, who, as the very tropes of his sexual descriptions emphasize, insists on the improved and heightened male orgasm. Evidence could be given indicating that Lawrence's demand included a peculiarly submissive sexual role for the female, but that, for him, is part of the heightening of male gratification. More generally, and leaving aside abstruse and disputed questions as to whether or not there are different kinds and degrees of orgasm, Lawrence's erotic situations generally insist on conditions that maximize, for both parties, the psychic and physical intensities of release.

18. *The Short Novels* (London: William Heinemann, 1956), I, 3–39.

19. *A Prelude*, ed. P. B. Wadsworth (Thames Ditton, Surrey: Merle Press, 1949), pp. 29–47.

20. *Stories,* I, 212–20.

21. *Stories,* II, 458–72.

22. *Stories,* I, 136–86.

23. See Eleanor Rackow Widmer, Love and Duty: The Heroines in Jane Austen and Charlotte Brontë (Ph.D. dissertation, University of Washington, 1958), chap. iv. She discusses, over the whole range of the nineteenth-century English novel, "the encroachment of duty over love," and the heroine as "a secular embodiment of the Christian ethos" in whom "all passion is subordinated to the domestic-moral order." This suggests the background in which Lawrence's fictions develop and which he seeks to invert.

24. *Stories,* I, 1–22. Another early story of Lawrence's, *A Fly in the Ointment,* in G. Stuart Gelder and Ada Lawrence, *Young Lorenzo: Early Life of D. H. Lawrence* (London: William Heinemann, 1932), pp. 183–94, concerns the muddled relation with a girl similar to Miriam of *Sons and Lovers.* The protagonist, a Victorian youth, catches a thief in his boardinghouse. The lower-class tough arouses

an excessive repulsion in the hypersensitive youth ("a blot fallen on my soul, something black and heavy which I could not decipher"), and he concludes that such knowledge of the hatred and repulsiveness of life (and masculinity?) blots out his idealistic girl friend's "purity."

25. *Stories,* III, 647–60. Lawrence's essays on love (*Phoenix* and *Assorted Articles*) help suggest what he was attempting in this story.

26. *Stories,* I, 197–211.

27. *Ibid.,* 234–43. The piece starts awkwardly with some imitative nineteenth-century moral rhetoric, usually subsumed under his own metaphysical or colloquial manner: "Trade, the invidious enemy; Trade, which thrust out its hand and shut the factory doors. . . ."

28. *Love among the Haystacks and Other Stories* (New York: Avon, 1949), pp. 44–53.

29. *Letters,* p. 143.

30. *Porcupine,* p. 178.

31. *Stories,* I, 117–35.

32. *Kangaroo* (London: William Heinemann; 1950), pp. 235–87, written long after the story, shows Lawrence's own revulsion to military authority. It, too, concludes with Somers (Lawrence) taking on the role of outcast from society: "Without a people, without a land. So be it. He was broken apart, apart he would remain." In both, the perhaps excessive sense of physical violation is crucial.

33. *Stories,* II, 366–78. Such fictions as this, I think, have not been given their due.

34. *Ibid.,* 334–46.

35. *Stories,* III, 605–29.

36. (New York, 1956), pp. 442–44.

37. This story emphatically reverses the perspective of *Sons and Lovers,* with the crude man now heroic, at the expense of the superior wife. The argument between the self-defining man and the literary man also appears in "What Is He?" *Complete Poems* (London: William Heinemann, 1957), II, 182–83.

38. Much of this appears in *Lady Chatterley's Lover,* throughout, and in many of the *Poems,* Vols. II and III.

39. *American Literature,* p. 79.

40. *Fantasia,* p. 124.

41. *Sex, Literature and Censorship,* pp. 89–122.

42. *Porcupine*, p. 18.

43. *Ibid.*, p. 41. Lawrence's view of marriage as conflict derives from principle and tradition as well as from family background. (Marital discord is sufficiently universal to be the ancestor of many attitudes toward marriage, and not just the Lawrencean one.) It is also doubtful if any of Lawrence's heroic men would write, as did Lawrence, "It is hopeless for me to try to do anything without I have a woman at the back of me." *Letters*, p. 93. Most of Lawrence's novels have an emphatically negative analysis of marriage, of which the most extreme is probably *Aaron's Rod*.

44. *Stories*, I, 244–66.

45. "Marriage, which on earth is a sacrament. . . ." *Phoenix*, p. 188. See *"A Propos Lady Chatterley's Lover," Sex, Literature and Censorship*, pp. 89–122, where Lawrence mainly propounds a paganized version of the Christian sacrament of marriage. The intense male ethos of miners is crucial. See C. Sigal, *Weekend in Dinlock*.

46. *Stories*, I, 45–53.

47. *Phoenix*, pp. 775–79.

48. *Stories*, I, 39–45.

49. *Stories*, II, 411–26.

50. *Virginia Quarterly Review*, XVI (Spring, 1940), 257–66.

51. *Stories*, I, 267–73.

52. Even such simple characters seem to illustrate Lawrence's principles of nonsocialized desire, such as "The more individual, the more does our blood cry out for its own specific answer, an individual woman, blood polarized with us." *Fantasia*, p. 160.

53. Yet again, the marital tragedy, like love passion, is not a question of rational or moral choice.

54. *Stories*, III, 779–89.

55. *Fantasia*, p. 170.

56. *The Lovely Lady* (New York: Penguin Books, 1946), pp. 139–56. Lawrencean marriage does not overvalue sex but does undervalue conversation and humor.

57. The Biblical manner and metaphors repeatedly appear in both Lawrence's fiction and nonfiction. For the causes, see "Hymns in a Man's Life," *Articles*, pp. 183 ff.; "[Autobiographical Fragment]," and "On Being Religious," *Phoenix*, pp. 817 ff. and 824 ff. Lawrence notes about his Congregational childhood, "I had the Bible poured everyday into my helpless consciousness" so that it "became an in-

fluence which affected all the processes of emotion and thought."
Apocalypse, p. 3. Among other possible effects of the Bible on him is
the repetition in his prose, the fine flavor of angry fanaticism,
patriarchal sexuality, some types of natural images, the prophetic
voice, and the search for the covenental religious flame.

58. *Sex, Literature and Censorship,* p. 109. Lawrence does not
mean increasing sexual intercourse but maintaining a sense of desire
and of physical and psychological polarity.

59. Or, yet again: ". . . this welter of pity, which is only self-
pity reflected onto some obvious surface." *Phoenix,* p. 407.

60. *Stories,* I, 23–38.

61. *Ibid.,* 221–33.

62. *Phoenix,* p. 694.

63. "Love," *Sex, Literature and Censorship,* p. 39. Also: ". . .
suddenly I lapse out of the duality into a sheer beauty of fulfillment.
I am a rose of lovely peace." *Phoenix,* p. 694.

64. In Lawrence's story, and in such other works as William Faulkner's *A Rose for Emily,* the traditional symbolism of ideal love has
been put in melodramatic juxtaposition with harsh emotional and
physical fact. Part of this comes from inversion of the traditional rose
image in modern literature. Where Burns insists on the comparison
—"My love is like a red, red rose"—Gertrude Stein inverts comparison
for particularity—"A rose is a rose is a rose." Where Edmund Spenser
draws the traditional duality—"Sweet is the rose, but grows upon a
brere"—Marianne Moore reverses it by questioning the rose's beauty
—"Your thorns are the best part of you." However, the iconography
of the rose in classical pastoral, Roman mystery religions (see
Apuleius, *The Golden Ass*), courtly love gardens (and Arabic love
poetry), Mariolatry, and romanticism has long been inverted by
demonic writers. William Blake's "The Sick Rose," "My Pretty Rose
Tree," and "The Garden of Love" emphasize delight in the thorns,
restraint turning the garden into a graveyard, and the sickness of love
brought about by secret (courtly) love. Corbière, and others, mocked
the traditional images. There is a significant dialectic with the cultural heritage, which is provided by perversity, as well as, probably,
mixed feelings toward the physical configuration symbolized by the
rose.

66. *Fantasia,* p. 124.

67. *The Short Novels* (London: William Heinemann, 1956), I,

3–46—the fourth, and final, work in the volume (page numbering is not consecutive).

68. "The real opposite of love is individuality." *Porcupine*, p. 175.

69. Intensity, insouciance, passion, self-sufficiency, vitality, rebellion, etc., but not peace, security, order, happiness, productivity, etc.

70. The "symbolic scenery" in *The Captain's Doll* provides another variation on that discussed in Chapter 1.

71. *The Captain's Doll* parallels part of *Women in Love*. Ursula, the true woman in the novel, like Hannele in the novella, identifies with the snowy mountain's "wall of white finality" and is ready to submit to "the mystic world . . . her consumation . . . oneness with all." The novel's hero, Birkin, like Hepburn in the novella, hates "the frozen eternality" and mystic dehumanization. He insists on the woman's submission and acceptance of his tortured individuality, and they flee to the valleys of the South.

72. *Sex, Literature and Censorship*, p. 104.

73. *Fantasia*, pp. 93 and 97.

74. *American Literature*, p. 102.

75. *Fantasia*, p. 179.

76. *Ibid.*

77. "He for God only, she for God in him." Milton—and the Old Testament. For Lawrence on masculine purpose and fidelity, see the citations given in note 43, Chapter 3.

78. Perhaps one should hasten to add that this kind of cosmic nihilism is drastically different from the contemporary pathological longing to "escape" into outer space, or other inhuman "frontiers" of technological fantasy.

79. *Porcupine*, pp. 103 ff. Lawrence argues about *Anna Karenina* that "all the tragedy came from Vronsky's and Anna's fear of *society*. The monster was social, not phallic. . . ." The same may be said of the Conrad, Hemingway, and Faulkner novels where the hero fails in "marriage" because he wishes to flee society. Lawrence's final fictions partly get around this issue by dealing with an absolute eros that cannot be reconciled with society, but also cannot have any social continuity.

80. *Sex, Literature and Censorship*, p. 103.

81. *Letters*, p. 773.

82. *Articles,* p. 26.
83. *Ibid.,* p. 56.

CHAPTER V

1. *Fantasia of the Unconscious* (New York: Thomas Seltzer, 1933), p. 60.
2. *The Letters of D. H. Lawrence,* ed. Aldous Huxley (London: William Heinemann, 1934), p. 190.
3. *Phoenix: The Posthumous Papers of D. H. Lawrence,* ed. Edward D. McDonald (London: William Heinemann, 1936), p. 734.
4. *Ibid.,* p. 726. That vital Christianity hardly exists has, of course, been held by both Christians and non-Christians in the past century: Sören Kierkegaard, *Attack on Christendom,* found Christianity as vanished as did Ludwig Feuerbach, *Essence of Christianity.* Kierkegaard's intellectual anti-intellectualism, in polemics like *The Present Age,* is markedly similar to that of Lawrence.

Achsah and Earl Brewster quote Lawrence as saying (1928): "You don't really believe in God. You can't in this age. No, no, it is a conception mankind has exhausted: the word no longer has meaning." *D. H. Lawrence: Reminiscence and Correspondence* (London: Martin Secker, 1934), p. 175. Brewster thought that Lawrence, who elsewhere talks of God, was being inconsistent. But, as many similar examples might also show, this misses the point. Lawrence was a religious atheist, who sometimes, inevitably, used the language of religion around him (though he most usually spoke of gods rather than God). He was religious but both anti-Christian and antimetaphysical in the traditional sense, always insisting that there was "no Ultimate Reality." Quoted in *D. H. Lawrence: A Composite Biography,* ed. Edward Nehls (Madison, Wis.: University of Wisconsin Press, 1959), III, 283. Lawrence would not allow for any fixed, ideal, ultimate, moral, transcendent, nonphysical god or gods but only for a religious view of the immediate and vital.

5. *The Letters of D. H. Lawrence,* ed. Aldous Huxley (London: William Heinemann, 1934), p. 604. Instead, he wants "the pagan many gods, and the animistic vision." Note that Lawrence also repeatedly yokes imagination and the Mediterranean ethos—"the artistic or pagan attitude." *Phoenix,* p. 724.
6. "I hate oneness. . . ." *Letters,* p. 604. "Oneness makes war.

. . ." "Future War," *The Complete Poems of D. H. Lawrence* (London: William Heinemann, 1957), III, 39. See also "Future States."

7. *Reflections on the Death of a Porcupine and Other Essays* (London: Martin Secker, 1934), pp. 135 and 137. See also "All Sorts of Gods," *Poems*, III, p. 109.

8. *"A Propos Lady Chatterley's Lover,"* Sex, Literature and Censorship, ed. Harry T. Moore (New York: Twayne Publishers, 1953), pp. 17–18. The "scientific" leads to "apartness" rather than to "togetherness." Lawrence prefers "chaos" to the "abstract" and the "mechanical." *Letters*, p. 605. However, as we discussed above, intelligence is not totally rejected; it is confined to its proper sphere: ". . . if barren idealism and intellectualism are a curse, it's not the head's fault." *Ibid.*, p. 671. It is codification and psychic rigidity, as well as intellectual hypostatization, that defeats responsiveness. Salvation consists of being "a man re-born from the rigidity of fixed ideas/ resurrected from the death of mechanical motion and emotion." *Poems*, III, 105.

9. *Poems*, II, 206.

10. *Porcupine*, p. 19.

11. *Ibid.*, p. 69.

12. *Mornings in Mexico* (London: William Heinemann, 1950), p. 79.

13. For example, Lawrence insists that everybody should be forced out of bed "early in the morning and put to work," otherwise they "will soon be nervously diseased." *Fantasia*, p. 160. In his rages and in his more petty moments Lawrence says many silly things. A man's heritage—in this case his mother's puritanical and genteel rigidity, the deadly restraint of English society, and nineteenth-century righteousness—is more likely to show up in daily habits and opinions than in his larger conceptions, where he can confront and pervert his sources.

14. *Poems*, II, 216. Subjectivity was always the key for Lawrence —just as it is the preoccupation of his work and the frequent burden of his style: "If God does not exist in my consciousness, then for me God does not exist." This early statement is quoted by "E. T. [Jesse Chambers]," *D. H. Lawrence: A Personal Record* (London: Knight and Co., 1935), p. 113.

15. *Porcupine*, p. 149.

16. *Sex, Literature and Censorship*, p. 105.

17. *Studies in Classic American Literature* (New York: Anchor Books, 1953), p. 112.

18. *Psychoanalysis and the Unconscious* (New York: Thomas Seltzer, 1921), p. 23.

19. *The Complete Short Stories of D. H. Lawrence* (London: William Heinemann, 1955), II, 451–57—hereafter cited as *Stories*. Because of numerous brief quotations, inclusive page numbers are cited at the start of each discussion. To the resolution of this story we might apply Lawrence's verse: ". . . nobody can be wise except on rare occasions, like getting married or dying." *Poems*, II, 226.

20. See *D. H. Lawrence: A Composite Biography*, ed. Edward Nehls (Madison, Wis.: University of Wisconsin Press, 1958), II, 468, note 219.

21. *Phoenix*, p. 245.

22. *Ibid.*, p. 350.

23. *Letters*, p. 769. Or, to put the point in Lawrence's most affirmative manner: "Man fights for a new conception of life and God, as he fights to plant seeds in the spring. . . . To plant seed you've got to kill a great deal of weeds and break much ground." *Assorted Articles* (New York: Alfred A. Knopf, 1930), p. 258.

24. *Fantasia*, p. 14. It "is man's own religious soul that drives him on beyond woman, to his supreme activity" (p. 90).

25. *Porcupine*, p. 4.

26. *Articles*, p. 142.

27. *Porcupine*, p. 89.

28. *Ibid.*, p. 96.

29. *Articles*, p. 123.

30. *Porcupine*, p. 211. See also the poem that starts, "Before Plato told the great lie of ideals," *Poems*, III, 129.

31. *Sex, Literature and Censorship*, p. 115.

32. *Fantasia*, p. 60.

33. *Pornography and Obscenity* (New York: Alfred A. Knopf, 1930), p. 35.

34. *Psychoanalysis*, p. 40. See also "Thought," *Poems*, III, 111. "Thought is the welling up of unknown life. . . ." Also: "Thought is not a trick, or an exercise, or a set of dodges/ Thought is a man in his wholeness wholly attending."

35. *Letters,* p. 94.

36. Yet tangible human being must always be overreaching the limits, transcending the ordinary, enlarging awareness: "Where do I pay homage . . . ? To the unknown, only the unknown, the Holy Ghost." *Phoenix,* p. 698. See Lawrence's intermittent discussion of the Holy Ghost as the appropriate phase of religion for the present (and, of course, as a rejection of Christology and the authoritarian deity), in *Twilight in Italy* (London: William Heinemann, 1950), pp. 54 ff. Also: "Man is only perfectly human/ when he looks beyond humanity." "Service," *Poems,* III, 85. This is but another form of characteristic Western heroic demand. But how restrained, in comparison with American and French literature of this time, Lawrence's break into the unknown appears to be. He never quite disintegrates.

37. *Letters,* p. 431.

38. *Ibid.,* pp. 197–98.

39. *Apocalypse* (New York: Viking Press, 1932), p. 190.

40. *Pornography and Obscenity,* p. 4.

41. *Phoenix,* p. 380.

42. For entertainment, see *Pornography and Obscenity.* For education, see *Fantasia,* pp. 61 ff. See also many of the polemical points scored off in "Pansies," *Poems,* Vols. II and III.

43. *Apocalypse,* p. 24. The "mass of people oughtn't even to try to think, because they *can't,*" says Mellors. "They should be alive and frisky, and acknowledge the great God Pan. He's the only god, for the masses, forever." *Lady Chatterley's Lover* (Florence: Privately printed, 1928), p. 305.

44. *Mornings in Mexico,* p. 100.

45. *The Short Novels* (London: William Heinemann, 1956), II, 3–81—this is the middle of three works in the volume (not continuously numbered). In reading this, we must "keep in mind always the near relationship between the religious motive and the sexual." *Fantasia,* p. 14.

46. The gypsies here are rather generalized and mythicized figures; possibly, Lawrence is drawing upon George Borrow, or upon the childhood tales so common then. Years earlier he had written, "I always remember the eyes of a gypsy woman. . . ." And he insists on "the gulf of dark hate and *other* understanding" that he saw in them. *American Literature,* pp. 106–7.

47. I suppose that we ought to add, for literalists, that Lawrence is not advising every young virgin to give herself sexually to a demonic stranger. "There is not and cannot be any actual norm of human conduct." *Fantasia,* p. 40. (I take it that he uses "norm" in this sense, not in the sense of a total lack of social pattern.) However, in some form or other, the separation from moral choices becomes necessary for the break into fuller experience. No moral norm can allow for fundamental transitions and changes. Amorality is essential at the crucial points.

48. *Stories,* III, 661–700.

49. Such as the use of the sun in Blake's poems and in Coleridge's "The Ancient Mariner." Kenneth Burke commented on this quality in his discussion of Coleridge in *The Philosophy of Literary Form* (Baton Rouge, La.: Louisiana State University Press, 1940). After arguing about it at some length, Mr. Burke and I seemed to agree that the ambiguities of romanticism (including Lawrence's) may often result in a double reversal that reaffirms ordinary life, morality, marriage, etc. (private conversation, April, 1956).

50. *Letters,* p. 685.

51. *Apocalypse,* pp. 199–200. "Oh what a catastrophe for man when he cut himself off from the rhythm of the year, from his union with the sun and the earth." *Sex, Literature and Censorship,* p. 109. The rhythm of the year and the sun become the dominant and organizing tropes in Lawrence's final fictions. The "loss" links up with Lawrence's repeated moral: man's alienation from the physical-cosmic unity produced a metaphysical loneliness and the anxious and willed systems of "slow death" exemplified by "science and machinery." *Apocalypse,* p. 41.

52. With M. L. Skinner, *The Boy in the Bush* (New York: Thomas Seltzer, 1924), p. 191. The passage and the whole motif are undoubtedly Lawrence's.

53. *Porcupine,* p. 229. See also the later and similar discussion in *Apocalypse,* pp. 41 ff.

54. *Fantasia,* p. 142. The sun and moon are also equated with fire and water. It would probably be specious to find an altogether consistent pattern in this symbolic imagery, with its mixture of pre-Socratic metaphysics and more-or-less Freudian motifs, forced through Protestant theologizing. Lawrence put the "Holy Ghost" of

unique individuality, which is based upon "our great negative center" (death), between the sun and moon polarities.

55. *Apocalypse*, p. 43.

56. *Fantasia*, p. 10.

57. "Aristocracy," *Porcupine*, pp. 223 ff.

58. *Poems*, II, 260–61. See also pp. 212, 213, and 263.

59. *Poems*, II, 260.

60. *Apocalypse*, p. 43. The malignity of the sun depends not only
upon the state of the individual being but also upon the metaphysical state of a culture: "The sun, the great sun, in so far as he is the
old sun of a superceded cosmic day, is hateful and malevolent to the
new born. . . ." *Apocalypse*, p. 114.

61. *Phoenix*, p. 131.

62. *Articles*, p. 189.

63. *Porcupine*, p. 229. Some of this material, in considerably dif-
ferent form and with other material, originally appeared as "The
Sacred Sun in Modern Literature," *The Humanist* (The American
Humanist Association, Yellow Springs, Ohio), XIX (November–
December, 1959), 368–72.

64. *Tales*, pp. 740–55.

65. *Letters*, p. 120.

66. *Porcupine*, p. 234.

67. I have not been able to examine a copy of this edition. The
final sentence is quoted by Harry T. Moore, *The Life and Works of
D. H. Lawrence* (New York: Twayne Publishers, 1951), p. 257.
Lawrence comments on this version of the story in *Letters*, p. 730.

68. *Apocalypse*, p. 150.

69. *Phoenix*, p. 761. This also implies one of Lawrence's major
aesthetic principles: "The business of art is to reveal the relation between man and his circumambient universe, at the living moment."
Ibid., p. 527. There is some contradiction between this avowal and
the repetitious and agonized insistence on difficult-to-communicate
subjectivity, which makes up a considerable portion of Lawrence's
prose, especially in the longer novels.

70. *Letters*, p. 628; see also p. 640. For Lawrence's criticisms of the
neutered modern image of Christ, see *Phoenix*, p. 84. Related remarks appear in "The Crucifix across the Mountains," *Twilight in*

Italy, pp. 3–26. Christ was one of Lawrence's obsessive subjects. For a number of Lawrence's remarks, see Witter Bynner, *Journey with Genius* (New York: John Day Co., 1951), chaps. xxxvi and xxxvii. The subject of Lawrence and Christ was taken up repeatedly by J. Middleton Murry. See, for examples of the running discussion, his *Reminiscences of D. H. Lawrence* (London: Jonathan Cape, 1933). Most of Lawrence's remarks about Jesus are emphatically negative, on sexual, social, moral, and religious grounds, and some are rather unjustified. Perhaps, to Lawrence, the worst failing of the Christ was that he represented Christianity.

71. *The Lovely Lady* (New York: Penguin Books, 1946), pp. 137–56. The marriage episode of this early story was discussed in the preceding chapter.

72. *Phoenix*, p. 23. The pagan gods were then made into the Christian demons, which suggests a substantial justification for the not-so-perverse reversals of later demonism.

73. *Apocalypse*, p. 26.

74. *The Short Novels*, II, 3–47—the last novella in the volume.

75. *Articles*, p. 130.

76. *Phoenix*, pp. 780–98. The dualism that Lawrence was dabbling with here may have had something to do with the piece not being finished.

77. *Ibid.*, pp. 808–10.

78. *Articles*, p. 130.

79. *Apocalypse*, p. 184. Lawrence also comments that "allegory can always be explained: and explained away. The true symbol defies all explanation, so does the true myth."

80. For typical comments of Lawrence's on Roman power and morality—negative, of course—see *Etruscan Places* (London: William Heinemann, 1950), pp. 13, 51.

81. Citation lost (from one of the essays).

82. For ". . . the way to immortality is the fulfillment of desire." *Phoenix*, p. 369. See also *Letters*, p. 361.

83. "What can a man do with life but live it? And what does life consist of, save a vivid relationship between man and the living universe that surrounds him?" *Phoenix*, p. 27.

84. In the sense indicated in the discussion, Lawrence shows the

characteristic *amor fati* of the serious nihilist, the atheistically religious. It results in the ecstatic affirmation, through pessimism, of "Life as it is!" *Porcupine*, p. 109.

85. *Apocalypse*, p. 145.

86. *Ibid.*, p. 79.

87. *Poems*, III, 118.

AFTERWORD

1. From verse in a letter to the author by Stewart Millpond, January, 1954.

2. *Studies in Classic American Literature* (New York: Doubleday-Anchor, 1953), pp. 73 ff.

3. *Reflections on the Death of a Porcupine and Other Essays* (London: Martin Secker, 1934), p. 59.

4. *Phoenix: The Posthumous Papers of D. H. Lawrence*, ed. Edward D. McDonald (London: William Heinemann, 1936), p. 42.

5. *Ibid.*, p. 680.

6. *The Complete Poems of D. H. Lawrence* (London: William Heinemann, 1957), II, 178.

7. *Assorted Articles* (New York: Alfred A. Knopf, 1930), p. 252.

8. "There is only life and anti-life." *Poems*, III, 118. The distinction here is an ultimate one. In one sort of application, it points to the common recognition that a lively "badness" is far better than a dead "goodness," a vital "wrongness" is more true than a mechanical "rightness," an intense "anger" far finer than a counterfeit "love," and so forth. These are not so much paradoxes, which are ideas, as perversities, which are realities.

9. *Porcupine*, p. 239.

Index to the Fictions of D. H. Lawrence

This index of Lawrence's fictions, including his full-scale novels, is intended as a rough chronological guide. The dates of composition given in parentheses are frequently approximations for stories written, or rewritten, over considerable periods of time. While it would be possible in some cases to suggest more exact dates by internal evidence and style, those given below are generally derived from references in letters and similar sources. Several stories received alternate titles from Lawrence, or final titles from his editors; the important alternate titles are indicated in brackets following the commonly used title.